RACE, NATIONALISM AND THE STATE IN BRITISH AND AMERICAN MODERNISM

Twentieth-century authors were profoundly influenced by changes in the way nations and states governed their citizens. The development of state administrative technologies allowed modern Western states to identify, track and regulate their populations in unprecedented ways. Patricia E. Chu argues that innovations of form and style developed by Anglo-American modernist writers chart anxieties about personal freedom in the face of increasing governmental controls. Chu examines a diverse set of texts and films, including works by T. S. Eliot, Katherine Mansfield and Zora Neale Hurston, to explore how modernists perceived their work and their identities in relation to state power. In addition, she sheds new light on modernist ideas about race, colonialism and the post-colonial, as race came increasingly to be seen as a political and governmental construct. This book offers a powerful critique of key themes for scholars of modernism, American literature and twentieth-century literature.

PATRICIA E. CHU has taught at the School of the Art Institute of Chicago, East-West University and Brandeis University.

RACE, NATIONALISM AND THE STATE IN BRITISH AND AMERICAN MODERNISM

PATRICIA E. CHU

CAMBRIDGE UNIVERSITY PRESS
Cambridge, New York, Melbourne, Madrid, Cape Town, Singapore,
São Paulo, Delhi, Dubai, Tokyo

Cambridge University Press
The Edinburgh Building, Cambridge CB2 8RU, UK

Published in the United States of America by Cambridge University Press, New York

www.cambridge.org
Information on this title: www.cambridge.org/9780521123815

© Patricia E. Chu 2006

This publication is in copyright. Subject to statutory exception
and to the provisions of relevant collective licensing agreements,
no reproduction of any part may take place without the written
permission of Cambridge University Press.

First published 2006
This digitally printed version 2009

A catalogue record for this publication is available from the British Library

ISBN 978-0-521-86966-9 Hardback
ISBN 978-0-521-12381-5 Paperback

Cambridge University Press has no responsibility for the persistence or
accuracy of URLs for external or third-party internet websites referred to in
this publication, and does not guarantee that any content on such websites is,
or will remain, accurate or appropriate.

For my parents, James and Barbara Chu

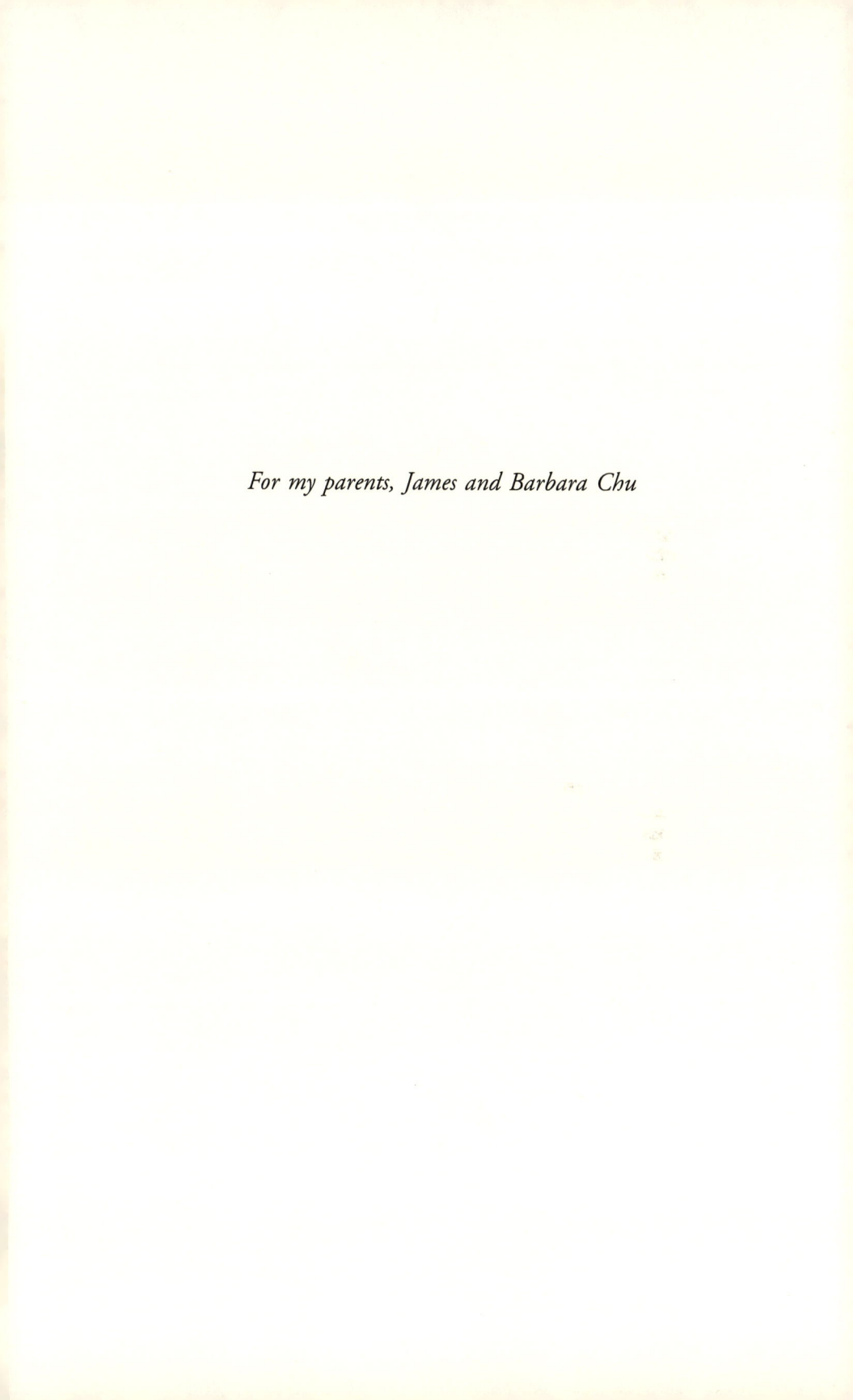

Contents

Acknowledgments	*page* ix
Introduction: white zombies, black Jacobins	1
1 White zombies in the state machinery	21
2 Set in authority: white rulers and white settlers	55
3 Soldiers and traitors: Rebecca West, the world wars and the state subject	79
4 White turkeys, white weddings: the state and the south	115
5 Modernist (pre)occupations: Haiti, primitivism and anti-colonial nationalism	145
Afterword: myths, monsters, modernization, modernism	162
Notes	169
Index	193

Acknowledgments

My earliest studies in modernism began at the University of Pennsylvania and I will always be grateful for the teaching and support of Vicki Mahaffey and David McWhirter. This book began as a dissertation at the University of Chicago under the guidance of my committee Lisa Ruddick and Curtis Marez and directed by Kenneth Warren. Although my work is far afield from his, Michael Murrin taught me much about literary methods. Ken Warren's challenging, creative and generous mentorship and example will always be my benchmarks for what scholarship should be. He has been a true ideal reader, and I have relied on his knowledge, humor and patience through all the time of imagining and writing this book.

A number of communities at Chicago influenced this book and nurtured me – my dissertation group Anne-Elizabeth Murdy and Victoria Olwell, the Gender and Society Workshop (especially Deborah Cohen), the Race and the Reproduction of Racial Ideologies Workshop, and the Department of English Association of Students of Color (DEASC), especially Terry Francis, Rolland Murray, Bill Orchard, Yolanda Padilla, Xiomara Santamarina and Jackie Stewart. Also at Chicago, I thank people without whom neither work nor laughter would have been possible: Deborah Cohen, Shoshannah Cohen, William Farr, Bonnie Gunzenhauser, Anita Houck, Kate MacNeill, Anne-Elizabeth Murdy, Greg Nosan, Victoria Olwell, Nayan Shah, Alicia Tomasian, Jeannie Yim and Paul Young.

I have been fortunate to find community in New England as well. I thank all of the staff, teens, peer leaders and board members of Teen Voices who have let me share in their work and camaraderie and who challenge and inspire me to act on issues of political agency it is easier to examine in history and fiction. For intellectual and other endeavors, I thank companions Min Song, Grace Kim, Tom King, Caren Irr, Josh Rosenberg, Kelly Ritter, Daniel Kim, Claire Buck, Roxanne Dávila, James Wu and Rajini Srikanth.

Lisa Pannella, Melissa Feiden, Linda Braga and Shannon Hunt have been generous with their attention, consideration, professional expertise and (very different) senses of humor. They have been oases in my workplace landscape.

I am grateful for the diligent and enthusiastic work of research assistants Roselyn Farren and Jackie C. Horne.

At the Cambridge University Press, I thank Ray Ryan for understanding what I wanted to do with this book, and for giving me the chance to do it. I thank my anonymous readers for their engaging and challenging comments. Maartje Scheltens, Jayne Aldhouse and Viji Muralidhar have guided me expertly through the completion process.

I can't imagine having written this book without help from patient, rigorous readers of wildly different philosophies over many years. Claire Buck, John Burt, Deborah Cohen, Shoshannah Cohen, Laura Doyle, Madhu Dubey, William Flesch, Andrew Hoberek, Caren Irr, Daniel Kim, Tom King, Curtis Marez, David McWhirter, Paul Morrison, Anne-Elizabeth Murdy, Victoria Olwell, Joshua Rosenberg, Xiomara Santamarina, Nayan Shah, Min Song, Jackie Stewart, Ken Warren, Laura Winkiel.

From among these readers, I am especially grateful to those who rallied around to offer different parts of this manuscript a home on their desks at a time when I didn't want them, and who insisted on giving them back, in improved form, after helping me get ready to receive them: William Flesch (who also sat through and discussed *White Zombie* and other films), Daniel Kim, Victoria Olwell, Min Song and Ken Warren (who has never wavered in either his kindness or his expectations).

During that difficult time, not a day went by but that I heard from Shoshannah Cohen or Daniel Kim or both. Roxanne Dávila, Deborah Cohen, Tom King, Anne-Elizabeth Murdy, Victoria Olwell, Nayan Shah (who reminded me to celebrate), Min Song and Alicia Tomasian provided more varieties of nurture than I could ever have imagined.

My family has carried the special burden of performing many of the care and feeding jobs I have described above without the "no biting" courtesies (often) extended to non-family members. My mother Barbara has taught me to aspire to the true rather than to the easily articulated and provided the caring and example that allowed me to try. This book is dedicated to her, and to my father James. My sister Sandi began teaching me from the moment she was born about the importance, joy and difficulty of collaboration and counterintuitive thought. My brother-in-law Derek Lustig's abiding intellectual curiosity about the backgrounds

Acknowledgments

to everything has been a refreshing example. My grandparents Helen and Jacob Young watched the earliest steps with loving interest I relied on. My aunts and uncle Jaylene and Edmund Chin, Joan Young and my godparents Ellie and Ted have all been deeply sustaining, as have all my cousins.

In addition to gifting me with more family to make the task of writing this book easier – that is, Natch, Audrey and Dawn Hoberek and Jody, Tom and Nadia Atkins – Andrew Hoberek, my *cha'Dich*, has watched every frame of this project in slow motion, even the most egregiously generated spectacles, without once wanting to close his eyes.

A version of Chapter 5 appeared, under the same title, in *Geomodernisms: Race, Modernism, Modernity*, ed. Laura Doyle and Laura Winkiel (Bloomington: Indiana University Press, 2005), 170–186. Reprinted by permission.

INTRODUCTION

White zombies, black Jacobins

The human monster. An ancient notion whose frame of reference is law ... the monster's field of appearance is a juridico-biological domain ... what makes a human monster a monster is not just its exceptionality relative to the species form; it is the disturbance it brings to juridical regularities (whether it is a question of marriage laws, canons of baptism, or rules of inheritance).
Michel Foucault, "The Abnormals" (1969)[1]

Certainly we no longer know, except that it is primarily a craft, what art is. A South American poet of sorts spent an evening excitedly trying to prove to me that only that which breaks the basic rules is art. ... But the apprentices to any craft first proudly acquire the tricks, then the deeper skills. This is only natural. But the young black who used to kneel in worship before the headlights on explorers' cars is now driving a taxi in Paris and New York. We had best not lag behind this black.
Jean Epstein, *Bonjour cinéma* (1926)[2]

Between roughly 1890 and 1945, elite Anglo-American and European intellectuals and artists described men of their status as being unable to maintain distinct personalities that could, because of their very distinctiveness, authoritatively affect social, economic and political life directly. The men in T. S. Eliot's crowd who flow over London Bridge to the financial district, each "fix[ing] his eyes before his feet," are on their way to Max Weber's bureaucratic organization. Once there, they will work with "[p]recision, speed, unambiguity, knowledge of the files, continuity, discretion, unity, strict subordination, reduction of friction and of material and personal costs."[3] The metropolis, a "social-technological mechanism" with a money economy and a division of labor, imposes "general, schematically precise form[s]" on its inhabitants in a way that exemplifies life under modernity:

The individual has become a mere cog in an enormous organization of things and powers which tear from his hands all progress, spirituality, and value in order to transform them from their subjective form into the form of a purely objective life. It needs merely to be pointed out that the metropolis is the genuine arena of this culture which outgrows all personal life. Here in buildings and educational institutions, in the wonders and comforts of space-conquering technology, in the formations of community life, and in the visible institutions of the state, is offered such an overwhelming fullness of crystallized and impersonalized spirit that the personality, so to speak, cannot maintain itself under its impact.[4]

According to Georg Simmel's, Weber's and Eliot's stories of the rise of twentieth-century modernity, men have been reduced to acting only within strictly delineated jurisdictions using strictly delimited authority. They become administrators of society's institutions rather than independent agents influencing those institutions.

In analyzing Anglo-American modernism's self-consciousness about its own modernity, I focus on this sense of limits created by jurisdiction, categorization and rational management as the center of modernist affect. The "new" subjectivities and identities imagined by Anglo-American modernist artists emerged in tandem with changes in how Western states were defining and managing the people within their jurisdictions. I argue that modernist alienation is most usefully understood as a response to specific characteristics of governance in the twentieth century.

It has become commonplace to describe literary modernism as a formal and narrative engagement with the conditions of modernity. The modernist period, approximately 1890–1945, is a time during which modern states developed unprecedented abilities to identify, track and regulate populations. I examine the ways in which Anglo-American modernism was shaped by the development and application of these state administrative technologies.

The nature of the modern Western state, and consequently the experience of being administered as a citizen–subject by such a state, changed significantly during the early twentieth century. Increased government oversight of the economy seemed justified. The second wave of industrial revolution, like the first, quickly and substantially concentrated capital, increased systematized factory production (which contributed to urbanization and the rise of commodity culture), and started a wave of transnational labor migration.[5] The scramble among the great powers for imperial territory before World War I was above all a competition among industrializing nations for economic modernization and expansion – the new basis of global power. Private production by individuals within each nation was now understood to have consequences for the nation as a whole. When Britain faltered in this competition, there were calls for an interventionist state that would promote national efficiency.[6] As Nikolas Rose and Peter Miller point out, the ensuing debate was thus not merely about attaining efficiency but also articulated general political ideals about the purposes of government.[7]

The first modern war necessitated further government management of national economies and populations. Noting the German phrase for battles of the 1914–1918 Western front – *Materialschlacht*, battles of materials – Eric Hobsbawm writes that one of the most significant characteristics of modern war is that it "used and destroyed hitherto inconceivable amounts of materials." The level of production suggested by the term, sustained over a number of years, required a large civilian labor force, a modern, highly productive and industrialized economy, and government organization and management of both.[8] Civilians and civilian life became objects of strategy for military operations and propaganda. Leaders needed the cooperation of civilians to fight the war, and made calculations in terms of populations as resources to be managed. After the war, the emergent world powers similarly counted on civilians to build expanding (inter)national economies and infrastructures. One of the war's lasting effects was the extension of expanded federal administration into peacetime everyday life.[9]

Twentieth-century Anglo-American political order, like twentieth-century war, was based on mass democratization. Initiatives such as extending the franchise increased the number of citizens who could claim the privileges attached to citizenship.[10] The discourses of mass democracy – representation, participatory government and consent – became more firmly established as the basis for rights, regulation, legitimate exercise of power and social identity. In practice, this new political order neither eschewed violence and coercion nor redistributed political or economic power in the way the phrase "mass democratization" might imply. In America, the number of labor injunctions issued by courts rose sharply after the war, as did violent anti-strike enforcement by private and government police. Company police forces had broad discretionary powers and could beat, evict and kill picketing or striking workers. Vigilante groups joined them. A particular twist of the rhetoric of democratization emerging from nationalist wartime production justified these measures by arguing that a society had the right to the labor of its workers.[11] Meanwhile, expansion of eligibility for the franchise in America was accompanied by sharp declines in actual voter participation – from 80 percent of those eligible in 1896 to under 50 percent in 1924 – and by regulations against the street parades to the polls and public meetings on election day that had provided avenues for lower-class (white) men to identify themselves as political actors. As Robert Wiebe explains it, nineteenth-century American electoral politics depended on collective fraternity but twentieth-century American electoral politics individualized the voter. New bureaucratic electoral rules (not limited to the south) including poll taxes, pre-election registration, and literacy tests were not merely exclusionary but also "atomized" the democratic electorate: "Government-prepared forms that each man used in secret became the norm – voting, once a loyalty-affirming public action, became a private act."[12] Across the Atlantic, the number of British voters tripled by 1921. But, paradoxically, the groups who were projected to benefit most by enfranchisement, women and labor, saw their movements stall after winning the vote. The Conservative Party won most of the elections from 1922 to 1940.[13]

Thus amidst what many historians consider a general political, economic and social "sinking" of the lower classes, immigrants and racial minorities, modernist elites such as Weber, Simmel and Eliot and other of my writers described their own loss of agency and authority. They decried the alleged redistribution of political power to a mass citizenship and depicted the new professionalized managerial class – including intellectual "experts" such as social scientists – as puppets and hollow men. In whose hands, then, did modern agency lie?

My exemplary text for this project is a film similarly populated by characters who cannot use their personalities to shape modern life: *White Zombie* (1932 dir. Victor Halperin), set in Haiti, starring Bela Lugosi, and released during the seventeenth year of the US occupation of Haiti. In *White Zombie*, the non-Haitian zombie master Murder Legendre uses non-white, Haitian zombies as labor for his sugar plantation. But, as the film's title suggests, the notable zombies of the film are white. Legendre's zombies are quintessentially twentieth-century figures that encapsulate and elaborate anxieties about whether white masculinity will still command what have heretofore been its prerogatives – free will, agency and authority – indeed, about whether it is possible fully to recognize the loss of these under increasingly mechanized and bureaucratized regimes of labor, state categorization and state regulation.

Roughly contemporaneous with the era I focus on, *White Zombie* pulls together elements whose theoretical elaboration in combination would be otherwise difficult to articulate. As I describe in more detail in my reading in Chapter 1, the film anxiously desires, but ultimately fails, to establish the boundaries between the living and the living dead in a series of cases: automaton-like manual labor in a cross between an assembly line and a sugar-cane mill, a bride turned into a zombie on her (white) wedding night, and Haitian nationals turned into zombies by a foreigner who has learned Haitian voudoun. The burden of each of these cases is slightly different (modern labor, marital consent as a model for democratic consent, and U.S. "democratic occupation") but they converge in the zombie, a monster that resembles a normal human, that has lost control over its own thoughts and actions and may not even realize its own loss of agency.

In other words, *White Zombie*'s horrors are political. In the case of the zombie master's laborers, the film references the period's increasingly frequent conflicts between labor and industry. As companies consolidated their power over labor with the support of the government, work lost its power to anchor (white, male) American freedom. The film uses the zombie bride – that is, the idea of marital consent – to map anxieties about whether consent as a social structure accurately models the exercise of a citizen's free choice. If consent is agreeing to terms to which there are no positive alternatives, then consent itelf may be inherently subordinating. In a Western political context of self-government and individual freedom, then, the zombie expresses doubts about the foundation of legitimate government: the freely consenting citizen–subject. Is such a creature merely giving the appearance, like a zombie bride or a zombie laborer, of participating willingly? Finally, against a backdrop of a country the United States was "democratically occupying," ostensibly with the consent of its nationals, a foreign zombie master raises the specter that domination lies at the core of U.S. democratic governance, whether practiced at home or abroad. As Foucault points out in his notes on monstrosity (see the first epigraph above), the most significant component of horror is not its distortion of the physical foundations of *humanity* but its suggestion that juridical and institutional assumptions about *personhood* have been undermined.

The zombie stalks the cities of modernism, where newly emergent methods of liberal-democratic interventionist government were becoming visible. Simmel's metropolis – a "vast, overwhelming organization of things and forces" – was a novel interarticulation of the nineteenth century's vast array of loosely coordinated and mostly voluntary social programs with the state apparatus.[14] Governance would now take place on the level of "social management" rather than direct coercion. The state would engineer its large-scale social objectives by influencing the behavioral choices of free individuals through mechanisms such as the establishment of social norms. But self-government, like twentieth-century representative democracy, offers a peculiar combination of agency and disempowerment. With regard to the voter, Lynnette Hunter describes this as "the condition of enfranchised subjectivity in the contemporary nation-state." Citizenship promises responsibility and agency, but one's actions as an individual (through, for instance, voting) seem only to lead to assent, through participation, to a nation-state that does not substantively represent all the people theoretically enfranchised.[15]

Nineteenth-century industrialization had first posed the problem of maintaining social and economic stability in a locale with a dense, constantly changing and heterogeneous population of people who were often detached from traditional community associations. Victorian Britain and America had both rejected the (Continental) centralized state. British liberal philosophy and ideology before World War I was anti-interventionist and anti-collectivist, emphasizing constitutional liberty, self-governance, and individuality. Centralized responses to social problems generated by industrialization and urbanization such as the 1834 New Poor Law or the 1848 Public Health Act were perceived as antithetical to the British national legacy of a free citizenry.[16] Americans similarly understood liberal laissez-faire government as part of their national identity and natural legacy. The cultural logic of American democracy at the start of the nineteenth century, Wiebe writes, was that "since all white men governed themselves equally as individuals, all white men combined as equals to govern themselves collectively."[17] American society came to describe American identity in terms of white men's right to an independent working life. The government had neither the capacity nor the public support to regulate or organize white men's productivity, and government policies and financial institutions (personal credit founded entrepreneurial prerogatives) became the greatest of social villains. Decision-making about the structures of social life was "relentlessly decentralized"; for example, poverty was not considered a federal problem.[18]

In the absence of federal intervention, British and Americans threw themselves eagerly into the now infamous voluntarism, philanthropy and social reform of the era, the foundation of modern social work. Many social theorists and historians have discussed the coerciveness of the Victorian reform enterprise. For the purposes of my project, what I would like to emphasize from those accounts here is the extraordinary scope of Victorian philanthropy[19] and the reformers' method of exercising power: establishing social norms for individual behavior. The poor, the unmarried, the intemperate, the uneducated, the spendthrift, the immigrant and the unskilled were to be personally addressed and then enlisted, rhetorically if not structurally, alongside their reformers in the great project of maintaining a socially stable yet economically expanding nation.

Such strategies characteristically, as Rose and Miller put it, draw people into "the pursuit of social, political or economic objectives without encroaching on their 'freedom' or 'autonomy' – indeed often precisely by offering to maximize it by turning blind habit into calculated freedom to choose."[20] Thus, the first step in altering people's behavior was inviting them to understand themselves as *having* an autonomous subjectivity. Reform rhetoric then invites people to imagine themselves as using the capacities of that subjectivity to govern themselves individually and as part of a whole society of self-governors as they "choose" to change their social behaviors. Without a Weberian monopoly on the legitimate use of violence to compel behavior, nineteenth-century non-governmental reform organizations invented social management.[21]

The oft-cited "rise" of the Western democratic interventionist welfare state of the first half of the twentieth century, Rose and Miller argue, is not a new form of the state, but "a new mode of government of the economic, social, and personal lives of citizens."[22] This mode of government inherits from classic liberal philosophy clear legal or constitutionally defined limits to the arbitrary exercise of state power. Laissez-faire government was designed to foster commerce: the state protected individuals' rights and liberties but did not interfere with "private" business or with the free play of market forces.[23] After the turn-of-the-century democratization of citizenship, freedom from the arbitrary imposition of state power came to mean a government that enacted rather than controlled "the will of the people." Government would act, with the people's consent, for "the good of society as a whole." Nineteenth-century social reform organizations provided strategies for such "non-arbitrary" yet powerful social management.[24]

Twentieth-century liberal-democratic Anglo-American government emerged as links developed between the non-governmental nineteenth-century network of reform organizations with their strategies of "maximizing subjectivity" and the apparatuses of the state meant to track and regulate "problematic" elements of the population (courts, reform institutions, schools, clinics).[25] This unprecedented alliance generated a vast, heterogeneous and contesting network of philanthropic individuals and organizations, state agents and institutions, professionalized experts and politicians, all working to define and articulate socially desirable outcomes and the best way to produce them. It was at this time that "social problems" were first treated systematically by imagining "the individual in society" as the object of governance.[26] To "govern" now meant to shape the beliefs, circumstances and environments of citizens, influencing their choices, which would in their turn produce particular social objectives.[27] As we can see from the history of Victorian organizations, government had not been the exclusive purview of the state, and it was not to be now. As Foucault has famously explained, understanding modern political power requires focusing "not so much on the State-domination of society, but the 'governmentalization' of the State."[28] The transformation of government during the first half of the twentieth century is not the story of a newly powerful state dominating a previously free and ungoverned private, social or civil sector, but rather the story of the growth of complicated connections between private social reform organizations already participating in government through the management of social life and the administrative and bureaucratic technologies of the state. The significance of this alliance at this time lies in the way the philanthropic techniques of addressing, individualizing, problematizing and normativizing the subject,[29] as Rose and Miller put it, "appeared to offer the chance, or impose the obligation, for [state] political authorities to calculate and calibrate social, economic and moral affairs and seek to govern them"[30] on the field of the social and without overstepping the (liberal philosophical) limits of legitimate political power. At the same time, private political authorities saw in an alliance with the state, with its capacities for revenue and information gathering and legitimate force, possibilities for achieving their organizations' ends.

But governing legitimately within the domain of an everyday life and culture interdicted from direct political authority by the limits of liberal democracy meant that the individuals governed must be, as Foucault explains, "free subjects." That is, they must be "individual or collective subjects who are faced with a field of possibilities in which several ways of behaving, several reactions, and diverse comportments may be realized."[31] Liberal states must go so far as to create and protect the freedom of these subjects; they are given "the task of shaping and nurturing that very civil society that was to provide its counterweight and limit."[32] The new subjectivities of the twentieth century, then, emerge from systems of authority and regulation. The much vaunted self-consciousness of this era is inextricably bound with anxiety about whether individual decisions, desires and the power to act on them were illusory. In other words, modern(ist) self-consciousness expresses uncertainty about the governed self and not only, as some critics would have it, the disappearance of unified perspectives.

My route through a low-brow American horror film and what has heretofore been understood as a minor site of colonial and postcolonial history may seem roundabout; I will say more about what this approach yields. In addition to figuring the zombie in terms of twentieth-century structures of political agency, *White Zombie* indexes Haiti's connection to *this representation* of zombies. That is, merely to have Haiti as the setting for a film about zombies is not notable, because the link between zombies and voudoun was popular knowledge. But the film also marks the Haitian zombies specifically as nationalist colonized subjects with relation to Haiti's history as a European colony, as the site of the first successful slave revolt and of the first black modern state, and as a nation occupied by the United States for, at the time of the film's release, seventeen years.

Haiti is also the site of an unacknowledged narrative of modernism: the back story of modern Western subjectivity. Critics and historians beginning with C. L. R. James have argued for Haiti's singular contribution to Western modernity. The modern Western subject – the individual and free citizen – was born economically, politically, culturally and metaphysically twice in the Caribbean. Caribbean development inaugurated an imperial commercial capitalism that held out the promise of entrepreneurial freedom from material poverty. This is not to claim that *all* Europeans inherited equally from this ancestor but rather that *only* Europeans were meant to benefit from this unprecedented transformation of economic production. The paradigm for this new economic order, as Hilary McD. Beckles puts it, was "African labor enslavement and European capital liberation." Plantation capitalists stood at the forefront of industrial technology and modern business practice. They were the first to establish and develop global networks to circulate labor (African slaves), raw materials, capital and credit, and commodities. The sugar mill was the most advanced and largest industrial complex of the sixteenth and seventeenth centuries. To run it, plantation capitalists developed the first industrial divisions of labor.[33]

The (economic) capacity of the European capitalist to recreate himself as a man of autonomy and authority depended on an enslaved labor force. As the capitalist economic system of slavery-linked global commerce expanded, Western nation-state power began to depend more directly on each nation-state's ability to participate in that system. This structural dynamic – in which European potential could fully develop only at the expense of colonized "natives" – became part of European cultural, juridical and political definitions of modern personhood. As the practice of slavery expanded, political philosophers theorized the foundations of modern citizenry as the capacity for self-mastery and self-determination. Enlightenment philosophers drew from the globalized master–slave economy their metaphors for political tyranny, their definitions of what made a free citizen, and in John Locke's case, the means to be a free citizen himself – as an investor in plantations in the Bahamas and in the Royal Africa Company. The modern individual stood in relation to the state; he must not be "enslaved" to the state but must directly participate in his own government. To do this he had to be independent and to have independent authority. The qualifications for modernity and civic participation were circular – to have authority one had already to have authority. In order to have the right not to be (literally) enslaved, one had already to be free.

The modern Western citizen was born as white in the Caribbean. It was only after the establishment of the Caribbean economic system that slavery took on its modern racial dimensions.[34] By the end of the eighteenth century, as David Theo Goldberg points out, Kant's notes to his readers about the parameters of modern citizenship (white, male, property-holding) underline both how firmly established and how deeply rooted in racial identity those parameters had become – as deeply rooted in racial identity as the Western economy was in enslaved labor.[35] The Western citizen of the modern state, regardless of his location, was a New World Man indeed.[36]

In or about 1791, the Caribbean – Saint-Domingue, to become independent Haiti in 1804 – again became the site for an unprecedented (re)construction of the modern, rational, autonomous and individualized citizen. This new New World man was a black, anti-colonial nationalist. The Western subject of modernity maintained his sense of modern self in part by locating unmodernity in various areas and peoples of the New World; the Haitian revolutionaries reversed those assumptions. For C. L. R. James, the Haitian Revolution, rather than the French and American revolutions, was the truer culmination of Enlightenment theories and ideals. Slave trade increased between 1789 and 1791. By contrast, the Haitian revolutionaries were the first post-Enlightenment people to write a national constitution declaring all citizens free. And though he was a Marxist–Leninist, for James the Haitian Revolution also historically upstages the Bolshevik Revolution as, as Beckles puts it, "that first moment in modernity when the alienated and dispossessed seized control of their destiny and emerged the subjects of a new world order."[37]

Haitian revolutionaries rewrote the established Western "order of things." Haitian slaves *as slaves* should have been incapable of conceiving freedom, let alone a revolution. As people lacking modernity, they should have been unable to comprehend the significance of the nation-state, let alone found the first Black republic in the world. Indeed, planters in Saint-Domingue never considered the possibility of any uprising more serious than a localized riot. The planters had no plans for countering an insurrection; their diaries and journals record their assumptions that no Negroes ever thought about revolution.[38]

The modernity of Europeans, on the other hand, is often asserted by noting that they seemed to think of little else but revolution during this period. Revolution was at the center of philosophical debates about individual freedom as a world historical force. But while the American and French revolutions *suggested* that the abstract ideals of the European Enlightenment were universal, it took the Saint-Domingue revolution, the first in which slaves overthrew their rulers and established a republic in which all citizens were equal and in which slavery was banned, to prove it.[39] The French revolutionaries, as Buck-Morss points out, undercut their own legitimating ideals of universal freedom by continuing to allow slavery after the revolution:

> The unfolding of the logic of freedom in the colonies threatened to unravel the total institutional framework of the slave economy that supported such a substantial part of the French bourgeoisie, whose political revolution, of course, this was. And yet only the logic of freedom gave legitimacy to their revolution in the universal terms in which the French saw themselves.[40]

Thus, it took Haitian revolutionaries to provide the conceptual framework for understanding the implications of the French Revolution. News about Saint-Domingue traveled across Europe via newspapers, journals and pamphlets and, Buck-Morss argues, finally provided the metaphor for Hegel's *The Phenomenology of the Mind* – the master–slave relationship.[41]

In other words, the Haitian revolutionaries did not merely join a new world order but actually created one. Both naturalist (enslaved and colonized peoples were permanently and essentially incapable of historical development) and historicist (the inferior position of enslaved or colonized peoples was due to their having progressed more slowly than European peoples) versions of European philosophies of humanity understood "history" as driven by European modernization. In inaugurating postcoloniality, the revolutionaries took the historical lead. If the foundation of twentieth-century citizenship and governance is the agency of the ordinary citizen, we might understand the Haitian revolutionaries as the first to lay a cornerstone. Beckles describes the "central paradigmatic feature of Caribbean modernity" as "the rise of the common citizen to institutional and cultural leadership."[42] Hegel followed postcolonial revolutionaries to limn the world-historical contours of modern subjectivity, not the other way round.

During the modernist period, Hegel's definition of the nature of the modern self in terms of power, race and governance remained trenchant despite the abolition of chattel slavery. The modern "black" Epstein describes in the epigraph above stands in stark contrast to the modern man whom Simmel depicts as fighting to retain his personality, whom Weber calls "the official" and whom Eliot portrayed as "hollow." Epstein's lines expose the inaccuracy of the assumption that primitivism always puts "the native" outside history.[43] He suggests that the native is the historical subject and that "we," presumably elite modernist subjects, may not understand modernity well enough. He emphasizes motion and location: the formerly subjected and immobile native viewer has not only moved to the metropole but also learned its routes. He now manipulates the object he once worshipped. "We," on the other hand, may "lag behind this black": has the leading edge of modernity become anti-colonial? Has the leading edge of modernity become politically "black"? As with Hegel and the Haitian Revolution, Epstein's lines should remind us of the marked rise in anti-colonial movements during the 1920s and 1930s. The "black" no longer worships Western technology but "drives" it, and has learned to map the metropolis. But unlike the administering and administered official, he actively fights state power.

I take the intersection of these contradictory creatures of modernism – the white metropolitan bureaucratized citizen–subject and the native revolutionary (or the white zombie and the twentieth-century "black Jacobin") – as provocation to emphasize the political foundations of the new subjectivities and identities modernist artists were concerned to describe.

Regardless of the accuracy of modernists' perceptions of themselves, natives and power, it is striking that for both black and white figures – and I deliberately make explicit the implicit whiteness of the bureaucratized administrator here – terms of agency derive from the relationship between the individual and large-scale systems of management and governance. The white administrator has lost the privileges of autonomous work and distinct personality and become a mere conduit for the impersonal markets of the capitalist city. Epstein's "young black" is reversing the early modern construction of human agency and world historical significance as white by challenging his place in the globalized economy.

In this book I emphasize the underlying histories of modernism and modernity I have outlined above to suggest ways modernist studies might re-theorize the relationships among the historical events of the modernist period, cultural understandings of the implications of those events, and "modernist aesthetics." Attaching postcoloniality to the modernity of modernism instead of to postmodernity sets geopolitical rather than merely geographical boundaries for imagining an "international arts movement."

"Modernism and empire" studies, at least thus far, have failed to engage the crux of postcolonial analysis: understanding the "native" rather than the "colonizer" as the subject of history. These studies tend to examine the relationship between the rise of artistic modernism and the historical phenomenon of Western imperialism, even when they are critical of the uses of imperial power, in terms of appropriation and inspiration. Imperialism provoked startling encounters with non-Western peoples and their cultural productions: social arrangements, religions and art. Western modernists derived new styles and forms from materials generated by these encounters: anthropological studies based on cultural relativism, artifacts displayed in Europe, personal travels through newly accessible territories. Globalizing capitalism, colonial violence, cultural and racial difference, and the national successes and failures of the great powers provided both content and metaphors for modernists describing their own phenomenologies of mind and experiences of modernity. Such analyses remain crucial to the task of refusing to accept modernism's self-definitions insofar as they analyze the power relations behind the narrative of modernist originality dealing subversive blows to established institutions. They nonetheless reiterate the logic of imperial economics: metropolitans use raw materials from the periphery to manufacture finished goods. In emphasizing work that reattaches Caribbean modernity to the Western philosophies of the self that would become modernism's legacy, I hope to index the anxiety not merely that there was "no one to drive the car" but that, as Epstein put it, the young black might be driving, with all that that implied.

I have chosen a motley assortment of artists for this study deliberately. The writers and filmmakers I discuss have different literary historical relations to modernist studies. Some (T. S. Eliot, Jean Toomer, and

D. W. Griffith) fit into traditional aesthetic definitions of modernism. But I also examine writers who have had limited claims to the label "modernist" based on particular works, themes or associations, or who are modernists under a "subset" of modernism such as feminist modernism or the Harlem Renaissance (Katherine Mansfield, Rebecca West, and Zora Neale Hurston). I have also included authors generally considered to be working in genres or periods inimical to modernism: Sara Jeannette Duncan and Ellen Glasgow (Edwardian novels of manners and American regionalism, respectively).

Perhaps more significantly, these artists have no obvious categorical relationships to each other. This, too, is deliberate. Analyzing modernism in relation to the history of governance also offers new theoretical possibilities for analyzing the significance of identity categories to modernist criticism. This topic in modernist studies, even in "the new modernisms," tends to analyze identity categories in terms of either how modernist writing represented, for instance, black people or women or how black people's or women's obviously constituted identities must be linked to "their" modernism. In reading "other" modernisms according to the predefined identity categories of its authors, modernist studies commits itself to an understanding of a primary (unmarked) modernism surrounded by (raced and gendered) satellite artists. Under the rhetoric of diversifying the modernist canon, "other" modernisms are discussed solely in terms of how their aesthetic techniques (or lack thereof) may be similar enough to mainstream modernism to be modernist, yet different in predictable ways related to their marginalization. The subject and agent of literary history is the white male artist; "other" artists only sociologically describe what he understood as a complicated *metaphor* for his experience under modernity. That the black person provided modernists a convenient symbol for rebellion, difference or alienation merges into the implicit assumption that Harlem Renaissance artists fell circumstantially into the aesthetics and subject matter (their modernism was mere realism) that primary modernists had to imagine and create. The great irony of the feminist refashioning of modernist studies in the 1970s and 1980s was that strands of it lauded Faulkner and Joyce for their mastery of *écriture féminine* – because revolutionary aesthetics derived from seeing from the margins were the provenance of mainstream modernism. Thus, although race and gender are analytically important for my project, the idea of women or racial minorities as pre-constituted groups is not. My focus is instead on the state's role in creating and sustaining administrable identities and subjectivities such as "women," "natives," "farmers" or "voters."

With this in mind, I have made my choice of historical incidents of state formation and state management wide-ranging in order to highlight the pervasiveness of the effects of state modernization and governmentalization across a broad swathe of cultural production. Overall, my aim is to show how several different and disparate areas of modernist studies might be critically connected through an analysis of state administration and the effects it had on cultural production in the first half of the twentieth century. For instance, this might allow us simultaneously to reconsider critical commonplaces about modernism's relation to sentimentalism and its relationship to professionalization.

I lay the ground for these counterintuitive connections in Chapter 1. In this chapter, I provide an example of how recognizing the significance of the state to modernism establishes links between such unlikely bedfellows as *White Zombie* and some of T. S. Eliot's practical criticism: the essays charting his change of opinion on Rudyard Kipling, "the poet of empire." I begin with a summary and detailed reading of the film that explores its overdetermination of the zombie in political and historical terms. The Haitian zombie is a figure that simultaneously evokes the laborer under an industrial regime, the native under a colonial regime, the (white) woman under a state-regulated marital regime, and the uncertainty of the twentieth-century subject's grasp on the free will that makes (white) (men) human. These contemporary questions of political agency and colonial history interarticulate with *White Zombie*'s aesthetic preoccupations, and I focus also on the film's relationship to new mass visual technologies and on its use of some of the very narrative strategies modernism is generally assumed to be separating itself from: melodrama, narrative coherence, realism, popular culture, and the gothic. I explore the ways in which a text such as *White Zombie* might be "modernist" not by cataloguing its formal features against a checklist of avant-garde characteristics, but by defining its approaches to form and style in terms of the way these respond to specific historical problems. Thus, I describe how the film's "sentimental" narratives and techniques, when read in the context of the particularly twentieth-century monstrousness of the zombie, respond to material, political and aesthetic modernization in ways that distinguish them from the genres to which they were originally attached.

The problem that Kipling poses for Eliot is very like the problem that a film such as *White Zombie* poses for modernist studies. Eliot wonders how to measure Kipling's artistic greatness, that is, how to put him into literary history, in formal terms. After all, Eliot wrote, "[Kipling] is not one of those writers of whom one can say that the *form* of English poetry will always be different from what it would have been if they had not written." In four essays written over a period of forty years, Eliot eventually cleared Kipling of this and other infractions against modernist critical values such as writing political verse. I argue that Eliot's change in position was not due simply to reconsidering the aesthetic qualities of Kipling's work but rather to the changing political function of "the man of letters" that accompanied changes in national identity, citizenship and the state management of these taking place at the time. I offer a reading of T. S. Eliot's engagement with Rudyard Kipling and with cultural geopolitics as an example of how considering the history of the Anglo-American state can reanimate the question of what is characteristically modern(ist) about Eliot's much-analyzed establishment of cultural value and authority for particular authors, styles, forms and critics.

This first chapter, then, establishes my interest in a particular set of problems modernism confronted that resonate both in Halperin's film and in the figures described by Weber, Simmel and Eliot. These figures and the zombie do not appear in every subsequent chapter. In this sense, the film and chapter are evocative rather than programmatic. At the same time, I mean the zombie to resonate as a reminder that there are reasons that Michel-Rolph Trouillot characterizes as those of (Western) epistemology that have kept Caribbean modernity from the modernist stage.

One of the outcomes, I hope, of such an approach is to help those of us in modernist studies to articulate more clearly what it is we accomplish intellectually as we expand the texts we consider under the aegis of "the new modernisms." I find equally unsatisfactory four common approaches: (1) declaring "modernist" any work written within a particular span of years. Modernism was an aesthetic commitment, despite our lack of critical agreement on the nature of that commitment; (2) describing the ways in which an author's work aesthetically resembles the work of authors whose place in the modernist canon is unchallenged. This seems to me to be a circular argument rather than a reconsideration of the aesthetics of modernism in a historical light. Moreover, in the case of non-Western writing, such an approach reinforces a condescending sense of the Western modernist as the privileged subject of literary history whom all the world strove to imitate; (3) establishing "special" modernisms (regional modernism, women's modernism, Harlem Renaissance modernism, and so forth) separate from an implicit "real" modernism. This segregation prevents any challenge to contemporary critical commonplaces of modernism – what might it mean that our definitions cannot cover these authors? – while again positioning the same group of artists as the ones whose strategies define the movement; and finally, (4) declaring modernist all texts with a particular cultural content, such as eugenics. Again, this begs the question of aesthetic commitment and effect.

In each of the chapters subsequent to Chapter 1, I explore a set of texts that take up what were then new sociopolitical understandings of nations, states and citizens. Taken as a whole, these chapters demonstrate the degree to which the myriad ways subjects have relations with the state became the foundation of the twentieth-century sense of self and then of a modernist aesthetic. I examine American, Canadian and British authors' textual integrations of issues of governance and the development of state administrative technologies such as the national map, marriage, the passport and other identity documents, the franchise, the treason trial, military service, colonial governance and the annexation of traditional regional farming to a federal managed agricultural economy.

In each chapter I reconsider a genealogical, formal or sociological critical commonplace of modernist studies to suggest how it might be better understood with relation to the historical phenomenon of increasing governmentalization. Thus, the chapters taken together link aspects of modernism often considered in critically separate areas of inquiry in modernist studies (for instance, the "crisis" in masculinity and modernism's relationship to American regional writing) to each other and to this history to form a broader theory of the relationship between modernism and modernization.

Chapter 2 focuses on early fiction by Katherine Mansfield and Sara Jeannette Duncan about white colonists in New Zealand and the British colonial administration of India. I discuss Mansfield's short stories and Duncan's novel in terms of the challenges they pose to "modernism and empire" criticism, and to definitions of modernism as grounded in the artist's conclusive rejection of realist technique. Mansfield and Duncan's insistence that empire can be described sets them, in typical modernism and empire genealogies, alongside realistic "adventure" literature (H. R. Haggard, Rudyard Kipling) or women's Victorian empire fiction (Flora Annie Steele, Maud Diver) rather than Joseph Conrad. Mansfield and Duncan, according to these literary genealogies, fail to comprehend their historical and literary historical moment and cling naively to a transparent literary authority, to a belief in the ability of the novel accurately to depict the world, and to a conception of the subject that were no longer historically viable. In other words, they do not *aesthetically* engage empire.

I argue instead that Duncan and Mansfield's particular uses of realist technique read as aesthetic engagements of modernization's implications when the imperial project is defined as a practical political problem of extending state authority, in its modern, rational, socially enforced and consent-driven form, across global distances. Rather than generating the ineffable of empire's indescribable expanses to assert the expansiveness of the human psyche, they focus instead on the non-representational elements in the realist languages of state management. In fact, Duncan and Mansfield's work reveals that modernism and empire readings, despite their claim to connect history and aesthetics, have been vulnerable to reifying precisely the idea these readings claim to unsettle: that modernist artistry consists of detaching techniques from their historical context.

In Chapter 3 I suggest ways in which several of the figures offered as contesting paradigms for the subject of modernity (the men of 1914, the suffragette or New Woman, the consumer, the anarchist, the nationalist) are more usefully understood as similarly sketching the ways state documentation, control and tracking of its citizens' identities, along with all state functions, increased markedly at the end of the nineteenth century. To do this, I take up the case of Rebecca West, who, despite now being listed consistently as a "woman modernist," continues to pose problems for modernist studies. Not an avant-garde stylist or a member of a modernist circle like Woolf, her work is not entirely, or even mostly, fiction. Neither she nor it is assimilable to any of these paradigmatic figures of modernity. Though she published a short story in Lewis's *Blast*, and followed this with a series of novels, she turned in the 1940s to writing on treason, war crimes, cold war spies, national histories (Yugoslavia and Mexico) and issues of government. Some critics have responded by treating her later work as separate from her earlier work. Bonnie Kime Scott writes: "After 1940, West did extensive trial and crime reportage, specializing in themes relating to treason that seem very distant from her modernist tendencies and her early socialist feminism."[44]

In contrast to this approach, I treat West's interests in trials, treason, crime and national identity – state forms – as "modernist tendencies." I trace their emergence in West's 1918 novel *Return of the Soldier* and their development in her account of William Joyce, hanged in Britain as a traitor, in *The Meaning of Treason* (1947). The trajectory thus described, I argue, echoes West's sense of the historical culmination of the process by which the subject's freedom to imagine his or her identity dissolved in the face of state documentation. I use accounts of the history of identity documents and of the legal history of treason to provide historical context here. Rather than reading court reporting and the close analysis of the legal and cultural constitution of the treasonous subject as a retreat from the intellectual concerns of modernism, I understand West's focus on trials themselves and on allegiances to political systems as an interest in twentieth-century forms and subjectivities that was present as well in one of her earliest works.

Chapter 4 is about modernization – economic, political and literary – in the American south. American regional writing, like American regional culture, is most often discussed as less modern than the rest of the country. "Local color" authors were imagined to be capturing the customs and dialects of regional areas before they disappeared into a rapidly homogenizing metropolitan culture. Regional writings' earliest practitioners, then, were associated with realistic depiction, domestic detail, nostalgia and sentiment. They were diminutive genres (the sketch, the peep) or at best serious in a non-literary sense (the slum exposé). They were certainly not art for art's sake. For regional writers clearly to establish their work as part of a modern arts movement – here the cases of William Faulkner and the criticism of the Agrarians come to mind – the most obvious kinds of sentiment and nostalgia had all the more clearly to be disowned, often by marking them as feminized.

Modernist studies currently has no way to place a work like Ellen Glasgow's novel *Barren Ground* (1925) in a constellation alongside regionalists currently recognized as modern stylists, such as Faulkner or Jean Toomer. This is true despite the fact that Glasgow self-conciously and calculatedly sets herself at odds with conventional strains of modernism while stating her intention to do something that sounds very like a New Critical agrarian program: "I would write of the South not sentimentally, as a conquered province, but dispassionately, as a part of the larger world."[45] Starting with this characterization of *Barren Ground* as a southern text, which, like the south, is confronting modernization, I examine the ways in which she imagines the southern text might modernize and to what ends. I define Glasgow against two conventional mappings of modernism: first, a masculine, agrarian and "high" or New Critical modernism and, second, a metropolitan feminist modernism. In place of these, Glasgow produces an account of modernization – both literary and material – using marriage. Glasgow describes both the allegedly private world of marital sentiment and the public world of modernizing agriculture and consumer culture as arenas where states exercise power by granting identity. She makes her heroine Dorinda both one of the "new [white] men" of U.S. agricultural business who are being integrated into a national economy and a woman who suffers that stock tragedy of the sentimental genres – she is jilted. Marriage, far from being obsolete, serves as a model for state-sanctioned consent and public identity in the twentieth century. I use accounts of the history of professional agriculture and of the legal history of marriage to discuss Dorinda's two functions. Thus, we find Glasgow's most intense engagement with modernism located in a trope usually associated with sentiment or realism but which in Glasgow's hands is eminently modern. I conclude with a brief consideration of how my reading of *Barren Ground* might produce a new sense of the source of both regionalism and modernism in Jean Toomer's *Cane* (1923). I argue that Toomer's aesthetic is not a stylistic reflection of the clash of urban and rural in the south so much as it is a reading of the planned uneven and racialized modernity inherent in twentieth-century regional planning.

In Chapter 5 I juxtapose D. W. Griffith's film *The Birth of a Nation* (1915) and Zora Neale Hurston's ethnography *Tell My Horse: Voodoo and Life in Haiti and Jamaica* (1938). I use the surprising similarities between these two works to argue that modernist primitivism and its construction of "natives" are not psycho-sexual fantasies but rather political ones. In a historical moment of rising postcolonial movements and changes in the rhetoric and modes of imperial governance, "natives" appeared to be the only people in the world who grasped the insidiousness behind promises of modern democratic enfranchisement well enough to wish to resist them. Elite Westerners had already lost the battle; U.S. "democratic occupancies" between the wars revealed how. World War I opens into modernism not only through the battlefields of Europe and the "men of 1914" but also through Woodrow Wilson's principles of ethno-linguistic determination for defining the boundaries and subjects of a modern nation-state, principles informed by anthropology's redefinition of "culture."

Griffith reaches back to Reconstruction, when the problem for white men was that black men were being enfranchised (theoretically) on equal levels. But he actually articulates and tries to solve a different problem: that enfranchisement didn't actually work in the way the liberal individualistic view of representative democracy claimed it would. Hurston rewrites the conventions of ethnographic narrative to describe "Haitian culture" not as a set of traditional practices independent of history but as the result of Haiti's colonization, the revolution in 1791, independence in 1804 and the more recent U.S. occupation.

CHAPTER I

White zombies in the state machinery

The horror of the 1932 Bela Lugosi film *White Zombie* (dir. Victor Halperin), released in the seventeenth year of the U.S. occupation of Haiti, lies in the anxieties it raises about the fundamental similarities of modern "democratic" colonial rule and ordinary twentieth-century governance of Western citizens "at home." The film articulates and resolves these anxieties using aesthetic strategies we usually associate with the popular and generic (sentimental, gothic, linear narrative) rather than with modernism. Halperin detaches these aesthetic strategies from their original genres to make of them historical responses to the problem of holding and recognizing individual agency in a modernizing world. Analyzing this film in these terms produces a definition of modernism that is neither merely a set of aesthetic requirements nor solely focused on cultural content.

To substantiate the ways in which this reading of Halperin's film allows for a rereading of modernist literary history, I follow it with a discussion of a problem T. S. Eliot set for his own criticism – how to value Rudyard Kipling, "the poet of empire," aesthetically. Eliot eventually comes to argue that the geopolitics in Kipling's work he originally claimed made it transitory actually marked it as prescient of how fundamental national identity and the state's uses of culture had become to the critical projects and social position of the "man of letters" in the twentieth century. In other words, my reading of *White Zombie* as modernist has a precedent in a little-noted avenue of Eliot's critical writing.

In *White Zombie*, a white and clearly non-Haitian zombie master named Murder Legendre (Bela Lugosi) uses Haitian people turned into zombies as labor for his sugar-cane plantation and mill.[1] In one of the most striking sequences of the film, zombie laborers walk around a bi-level mill inside a large stone building. On the top level, zombies carrying baskets of what is presumably sugar cane balanced on their heads walk slowly, staring into space, stiff-legged. As they pass the mill, they dump the contents of their baskets. A shot from above shows that there are two sets of gears, one on top of the other, turning in opposite directions. The sugar cane falls onto the gears to be ground. Below the zombies carrying baskets is another circle of zombies, each pushing on a spoke of a larger wheel that moves all the gears above them. They too stare unseeingly into space as they walk their endless circle. The shots from above emphasize the concentric and interrelated circles around which the perfectly aligned and evenly interspersed men are oriented. The soundtrack consists of the mechanical sounds produced by the mill.

The viewer tours the mill through the movements of Beaumont, a wealthy white planter who has fallen in love with Madeline, a beautiful white woman who has come to Haiti to marry her white fiancé Neil. Beaumont has lured the couple to his mansion on the pretense that, having met Madeline on the boat coming over, he likes her so much he wants to host their wedding and give Neil a job. Beaumont plans, however, to have the zombie master kidnap Madeline; he thinks he can make Madeline love him if he delays the wedding.

The shot/reverse shot pattern in this sequence makes it clear that the viewer is both seeing what Beaumont sees and witnessing the beginning of his entrance into the zombie master's machine. We see his moving body surrounded by different frames: sometimes angles and parts of the mill building, sometimes shadows cast by the machinery or the machinery itself. These shots clearly foreshadow Beaumont's eventual fate as a zombie. The emphasis on how deeply into an implausibly labyrinthine mill he must penetrate to reach the zombie master illustrates his slow capitulation to what will become a plan to turn Madeline into a zombie.[2] Beaumont has never been inside the mill and wears an expression of shock as he observes the workers. He sees a man coming up to put his sugar cane into the mill fall into the machinery and disappear. The other zombies around him keep working without responding; the fallen man does not even cry out.

The horror zombies index at this moment in the film is the possibility that a human can be alive but without the essential characteristics of humanity, in the popularly understood sense of what distinguishes humans from animals, who are *merely* alive. Beaumont confronts the idea that there can be living humans who can't comprehend or control their own actions, recognize their bonds with others like them, or value their lives. To put this another way, what horrifies Beaumont is a particular kind of subjectivity.

His horror doesn't immediately translate into fear (though given the movie's overexplicit foreshadowing it probably should) but rather into an outrage that reveals all kinds of implicit and explicit investments in what kinds of humans actually live or should continue to live as non-zombies. Upon being ushered at last into the zombie master's presence, Beaumont refuses to shake hands with Legendre, looking significantly back at the mill workers when the zombie master holds out his hand. Maintaining his composure and exaggerated politeness (other than clutching his rejected hand into a claw before pulling it back), the zombie master refers to a journey he has taken, "looking for men for my mill." "Men?" Beaumont sneers at the zombie master for being the kind of man who would make or use zombies. He bases his claim of superiority, despite the fact that he is there to hire the man to kidnap Madeline, on his commitment to recognizing the subjectivities of others. The punishment (denial of the handshake) therefore fits the crime in the sense that he will pointedly refuse to acknowledge that Murder is a man like himself. That is to say, he is better than the zombie master both because he wouldn't use zombie labor and because he understands that even if one does use it, one shouldn't call it human. Perversely, the zombies allow him to feel self-righteous about kidnapping. While he plans to imprison Madeline against her will, his goal would not be to take away her will. Eventually she would come to want what he wants. Beaumont claims kidnapping is not coercive, but merely gives him a sort of sporting chance. "Give me a month," he says, to get her to change her mind and fall in love with him. The zombie master insists that Beaumont's plan will never work. "Do you think she will forget her lover in a month? ... Not in a month, nor even in a year. I looked into her eyes. She is deeply in love, but not with you." Legendre is the one who insists on the integrity of Madeline's desires. Beaumont, despite his sneer at the zombie master, and despite his avowed respect for what makes *men* men, is willing to believe that Madeline does not know her own will or that he could change it. And ultimately, despite his insistence that making Madeline into a zombie in order to have her is something repugnant to him, when he is unable to change her mind by wooing her (as he walks her down the aisle!) he gives her the poison.

What is fascinating about this is that it takes so long for Beaumont to recognize that a woman who is of the living dead will be as horrifying as the men who so shock and disgust him that he will not shake the zombie master's hand. How is it that Beaumont can possibly imagine, even briefly, that a zombified Madeline might be satisfying to him in his house when he is outraged by the very suggestion that he might have come to the zombie master in order to get zombie labor for his plantation? When isn't simple slavery enough horror for a Caribbean horror movie? When zombies can be white men.

This is not to say that the film advocates Madeline being turned into a zombie because she is a woman. On the contrary, as I will argue shortly, our ability to recognize her consent to institutionalized heterosexuality as an act of free will is the centerpiece of the film's resolution. My point is that Beaumont has to learn that female loss of will is horrifying – he does not simply know it. Nor do I claim that Beaumont identifies simply with "men" – and this is significant too. His subsequent battles with the zombie master never again make the position of black zombies (male or female) the center of a moral claim. The film shifts dramatically, in other words, from using the loss of black male subjectivity to using the loss of white female subjectivity to invoke horror at what zombification entails. Later, the film shifts its focus again, from the horror of Madeline's zombification to the horror of Beaumont's. Beaumont's subjection is more horrible partly because it is more drawn out and detailed. Moreover, it seems more unnatural than Madeline's zombification because a compliant white man can't be eroticized within the heterosexual economy of this film in the way a compliant white woman can be. Whereas Madeline simply falls "dead" at her wedding dinner, unaware of what is happening, Beaumont knows what is coming. He struggles vainly, his movements becoming clumsier and clumsier, as the zombie master's manner becomes more and more gentle, soothing and solicitous. The contrast between Legendre's attractive and seductive offer of comfort and empathy that makes "giving in" seem desirable and what giving in to the zombie master entails adds intensity to a scene that might otherwise seem far too long. The spuriousness of the master's proffered warmth is apparent only in his reference to an earlier moment. His tone of voice and gestures are oddly kind. Beaumont struggles and finally manages to place his hand pleadingly on Legendre's. Legendre looks at him and says gently, "You refused to shake hands once, I remember. Well, well. We understand each other better now." He pats Beaumont's hand. It is more agonizing to see Beaumont succumb than to see Madeline succumb in ways that secure the greater importance and interest of his subjectivity as well as its greater original distance from the state of being a zombie. If one renders unconscious or kills the zombie master his zombies are released. Beaumont mysteriously has the mental wherewithal to struggle out of a zombie state long enough to redeem himself by preventing the zombie master's last stand; they both plunge off a cliff into the ocean. Even the zombie master himself acknowledges the importance of Beaumont's subjectivity as he watches him succumb to the drug, saying that it is too bad Beaumont has lost the power of speech because he (the master) would be very interested in hearing an account of his symptoms: "You are the first man to know what is happening. None of the others did."

White male subjectivity becomes the ideal vehicle through which to articulate the pathos of zombification and to convey the danger of eliding the difference between the living and the living dead. The scene of circular movement by the zombies incorporates commonplaces about the mechanization of the body under regimes of modern labor even as it references the earlier regime of slavery in the Caribbean by depicting black male bodies in a sugar mill. With this, the film somewhat circularly asserts not only that simple slavery is not horrible enough to create this horror film (they aren't just slaves, they're zombies!) but also that the similarities between the situation of these zombies and the situation of slaves prove just how horrible it is to be a zombie. The film rests its case on the idea that a barbaric past practice has intruded into modernity while contradictorily asserting that the modern laborer (automaton) and the slave may come from the same moment. It nonetheless represents its moment as one in which the most fundamental structures of individualism and free will, most easily recognized when white people, especially white men, lose them, are in danger. But the film does not articulate these losses *only* in terms of racial and gender fates that "should be" incompatible with whiteness, though it does do this. After all, the title appeals to the same titillating logic whereby nineteenth-century sensational narratives about "white slave traffic" appealed to their assumed white audience: a *white* slave is of special interest because s/he is illegitimately overpowered and out of place under a particular kind of subordination, and suggests that the reader might not be as secure in his/her place as s/he thought.

My point is not that the film is politically retrograde in its gendered and racial codings – an ahistorical reading with low stakes – but rather that the way it holds (seemingly) asynchronous cultural codings of labor in tension (whether intentionally or not) acknowledges that "free" labor, like marital "consent," is not the pure product of increased rationality. As Gilroy puts it, modernity must be understood in terms of the "complicity of racial terror with reason." He continues "whether [slavery] encapsulates the inner essence of capitalism or was a vestigial, essentially pre-capitalist element in a dependent relationship to capitalism proper, it provided the foundations for a distinctive network of economic, social and political relations."[3] That is to say, the debate on where to draw the temporal and geographical boundaries of "modernity" may function to disguise modernity's essential heterogeneity. While in many discussions about abstract modernity the fragment gets cited as characteristic, the debate about slavery (or imperialism), capitalism and modernity often seems strangely unable to imagine these as part of modernity's fragments but only as symptoms, exceptions, causes or effects.[4] *White Zombie* may not resolve the problem of a racialized modernity in which history does not play out as progress, but it vividly visually marks this problem as central to its assumptions.

The colonial living dead of *White Zombie* have special significance: they perpetrate even while grossly parodying and exposing the illusion of free (national) will. "Blackness" is not only racial but also national. Some of the zombies are possibly "white" but all are understood to be Haitian. "Natives" are not understood in this film as strictly racial, nor is zombification understood as a native practice.[5] The zombie master is white and foreign, but the point is not so much that he is a white man turning blacks into zombies. Rather, he is a foreigner turning Haitians into zombies. In one scene he introduces a crew of zombies to Beaumont as a demonstration of his power:

In their lifetime they were my enemies. Latour, the witch doctor, once my master. The secrets I tortured out of him! Von Gelder, the swine, swollen with riches he fought against my spell even to the last. . . . Victor Trisher, Minister of the Interior; Scarpia, the brigand chief; Marquis, captain of the gendarmerie; and this – this is Chauvin, the high executioner, who almost executed *me*!

In a metaphor for Haiti's status, a foreign man came to Haiti, became a zombie master and subdued leading figures of the formerly independent Haitian administration, the anti-U.S. nationalist movement, the Haitian elite and a native religion that would have been popularly understood as a powerful force in national life. Natives have no defense against or useful practical knowledge about zombification. When Neil and Bruner, the local missionary, try to find out what really happened to Madeline (Neil goes to her tomb and finds it empty), Bruner develops his theory from a law statute. If it is against the law to perpetrate living death, there must be such a thing as living death. But he finds that the native witch doctor can give him no further information beyond the (staggeringly) obvious: "It is dangerous to go to the land of the living dead."

The nationalist representatives the zombie master conquers do not die as national martyrs but live on as poor imitations of Haitians in a kind of technical relation to their previous identities as citizens. They appear alive in their national identities but are "really" "voluntarily" doing what the zombie master wants. This technical relation echoes the form and style of U.S. imperialism in Haiti. The United States, rather than literally taking over Haiti by administering it as a colony, tried to maintain an appearance of Haitian independence and volition. For instance, Haiti would elect its own president, even though that president was selected by the United States. Rather than simply setting aside the Haitian constitution and seizing land, the United States wrote a new constitution permitting foreign investment, so that Haiti would still technically be a republic. The United States needed to put down resistance by the Cacos, nationalist guerilla fighters, and to police the cities. After all, Legendre tells Beaumont, if the zombies regain their souls, they will tear him apart. But the United States used the Haitian *gendarmerie*, a Haitian military force invented, trained and officered by U.S. Marines in addition to the marines' expeditionary forces.[6]

The zombies and the zombie master symbolically replay the central problem of a so-called "democratic occupancy" – indeed, of liberal democratic governance itself. Democratic governance is not supposed to force interests on but rather engage and enlist the willing participation of governed individuals.[7] Juxtaposing a white male zombie against the black Haitian zombies in *White Zombie* expresses the dilemma of the white, elite twentieth-century citizen–subject. The zombie figure gestures at slavery in its comparison of coerced labor with the kind of automaton-like routines and material positions demanded by modern industrialization. However, particularly in the context of Haiti, slave labor implies the capacity for revolt. The zombie is not simply a slave. Slaves know which of their actions are coerced. The zombie, on the other hand, encapsulates a different subject(ive) position. The living dead act without being overtly coerced but are not acting of their own volition. More significantly, a zombie does not understand his own condition. He is not forced to act against his will; his will has been changed.

The zombie is Haiti's enfranchised subject:[8] the modern worker, the modern voter and the modern bureaucrat or administrator whose "field of responsible freedom was shrinking," as Weber understood it, because of the historical development of state bureaucratic management.[9] The alienation the zombie represents does not emerge, as Marx would have it, solely from the separation of the worker from the material means of production. According to Weber, the historical dynamic Marx describes is not a fundamental cause, but one of a number of analogous expropriative historical processes that effectively decrease individual agency:

> The whole process [of the development of the modern state] is a complete parallel to the development of the capitalist enterprise through gradual expropriation of the independent producers. In the end, the modern state controls the total means of political organization, which actually come together under a single head. No single official personally owns the money he pays out, or the buildings, stores, tools, and war machines he controls. In the contemporary "state" – and this is essential for the concept of the state – the "separation" of the administrative staff, of the administrative officials, and of the workers from the material means of administrative organization is completed. Here the most modern development begins.[10]

The citizen experiences this as inexplicable (which may explain the modernist turn to the supernatural, the primitive and the psychological) because political expropriation and the development of bureaucracy as Weber describes them here are accompanied by and supposedly depend on democratization – redistributing political power. This would include measures such as mass enfranchisement, equality before the law and the end of "notable rule" (the distribution of employment and authority based on personal connections or class identity rather than training and expertise). But, Weber cautions, mass democratization "does not necessarily mean an increasingly active share of the governed in the authority of the social structure."[11] Instead, democratization makes a passive electorate necessary: "It is unimaginable how in large associations elections could function at all without this managerial pattern. In practice this means the division of the citizens with the right to vote into politically active and politically passive elements."[12]

The establishment of administrative form and ritual, that is, bureaucratized electoral or constitutional procedures, seems to initiate two opposed effects on citizens' political power. On the one hand, these state forms are supposed to provide a structure for converting the passive *governed* into an active *electorate*. In a representative democracy with universal franchise, citizens act through the decisions, actions and policies of elected officials. This presumes that the more general meaning of "enfranchise," "to set free," permeates the more technical "to give citizenship, political privileges or rights to," and the more specific "to grant the right to vote." The logic here is that form, in addition to keeping citizens equal to one another in their exercises of power, circumscribes what would otherwise be the arbitrary exercise of state power.

On the other hand, as many of his readers have recognized, Weber places legitimation at the core of twentieth-century state power. The state is a "compulsory association which organizes domination," and has an "especially intimate" relationship with violence, but it must over the long term "(successfully) claim ... the *monopoly of the legitimate use of physical force* within a given territory."[13] What the modern state manages most adroitly is presenting the coercion at the heart of governance as at worst consensual and ideally participatory – but in any case derived from the will of the governed. This too is accomplished through consistent and preexisting forms. The stability of state forms underscores their inaccessibility to individual negotiation. It would be impossible to maintain a state in which each citizen negotiated his or her particular terms of citizenship. State forms collect and organize power rather than redistributing it. In the twentieth-century liberal democratic state, the social contract must be continuously reenacted in plain sight. State forms provide a way for citizens *publicly* to agree that the state is exercising their power properly and that they have been active in their representation. It should be clear that both tendencies of state form – to create autonomous and active "citizens" out of the passive governed *and* to display and redefine the powers thus granted – work simultaneously. This is consent-as-agency.

The degree to which the field of responsible freedom shrinks, then, is in inverse proportion to the degree to which agency and choice are successfully redefined at this historical moment in terms of the power merely to legitimate, through consent, already existing institutional and structural arrangements for the exercise of political power. Seemingly possessed of agency derived from the secularism, rationalism and individualism which characterize modern institutions (liberal contractual labor, enfranchisement, consumption, self-consciousness) the elite citizen nonetheless finds, despite the state's assertion that the modalities of power are in plain sight, that enfranchisement conceals its contradictions.[14]

The figure of the zombie in Halperin's film visually renders these structural politics as the fear of becoming nothing but a body endlessly consenting to its own lack of autonomy. Zombies are not frightening as predators. On that level, they function simply as Legendre's goons, even if it is inconvenient and shocking that they cannot be killed with bullets. Significantly, fear of becoming a zombie does not encompass any kind of painful physical transformation, nor does "living" as a zombie entail emotional pain from being forced to perform actions against one's will. Zombies, with the exception of Beaumont, do not even realize what is happening to them until it is over, at which point they no longer have subjectivity. When Legendre displays his formerly nationalist but now colonized zombies to Beaumont, they are not humiliated by his gloating.

They feel nothing. The fear and horror Beaumont experiences come entirely from imagining himself as being that kind of puppet and *not knowing* that he is. In other words, horror is the modality of state power in plain sight. Is he now a zombie without knowing it?

I have already argued that Legendre's zombie mill workers and personal servants describe shrinking fields of freedom with regard to modern labor and to colonial peoples. On the crudest level, the film expresses this in terms of race – horror is treating a white Western man as if he were a black Caribbean man. The elite, enfranchised Western citizen is a *white* zombie and notable as such because his position should have exempted him from the kinds of coercions historically reserved for non-whites.

But the horror of Beaumont's transformation is also gendered. Halperin asserts that it is more significant to violate Beaumont's self-conscious subjectivity than Madeline's with his visual effects. Remember not only how ridiculously long it takes for Beaumont to realize that it is wrong to turn Madeline into a zombie (even though he realizes immediately that it is wrong to turn men into zombies) but also how much more visually natural, even beautiful, Halperin is able to make Madeline-as-zombie in comparison to Beaumont-as-zombie. Madeline first appears as a zombie in a long shot of the castle interior. The shot is so long, in fact, that it is impossible to tell that she is a zombie. Beaumont listens to her play the piano from far across the room. In comparison to the mill scene, which immediately and sharply distinguishes the male zombies from normal men, the opening of this scene underscores the way in which a zombie bride *resembles* a normal bride.

The long shot, coupled with the way Beaumont watches her from such a distance, also emphasizes the way in which this normalcy is an effect of women's visuality. Men become monstrous and grotesque upon losing their individuality and agency and appear as spectacular monsters. Women's spectacularity as zombies, on the other hand, is harder to distinguish from their spectacularity as women. Madeline is still beautiful as a zombie rather than appearing awkward, grotesque and out of place. Her face is unaltered, her hair is styled and she wears beautiful clothing. Many of the male zombies have cadaverous faces; they all have rough sackcloth-like clothing. Some have injured limbs tied up in makeshift braces. Their eyes seem to bulge out of their heads. All move clumsily, as when the zombie leading Beaumont to his meeting with Legendre paws at his shoulder to catch his attention. Madeline's movements, though slower, are graceful. Her white dresses billow around her; even as a zombie she is meant to produce visual pleasure. When Legendre summons her, she glides through the castle, holding her arms out gracefully; that is to say, she moves in a way that should make us realize that "feminine grace" is constructed from non-functional, unnatural movement.

Eadweard Muybridge's famous late nineteenth-century stop-action pictorial motion sequences included naked or nearly naked men and women performing everyday activities chosen to show a wide range of human movement. But, as Linda Williams points out, he did not have his men and women perform the same tasks the same way. Women added excess and non-functional actions to their activities:

When the women perform the same activities as the men, these activities are often accompanied by some superfluous detail, such as an inexplicable raising of a hand to the mouth. ... If a woman runs, her run is marked by a similarly gratuitous gesture of grasping her breast ... the physical business of the women is less clearly defined and their self-consciousness in its performance is much greater; they blow kisses, narcissistically twirl about, endlessly flirt fans, and wear transparent drapery that emphasizes the nudity underneath.[15]

This underscores the chief difference between Madeline and the male zombies: they are laborers and she is not. Their motions look "wrong" because the male body is supposed to work efficiently. Male grace derives from function. Madeline, on the other hand, does not work. As she moves through the castle, doors mysteriously open before her. When she plays the piano (a task which, in the hands of women, is leisure rather than work) we don't see her hands. Moreover, while Beaumont is explaining and apologizing to her unresponsive and beautiful form, her image appears as a reflection on the piano's polished and raised top – she has become, as she always was for Beaumont, a pure, infinitely reproducible image.[16]

Nonetheless, the male white zombie, for all that he alone of Legendre's zombies is able partially to resist Legendre's power, can neither be redeemed nor resolve the film. Beaumont struggles against Legendre's power and helps Dr. Bruner to defeat him, but then tumbles over the cliff to drown with Legendre and the other zombies. The film never offers any explicit explanations for why Beaumont is so exceptional (or so typical). But, as I argued above, it identifies the endangered white male subject as the vehicle that most clearly conveys the seriousness of the modern threat to individual political agency. As many political theorists have made clear, maintaining the paradigmatic liberal subject's existence as "free" requires understanding (and compensating for) any elements of subordination to the state as not actually characteristic of the true liberal subject. Thus, as Brown explains it, the ur-liberal subject is masculinist: "the attributes and activities of citizenship and personhood within liberalism produce, require, and at the same time disavow their feminized opposites ... the liberal subject emerges as pervasively masculinist not only in its founding exclusions and stratifications but in its contemporary discursive life."[17] As a man who resists the zombie master, Beaumont remains a sovereign subject who has never consented (unlike Madeline or the non-white laborers), and thus offers the ideal of autonomous personhood for the film. The historicized horror of *White Zombie* is that the exclusions of liberalism no longer work. The colonial citizen, the worker and the voter are all consenting citizen-subjects, rather than citizens. Beaumont is dead and the bumbling, hapless Neil is "alive" (so hapless he doesn't need to be turned into a zombie). *White Zombie*'s ending does not alleviate anxiety about the possibilities for modern masculinist political agency (even though Legendre dies) so much as it offers structural metaphors for creating the undead *legitimately*.

This is why the film must also stage the freedom and desire of a female marital subject, the zombie bride. Madeleine's white wedding lasts the length of the film and provides the film's narrative motive and structure. Action in the first part of the film revolves around Beaumont's plots to stop Madeline and Neil's wedding. He is unsuccessful, and Madeline and Neil complete their wedding ceremony off camera. In the next scene, she falls "dead" at her wedding dinner. After this, the film's impetus is to fulfill the marital form suggested at the first sequence: a bride meets her groom at the altar of her own free will. The ceremony is familiar and incomplete; the audience knows both that it must be completed and how it should be completed. Madeline must reclaim her subjectivity so that she can return to Neil as a fully sentient and fully desiring bride.

The zombie combines horror and melodrama in the female – the bride's – body because women, in giving their consent, are presumed not to have the same kind of agency at stake as men. Even when Beaumont realizes the meaning of the fact that Madeline cannot appreciate his gift of a necklace and regrets his actions ("Foolish things [the jewels]. They can't bring back the light to those eyes"), he reiterates the idea that Madeline could have made his act unnecessary by consenting to an equivalent of it: "I was mad to do this but if you'd smiled on me I'd have done anything, given you anything! I thought that beauty alone would satisfy, but the soul is gone! I can't bear those empty staring eyes. Oh, forgive me

Madeline, forgive me! I can't bear it any longer! I must take you back." Signs of feeling that can be read (eyes, smiles) could legitimate subordination. Note here that Beaumont says he can't stand looking at a blank face. The problem is not that Beaumont forced Madeline to do something against her will. Rather, it is that she forced Beaumont to acknowledge that it was against her will, or, in the context of the larger argument I am making about the consenting citizen, her eyes force him to see that consent is always a product of unequal power and mediated by authority.

As other critics have noted, the men in the film all have Madeline as a sexual object, even as she triangulates changing relationships among the men. More significant is that these sexualized relationships with Madeline are all defined in terms of consent, freedom, coercion and readability rather than in terms of purity or property. Within the morality scheme of the film, Neil has her legitimate consent and is therefore her rightful lover. Upon learning that Madeline may have been abducted alive from her tomb, Neil exclaims, "You mean she's in the hands of natives? Better dead than that!" The audience knows he is on the wrong track, and moreover, an outdated track. Illicitness consists now of tampering with the transparency of desire. "Illicit" practices such as bondage are illicit because they make something that is voluntary look coerced. Beaumont and Legendre's illicitness comes from the same idea of distorted transparency: both want to make something coerced look voluntary. Beaumont and Legendre differ in degree rather than kind. Beaumont wants to replace Neil in the domestic fantasy of a marriage in which the bride shows with her eyes and smiles that she wants to be a/his bride; Legendre wants Madeline to kill Neil.

The final scene of the film completes the wedding ceremony Beaumont and Legendre interrupted to emphasize both the significance and transparency of bridal desire. After Legendre dies, Madeline once again turns to Neil ("Madeline, my darling!" "Neil, I ... I dreamed ... "). Neil and Madeline play out a version of a wedding ceremony with their clear statements of each other's names (recognition) and clear visual cues about how much they love each other. Madeline's expressions, especially, demonstrate that she is fully consenting and desiring. They have finally properly and transparently and ceremoniously taken each other. Bruner interrupts their kiss by tapping Neil on the shoulder to ask whether he has a match – the film's running joke about Bruner and his pipe. Making this the last line (and shot) of the film emphasizes the degree to which the wedding ceremony ("the match") can be conclusive. Thus, the film opens with the problem of zombies, a question of labor and colonization, puts this problem in terms of marital form, and then offers a formal solution. The zombies simply tumble off the cliff like their master, leaving the "wedding" to stand as the answer to the larger problems these zombies raised about modernization and laboring bodies at home and abroad.[18]

This conclusion can resolve the film's political anxieties about modernization, labor and American imperialism because marital consent, particularly bridal consent, has a political history of acknowledging, recuperating and legitimating the subordinating nature of structures of consent in political life. As with eighteenth-century theories of social contract, consent legitimated the structures of rights and responsibilities people accepted when they married. The material and symbolic importance of the concept of legitimate consent and voluntary association increased when the end of slavery supposedly eliminated involuntary labor contracts, reinforcing the idea that American economic systems and political values were grounded in individuals' free choices.[19]

This may have, as Nancy Cott puts it, "consecrated" the aspect of consent in the wage labor contract. Indeed, it may have consecrated the American (male) laborer as the exemplary citizen. But American women's rights activists frequently compared women with slaves during the nineteenth century. Though the two statuses were hardly the same, the comparison allowed these critics to theorize marriage contracts as revealing deeply embedded contradictions in the consent model and, thus, in the American social contract generally.[20]

This explains why the bride has served as a more intuitive symbol for the citizen's relationship to the state than the groom. The paradox of her relationship to marriage is the same as that of the citizen to representative government: her ability to consent is precisely what constitutes and legitimates her subordination in the (social) contract. The figure of the bride differs from the male zombie-citizen in that the naturalization and privatization of women's subordination through romance sets up a cycle that continually produces and then alleviates anxiety about whether we can discern bridal agency and what it would mean if the bride did not have agency. Madeline as zombie raises the specter of unfree consent to forms; Madeline as bride recuperates modern consent and citizenship.

Courts and legislatures modernized American marriage regulation at the turn of the century to redefine marriage as a matter for public interest and state intervention rather than, as formerly, a private contract between two individuals. This redefinition reflected a broader social agreement that intimate romantic love was the foundation of marriage and that the courts should not "sully" it with the kind of adjudication they applied to commercial contracts. At the same time, sociologists and other social scientists publicized theories about marriage's role in creating stable societies. A new sense of a public interest in supporting marriage and in preventing divorce developed.

In his work on the judicial and cultural history of the breach-of-marriage-promise suit, historian Michael Grossberg connects this developing public interest in marriage to a greater willingness on the part of citizens to understand their identities as state-generated. People began to accept state interventions into everyday life such as information gathering and to allow the state to define which events would be considered significant, that is, which events would require legal documentation:

[M]any reformers ... couched their proposals [about regulating marriage] in nostalgic terms. Yet their calls for more stringent state intervention rested on a new relationship between the individual and the state which bore little resemblance to the colonial bonds to which many reformers referred. The hierarchical, patriarchal family no longer served as a buffer between people and public authority. Each citizen's legal identity now had its source in his or her individuality, not in family or community membership.[21]

Here Grossberg draws attention to the way early twentieth-century descriptions of institutionalized marriage used the rhetoric of anti-modernity and of the sentimentalized pastoral family structure to advocate the kind of statism we usually associate with modernizing industrialization.

In her study of the public and political functions of marriage in forming and maintaining the American nation, Cott similarly examines how marriage's associations with authentic desire, mutual benefit and voluntarily relinquishing individual authority made it a model for explaining the citizen's relationship to the nation. These were so tightly intertwined, she argues, that immigrant groups whose marriage practices resembled arranged marriage in any way were categorized as unfit to be Americans because they lacked a fundamental understanding of the free consent that grounded American democratic government and civic participation.[22]

Both Grossberg and Cott locate marriage's utility for describing modernity in its ability to organize contradictory associations. The institutionalization of marriage demonstrates that individual personal desires can be formally equated for purposes of rational administration. But erotic heterosexual love also represents desire so personal and authentic it counters the rationality of modern institutionalization.

Thus, twentieth-century marriage provided a metaphor for the contradictory production of modern selfhood in the context of instrumental rationality. The definition of the term "modernity," Rita Felski writes, "typically includes a general philosophical distinction between traditional societies, which are structured around the omnipresence of divine authority, and a ... secularized universe predicated upon a individuated and self-conscious subjectivity."[23] I have been using the term "modernization" to refer to the spread of modern large-scale systems of social and economic organization, including capitalist markets, industrialized production, bureaucratic institutions, scientific and technological development and systems of representative government. All of these tend, as Weber might put it, toward impersonality and standardization. Modernization threatens the very "individuated and self-conscious subjectivity" it produces. Brown explains this as a logical consequence of the development of this liberal self:

[T]he state rises in importance with liberalism precisely through its provision of essential social repairs, economic problem solving, and the management of a mass population. ... As the social body is stressed and torn by the secularizing and atomizing effects of capitalism and its attendant political culture of individuating rights and liberties, economic, administrative, and legislative forms of repair are required. Through a variety of agencies and regulations, the liberal state provides webbing for the social body dismembered by liberal individualism and also administers the increasing number of subjects disenfranchised and deracinated by capital's destruction of social and geographic bonds.[24]

The social and regulatory history of marriage is a nearly perfect example of how the liberal state treats subjects entering marriage individually and self-consciously, as opposed to sacramentally or socially. The first sentence could describe the ways in which the state uses marriage to disburse economic benefits (or shift the responsibility for providing them), grant citizenship rights, regulate the biological composition of a population and define the public, the public good and public authority. But the figural aspects of Brown's language in this passage contain a narrative in excess of its political and historical analysis. In rendering the social as a body "stressed," "torn" and "dismembered," Brown describes these political changes in terms of the "injury" of her book's title despite her criticism of injury as a foundation for political change or analysis.[25] The artificial "webbing" is the first of the words that establish society before the rise of the liberal state as natural and unconstructed – again, despite Brown's actual anti-nostalgia. Finally, the state presides over a collection of bodies within this violated social body, and these, despite being "disenfranchised and deracinated" (a combination that describes a political condition in terms of violence and unnaturalness), are still alive, but without their former connections to society. They are monstrous; they are the living dead. This passage gestures back to similar narrative excesses in Weber's and Marx's great analyses of modernity upon which Brown draws. Weber, in setting erotic love against modern rationality, departs from sociological style:

This boundless giving of oneself is as radical as possible in its opposition to all functionality, rationality, and generality. It is displayed here as the unique meaning which one creature in his irrationality has for another, and only for this specific other. ... The lover realizes himself to be rooted in the kernel of the truly living, which is eternally inaccessible to any rational endeavor. He knows himself to be freed from the cold skeleton hands of rational orders, just as completely as from the banality of everyday routine.[26]

Animated skeleton hands and a distinction between the "truly living" and, implicitly, the walking dead raise the idea of excess meaning conceived as monstrosity, as if one of the problems of large-scale rationalization is that it has no language to describe itself. This rhetorical turn poses the problem of analyzing modernity as the problem of identifying and describing dismembered subjects. This is an aesthetic problem that cannot be solved by (to put it in the traditional modernist studies terms) countering the insufficiency of modern functionalism with the expansive irrationality of art. The excess and the monsters are as historically contingent as the cultural circumstances that conjure them.

When we understand modernist aesthetic excess and monstrosity to emerge from the state's consolidation of its subjects through administrative forms, we can see that *White Zombie*'s modernism lies precisely in the characteristics that might seem to mark it as so conventional (horror, melodrama, sentiment) as to be unconscious of its aesthetic and its historical moments and the implications of its medium.

Halperin's zombies are far from generic. As my readings of Brown and Weber's passages suggest, the zombie, no less than the bride, is a historicized figure. The zombie is a characteristically twentieth-century monster (as, perhaps, the vampire is a nineteenth-century one) lurking as an excessive irrational metaphor at the edges of the democratized, institutionalized and mechanized citizen's peripheral vision. As for Brown and Weber, supernatural monstrosity emerges alongside rationalized production and organization.[27] This echoes actual media coverage and other writing about Haiti during the U.S. occupation: the standard story was either about the most recent changes guided by U.S. modernization, or about voodoo or other native practices.[28] Halperin's aesthetic and formal engagements with horror and sentiment in *White Zombie*, moreover, draw attention to film as a technological, eminently modern, even rational and realistic medium that has incalculable and inexplicable excess narrative.[29]

White Zombie persistently intertwines the technological or mechanical and the primitive.[30] In the case of horror, the paradox is that the technology of realistic depiction makes the supernatural plausible. Halperin places mechanized production and labor alongside earlier modes of production, "native" ritual and supernatural or "magical" causes and effects. Legendre's mill is both plantation and modern factory. His workers are both slaves and reified capitalist laborers. The zombie's jerky and unnatural movements reference the bureaucratic or factory-conditioned modern automaton, the supernatural undead and the way photography (the mechanical eye) functioned (most famously in the case of Muybridge's animal locomotion pictures) to demystify motion too fast for human vision to see.[31] But instead of learning how a horse runs, we see the relationship between capital and labor or between colonizer and colonized. The process by which a person is turned into a zombie is both scientific (the person must ingest or inhale a powder) and magical (Legendre uses wax figures of his victims).

In the course of explaining to a disbelieving Neil that Madeline may not be quite dead, Dr. Bruner makes distinctions between "superstition" and "practice," and between what one sees and what one *believes* one sees. Neil saw her die, he insists, and a doctor signed the certificate. He saw her buried. Bruner replies:

"I've lived in these islands for a good many years and I've seen things with my eyes that made me think I was crazy. There are superstitions in Haiti that the natives brought here from Africa. Some of them can be traced back as far as ancient Egypt and beyond that yet into countries that were old when Egypt was young.... Wherever there is a superstition you will find there is also a practice. Now do you remember what your driver told you the night he took you to Beaumont's house?"

"About those horrible creatures we saw. He said they were corpses taken from their graves." "... That's the superstition. Now for the practice. ... Your driver believes he saw dead men walking. He didn't. What he saw was men alive in everything but this [points to head] and this [points to heart]."

In order to accept Bruner's argument, Neil must learn to define a "superstition" as the irrational version of a scientifically explicable "practice." ("There's been lots of people who have been pronounced dead and came alive and lived for years. Now if nature can play pranks like that, why isn't it possible to play pranks with nature?") He must also admit that like the driver (or Muybridge), he cannot rely on what he thinks he sees. Dr. Bruner finally convinces him with Haiti's Penal Code: "Article 249: The use of drugs or other practices which produce lethargic coma or lifeless sleep shall be considered attempted murder. If the person has been buried alive the act shall be considered murder no matter what result follows."[32] What makes zombies "real" is juridical categorization – state narrative. The juridical version of state narrative focuses on reducing zombies to the legal consequences for creating zombies – attempted murder or murder. Zombies simply become equivalent to dead bodies. But like the ironic narrative of national "sovereignty" buried alive in the title "The Penal Code of Haiti," a nation occupied by the United States whose constitution had been authored by the U.S. government, Article 249 avoids confronting the impact of the walking dead. The rational term "practices" that Bruner counters earlier to "superstition" reverts to being a catch-all term for what the penal code can neither see nor make visible. There are thus two political technologies in Halperin's film. The first, as I have discussed above, is marriage. This second is that of the image, "modernity's most prominent fetish."[33] Only the *image* of the living dead could be so overdetermined. And only the camera can provide that kind of image.

Cinematic technology uses horror and monstrosity to reveal part of what we believe we can see about modernizing subjects and bodies. The visual power of the zombie lies in its shocking presentation of the human body automatized, caught in "the machine" as an apparently consenting citizen-subject. Rey Chow writes of cinematic technology that it

> exaggerates and deconstructs pre-filmic materials, in particular the human body. What becomes clear in the film [*Modern Times*] is how a perception of the spectacular cannot be separated from technology, which turns the human body into the site of experimentation and mass production. . . . In Chaplin's assembly line worker, visuality works toward an automatization of an oppressed figure whose bodily movements become excessive and comical. Being "automatized" means being subjected to social exploitation whose origins are beyond one's individual grasp, but it also means becoming a spectacle whose "aesthetic" power increases with one's increasing awkwardness and helplessness.[34]

In *White Zombie* Halperin converts the excess to monstrosity rather than to comedy, but Chow's point about how cinematic technology generates its aesthetics still applies. One might argue that the kind of bodily distortion Chow finds in comedy is a form of physical monstrosity. The instrumental mechanics of the camera with relation to human bodies parallels the instrumentality of human bodies under industrial capitalist modernity. Paradoxically, this instrumentality generates excess expressivity in the form of cinematic spectacle. But this expressivity is by no means "authentic" or "subjective" with regard either to the subjects it depicts or to the camera's viewpoint. For both Benjamin and Epstein, the significant characteristic of the camera was that it was *different* from a human eye. It was "the camera's perceived ability to circumvent human mediation that gave it such unnatural power."[35] Chow's reading of *Modern Times* suggests that we can think of early cinema and the state as similarly drawing their power (administrative or aesthetic) from the ability to automatize and detach individuals from their social origins, that is, to establish them as primarily related not to other individuals but to a central power – the state and/or the camera.

Halperin uses this function of the camera in *White Zombie* to depict the bride in the same way as he does the zombie. He uses a marriage narrative to question the privacy, authenticity, and agency of even the subject(ivitie)s we think we see. By linking the bride to the zombie, he invokes the most naturalized of sentimental narratives of authority, the consenting bride, alongside the most coerced and unnatural of horror genre monsters. With this juxtaposition, Halperin stresses the technological and mechanical qualities the two have in common. The bride is as administrative a monster as the zombie. Indeed the bride, because of her connection with desire and willingness, can act as an administrator and organizer of modern subjectivity.

The close-up in *White Zombie* is not, then, strictly "sentimental," that is, committed to the idea of expressing and evoking genuine emotion. Halperin is conscious of the camera as a mechanism that reproduces the "truth" and significance of emotional processes while revealing them (and reproductions of them) as manipulable mechanisms themselves. When Dr. Bruner knocks Legendre unconscious, he and Neil rush back to Madeline. She has not been able to recognize Neil, but now she looks around and then, when Neil takes her hand, turns to face him and looks into his eyes. Four close-up shots alternating between Neil and Madeline suggest that Madeline can finally see Neil (the first close-up of Neil is blurry and the second significantly clearer); in the fourth close-up of this sequence, Madeline begins to smile. Neil and Bruner have been watching her intently, Neil with tears in his eyes. Shortly after this, she raises her hand and touches Neil's face. Behind Neil and Bruner, Legendre regains consciousness and raises himself to his feet; Madeline resumes her "zombie" stare and turns away from Neil. Bruner interjects, "I could swear for a moment she recognized you." The close-up of Madeleine's face asserts that it is the self-evidence that founds subjectivity free from outside coercion or construction. Significantly, though, evidence of Madeline's independent subjectivity is not that she recognizes herself or her surroundings (think for instance of the convention of asking people who have regained consciousness whether they remember their own names) but whether she knows her husband or not.

Dr. Bruner's comic interruption of their reunion to ask whether they have a "match" so he can light his pipe underscores the idea that Madeleine's authentic subjectivity and her consent to marriage secure each other. Cott has argued that new twentieth-century media such as film and advertising worked to influence American understandings of marriage by infusing "the notion of consent in marriage with awareness of the magnetizing power of sex." This, she claims, worked to establish "true love"and authentic passion as the only moral basis for marriage and defined this kind of love as utterly resistant to rational considerations. It could not be produced or influenced.[36] As Legendre tells Beaumont, Madeline will never love him: "Not in a month, nor even a year. I have looked at her eyes. She is deep in love, but not with you."

Film technology may mystify emotions by rendering them as irresistible forces with inexplicable origins, but it also demystifies them by claiming that they are readily discerned and mechanically constructed. Legendre, like the audience, knows what he knows because he "looked at her eyes." But of course, there are also the famous shots of *Legendre's* eyes isolated from his face and burning out of the screen. Far from being windows to the "truth" of his soul, his eyes mesmerize and control his victims. Shots of Legendre's eyes in extreme close-up indicate when he is giving instructions to his victims, and have no connection with what Legendre could actually see from where he stands. When he instructs Madeline to come down to the table, take the knife, and go back and kill Neil, she is upstairs in the bedroom. The extreme close-up of his eyes would conventionally imply that he sees her, but this is physically impossible. His "view" is not merely a perspective but *the film itself.* At first he is concerned and annoyed when he learns that Neil is in the castle.

He rises from the table and runs up the stairs when he hears the noise. But as he stands over Neil's unconscious body (Neil has fainted from illness), Halperin cuts from the close-up of Neil's face to Legendre. Lugosi produces a series of facial expressions: he has a problem, he thinks, he gets an idea, he smiles diabolically. He then clasps his hands (a gesture he uses when issuing orders to his zombies) and Halperin gives us an extreme close-up of his eyes. The dissolve is to Madeline lying on a bed; she rises and responds to Legendre's signal. She is, as ordered, about to go to the table where Legendre had been sitting with Beaumont and take the knife. Legendre's idea is that she will kill her own husband. Legendre's eyes see something that is not there and have the power to make it seen.

This perspective is that of the cinematic eye. Note a difference between Legendre looking into Madeline's eyes and the audience looking into her eyes or into Legendre's eyes. The first is supposedly unmediated – Legendre doesn't look at Madeline *through* a camera. These floating eyes are, instead, *like* a camera – inhuman, detached, controlling, unnatural. Legendre presides over the field of visual aesthetic power, of seeing and of producing images. His "close-ups" only seem to accede to the authenticity of human emotions by simply depicting them. In reality he uses his eyes to alter those desires as people turn into zombies under their gaze or perform seemingly voluntary acts at his command.

Jean Epstein explained the significance of the close-up by emphasizing the way it depicted expression about to happen as a gathering, inevitable power. But his metaphors complicate Cott's reading of the close-up as reading sentimentally because they refer to progressive phenomena formerly understood as supernatural transformations before scientific "close-ups" defined them as explicable processes: a disease incubating, pregnancy, liquid coming to a boil, fruit ripening.[37] Early cinematic melodrama, then, naturalizes *in a scientific technological sense* what might have been a narrative of pure inviolable sentiment.

This technical question about the aesthetic-historical meaning of the close-up – is it sentimental/melodramatic or modern(ist)? When? Why? – maps onto *White Zombie*'s critical reception and its use of solidly (some critics might have meant "stolidly") generic styles. Critics faulted Halperin for using out-of-date acting styles ("Its idiocies, moreover, are emphasized by a brand of acting that might have been understandable twenty years ago") and worn-out generic codes ("a potpourri of Zombies, frightened natives, witch doctors, leering villains, sinister shadows, painted sets, and banal conversation. . . . I can think of few films so nicely compounded of tedium and banality in equal parts"). Some critics were willing to rate it slightly higher but only if it were clear that this was in comparison to other horror films. The "kinds of people" who like horror films or the people who liked "those kinds of films" would enjoy it ("*White Zombie* is the latest jitter and gooseflesh cinema ... all have been box office successes"; "The acting of the principal players is uniformly terrible. But that doesn't matter. For you aren't expected to believe in their bizarre adventures. You merely are to be thrilled and appalled by them").[38]

These comments echo both contemporary and modernist-era criticism defining modernist style as a departure both from sentiment and melodrama (genres which emphasized the primacy of feeling and were connected to femininity) and from realism (a style that assumed the transparency of language and images). They also assume that film art was separate from a vulgar market of popular taste and profit-motivated production. I am leaving aside for the moment critical reconsiderations of how effective these "great divides" actually were. I do not argue here that modernism is "really" sentimental, mass culture influenced and so on. My point is rather that this film emerged, and perhaps continues to be read, into a critical paradigm that categorizes its genres and styles as aesthetically archaic because we have not sufficiently marked the presence of the modern state behind monstrosity and marriage's administrative symbolics during this period.

The type of non-human, centralized and centralizing camera eye that Epstein describes in his film theory does not so much make "true" feeling available as create mechanized feeling and pleasure in illusion. As Williams describes happening with instantaneous animal locomotion photographs and the human body, the camera reveals what humans cannot see in a way that defines the thing filmed as a mechanism itself. Moreover, although the initial impulse is to see a previously unseeable "truth," the more significant outcome is that this truth becomes eventually less important than the previously "unsuspected visual pleasure" also delivered.[39] Chow follows a similar line of argument in her description of how the camera functions in melodrama:

Cinema, then, allows us to realize in an unprecedented way the mediated, i.e., techonologized, nature of "melodramatic sentiments." The typical features of melodramatic expression – exaggeration, emotionalism, and Manichaeanism – can thus be redefined as the eruption of the machine in what is believed to be spontaneous. Gestures and emotions are "enlarged" sentimentally the way reality is "enlarged" by the camera lens.[40]

Note here that, as for Williams, the point becomes precisely the opposite of establishing the immutability of the authentic, unconstructed and spontaneous subject. Both Williams and Chow insist that the pleasure taken in the cinematic spectacles they analyze ultimately derives from the exercise of technological power over human bodies and feelings. The visual pleasures of *White Zombie* are organizational and administrative. Zombies and brides/weddings, horror and sentimental melodrama all make something the human eye cannot see available: citizen consent and democratic subjectivity. In the process of doing so they also render it vulnerable to administrative mechanization.

A mocking *New Yorker* review of *White Zombie* may thus have unintentionally come closest to articulating the film's aesthetic:

Whether *Rebecca of Sunnybrook Farm* or *White Zombie* is the more gruesome movie I cannot say with any exactitude. In fact, at times one seems very much like the other. ... I need hardly add that no such similarity was the purpose of the producers of these two films. One was to be the embodiment of sweetness and light, the other the essence of horrors. Nothing in the zombie picture, however, was as creepy to me as the "sunniness" of that Rebecca as she runs about adopting stray infants, bringing them right into the house, reconciling married couples, softening the temper of that rich aunt of hers. ... On the other hand, the mooniness of Mr. Lugosi commands at times a welcome, refreshing titter.[41]

As Rey Chow points out, the medium of cinema allows us to "realize in an unprecedented way the mediated, i.e., technologized, nature of 'melodramatic sentiments.'" Rebecca might well appear creepily like Madeline when we no longer believe in her "sunniness" as she plays her role. Unfortunately, with the archly ironic and superior *New Yorker* house style, J.C.M. (John C. Mosher) reduces what could have been an insight into the aesthetics of modern media to a simplistic attack on sentimentalism and popular culture. "Sunniness" is "creepy" not in the disquieting sense of transposed genres or interarticulated styles (zombie movement as modern movement à la Bresson)[42] but because it is laughably conventional and generic – the close-up is tired, and no one reads *Rebecca of Sunnybrook Farm* anymore: "Rebecca, of course, is Kate Douglas Wiggin's heroine and she moved into the zombie class about twenty years ago."

Following the modernist criticism contemporary with his review, J.C.M. dismisses the sentimental as a form, a set of tropes and a rhetorical stance that can never be unpredictable or transgressive.[43] Ultimately, the point the review makes is that both *Rebecca of Sunnybrook Farm* and

White Zombie are *gruesomely popular*. Both become parodies of their genres: "Mr. Lugosi is now the official interpreter of the macabre on the screen, but he seems, at least in this picture a stagy old party ... as he stalks about in the gloom with contracted pupils, presumably of hypnotic powers." A zombie is an out-of-date product, or someone who doesn't know when things are played out: "[T]he dead can be raised from the grave.... These dead things ... are the zombies and I am by no means uncertain that I haven't seen one or two of them running about New York, grabbing up a few bargains at the Liquidation Sales." J.C.M. understands that something about the sentimental and its techniques in a modern medium and context may demand a comparison of Lugosi's character to Rebecca, but does not consider how narratives (or genres) that explain and legitimate feeling or that create monstrosity might be responsive to material, political and aesthetic modernization.

In the literary reviews that established the standards for this type of anti-generic and anti-popular criticism, T. S. Eliot partook as liberally of the arch, superior and ironic as J.C.M. did. But in the case of Rudyard Kipling, he publicly reconsidered his original judgments about Kipling's aesthetic choices in terms of their proximity to larger questions about the cultural effects of twentieth-century representative democratic governance.

I juxtapose this episode in Eliot's critical career with Halperin's film to suggest that we might understand Eliot and a "B" horror movie as attempting *formally* to understand and manage the same sociohistorical crises of individual agency. In emphasizing the formal here, I mean to claim that there is a way to encompass both "central" and "marginal" texts (or "high culture" and popular or generic texts) in our understanding of modernism's aesthetics without recourse to either a simple temporal definition ("all texts between 1890 and 1945 are modernist") or a merely thematic one.

During roughly the period my study covers, T. S. Eliot wrote about Rudyard Kipling four times (1919, 1928, 1941, 1959). Though he began derisively ("the arrival of a new book of his verse is not likely to stir the slightest ripple on the surface of our conversational intelligentsia"), he eventually claimed that traces of "the amazing man of genius, every single piece of writing of whom, taken in isolation, can look like a brilliant *tour de force*; but whose work has nevertheless an undeniable unity" could be found in his own (Eliot's) work.[44] Kipling's aesthetics ultimately take second place to Eliot's attempts to outline a place for a modern "man of letters" amidst the new global order. Nonetheless, Eliot's engagement with Rudyard Kipling reanimates the question of what is characteristically modernist about his much-analyzed establishment of cultural value and authority for particular authors, styles and forms. Essays Eliot wrote on other topics suggest that what he earlier condemns as Kipling's improper mixing of "art" with "politics" he later comes to understand as a response to the nation-state's increased administration of culture.

What is wrong with Kipling in 1919? Like Swinburne, he has only "a few simple ideas" rather than, like Conrad, a "point of view" or a "world." Eliot characterizes authors who have (simple, abstract) "ideas" as "producing" them out of events and influences. His use of the word "production" clearly alludes to the mechanistic. Eliot sees this kind of author as generically stamping out the most likely art from his given aesthetic and historical circumstances without infusing it, as Conrad does, with a point of view that transcends historical circumstances. Conrad would be himself in any time or any place, but artists such as Swinburne or Kipling are merely conduits for the events of their time:

> Swinburne had the Risorgimento, and Garibaldi, and Mazzini, and the model of Shelley, and the recoil from Tennyson, and he produced Liberty. Mr. Kipling, the Anglo-Indian, had frontier welfare, and rebellions, and Khartoum, and he produced the Empire. . . . Mr. Conrad is very germane to the question, because he is in so many ways the antithesis of Mr. Kipling. He is, for one thing, the antithesis of Empire (as well as of democracy). . . . Mr. Conrad has no ideas, but he has a point of view, a "world"; it can hardly be defined, but it pervades his work and is unmistakable. It could not be otherwise. Swinburne's and Mr. Kipling's ideas could be otherwise. Had Kipling taken Liberty and Swinburne the Empire, the alteration would be unimportant.[45]

The individual point of view with which Conrad infuses his work, Eliot argues, is different from the merely "personal," in which an artist's technique depends on his presence as a "public speaker" "throwing himself in and gesturing the emotion of the moment," "imposing himself" on the audience through "emphatic sound" rather than reason. Kipling does not lay the emotion before the reader "simply, coldly independent of the author, of the audience, there and for ever."[46] The "ideas" create another problem here, in that they seem to compel work whose point is not simply to state an emotion but to "stimulate a particular response in the reader."[47] Kipling makes no discoveries about syntax, vocabulary or structure. His reliance on the Revised Version hampers him, since "it is not a style into which any significant modern content can be shoved."[48] Because he has no overarching point of view, or clear history of technical development, his "poems no more hang together than the verses of a schoolboy."[49]

In 1928, as he challenges Julien Benda's reading of Kipling as part of a review of *The Treason of the Intellectuals*, Eliot is willing to rework his summary of how much imperial politics might be too much: "there is, no doubt, a bit of political jingoism in Kipling, but it does not affect his best work. The imperialism which is in all of Kipling's work, and in the best of it, is not a political passion at all; it has no practical aim, but is merely the statement of a fact: and there is all the difference in the world between the vision of an Empire which exists, and the incitement to passion for an Empire in the future."[50] In not having a "practical" aim, Kipling is no longer the vulgar public speaker of the 1919 essay. Rather, his work illustrates Benda's failure to explain accurately, let alone analyze, what constitutes an improper venture of the artist outside the realm of pure art and thought.

Eliot's introduction to his Kipling collection in 1941 addresses the thin line between political jingoism and the vision of an Empire apart from the material world. Eliot uses this essay to make a case for Kipling as an important writer, perhaps even a poet, despite the fact that Kipling's work does not meet Eliot's own criteria for great poetry. He frames this as an attempt to answer a question "everyone" asks: "whether Kipling's verse really is poetry: and, if not, what it is."[51] The essay itself consists of a series of accusations and defenses. Eliot sometimes uses the passive voice to suggest that he defends Kipling from what "people" think and sometimes displays honest bewilderment about why he thinks Kipling is "great" when his writing so clearly flouts Eliot's own standards. The problems with Kipling are that he wrote topical, occasional or "political" verse, that he is "excessively lucid" and that when Eliot examines his verse over time, there is no "unity," "development" or "experimentation."[52] Eliot's quandary as he describes it is that he *knows* Kipling is great, but he can't use the normal standards for proving greatness: traditional criticism and his own work. "I confess ... that the critical tools which we are accustomed to use in analysing and criticising poetry do not seem to work; I confess furthermore that introspection into my own processes affords no assistance."[53]

Continuing the argument he began in 1928, Eliot rescues Kipling from the charge that he is "in a denigratory sense, 'political.'"[54] He distinguishes between an artist who writes "in the service of the political imagination" and one who is "a doctrinaire or a man with a programme."[55] The political imagination goes beyond the moment of a political opinion to become permanent enough to speak to future generations. As with Matthew Arnold, Kipling's occasional verse[56] can be read as transcending the occasion of its writing by expressing a moment in history in the voice of "its most representative mind."[57] Note how far Kipling has come since 1919, when he was too obviously a product of his time. Eliot finds it more difficult to sidestep the charge of "writing jingles"; the phrase suggests that Kipling's forms are, first, too close to those of mass cultural advertising and political advocacy, forms that "act" rather than exist for their own sake. "I know of no writer of such great gifts," Eliot writes, "for whom poetry seems to have been more purely an instrument."[58] Second, Kipling adopts forms arbitrarily. They are not forms that "necessarily" emerge from his subject matter. He moves from one form to another not out of artistic instinct, but with conscious craftsmanship. His versatility is his undoing because he moves so easily from form to form that "we are aware of no inner compulsion to write about this rather than that. ... We expect to feel, with a great writer, that he *had* to write about the subject he took, and in that way. With no writer of equal eminence to Kipling is this inner compulsion, this unity in variety more difficult to discern."[59] Kipling uses too many forms to have developed a sense of the proper relations between form and content. "[V]ariety is suspiciously great. We may ... fail to see in it more than the virtuosity of a writer who could turn his hand to any form and matter at will."[60]

Eliot is able to clear Kipling of charges of being political and to establish his formal resemblance to Dryden. Yet toward the end of this essay Eliot comments in a way reminiscent of his 1919 criticism of Kipling, without the sneer:

The late poems ... do not show any movement from "verse" to "poetry": they are just as instrumental as the early work, but now instruments for a matured purpose. Kipling could handle, from the beginning to the end, a considerable variety of metres and stanza forms with perfect competence; he introduces remarkable variations of his own; but as a poet he does not revolutionize. He is not one of those writers of whom one can say, that the *form* of English poetry will always be different from what it would have been if they had not written.[61]

Eliot resolves this problem of form by questioning the implicit literary valuation with which he began – does Kipling ever move from "verse" to "poetry"? Verse, Eliot argues, must not be thought of as "failed poetry"[62] but should be understood as encompassing the ballad, the hymn and the epigram. These are, he writes, difficult forms in their own right (Eliot asks the reader to look "attentively" at "Epitaphs of the War, 1914–1918") but more significantly they are public forms.[63] Eliot says differently in 1941 what he said in 1919: "For Kipling the poem is something which is intended to *act* – and for the most part his poems are intended to elicit the same response from all readers, and only the response which they can make in common."[64] In 1941, he argues that a work's having a "public purpose" does not necessarily lower its value on the grounds that a critical approach unable to accommodate whatever kind of greatness Kipling had (or that Eliot sensed he had) might be asking the wrong questions. "If we belong to the kind of critic who is accustomed to consider poems solely by the standards of the 'work of art' we may tend to dismiss Kipling's verse by standards which are not meant to apply."[65] Later, "Kipling certainly thought of verse as well as prose as a medium for a public purpose; if we are to pass judgment upon his purpose, we must try to set ourselves in the historical situations in which his ... work was written ... we must not look at his observations of one historical situation from the point of view of a later period."[66] Valentine Cunningham compares this critical move to Jane Tompkins's now famous argument challenging the relevance of the question "But is it any good?" to sentimental novels such as *Uncle Tom's Cabin*. He argues that our interest in this move for the modernist period should lie in Eliot's having, perhaps unintentionally, written "a defence of what Randall Swingler and Alan Bush were about in their Workers' Music Association and Left Book Club Musicians' Group work ... an effective defence too of many a Spanish Civil War propaganda ballad ... a sturdy sticking up for a great deal of thirties left-wing poeticity of the kind that can only be accorded high value if we grant it merit in Eliot's Kiplingesque terms." To put it another way, another of the great divides between high modernism and something tainted by public life or political advocacy (Thirties literature as crudely ideological) may not be critically sustainable.[67]

I take Cunningham's point, but I also find it telling that Eliot's trajectory toward bridging this divide seems to have been directed by his interest in how the "man of letters" should engage with "passions of race (e.g. the Nordic theory and the Latin theory), passions of nations (e.g. fascism) and passions of class."[68] Reevaluating Kipling is a secondary effect of the way Eliot was beginning to define how the man of letters might claim political authority. Note that he begins to think of Kipling differently in 1928 when he wants to argue against Benda's account of the intellectual and artistic "treason" inherent in involvement with political passions. In 1945, in "The Man of Letters and the Future of Europe," we find Eliot arguing against Benda again:

> He [the man of letters] differs from other artists, in that his medium is his language: we do not all paint pictures, and we are not all musicians, but we all talk. This fact gives the man of letters a special responsibility towards everybody who speaks the same language, a responsibility which workers in other arts do not share. ... there are matters of public concern, in which the man of letters should express his opinion, and exert his influence, not merely as a citizen but as a man of letters.[69]

State forms and consciousness intersect in ways that make the forms more important than the content – "[e]veryone is conscious of nationality and race (our very passports impress that upon us), but no one is sure who or which or what is what or which race."[70] The man of letters in 1945 also has special insights into how to maintain a European culture (that is, a culture that is neither too local nor too internationalized/industrialized) because his habit of thinking in and about forms gives him facility in dealing with the already established formal habits of political thought. In this essay, Eliot identifies the contribution the man of letters could make as being to "the cultural," rather than to the political or economic, peacetime map of Europe. The post-World War I ideal of the (Wilsonian) self-determined nation ("nationalism") and the current ideal of the efficient (for industrial purposes) establishment of nations ("internationalism"), according to Eliot, have equal and opposite problems. The first puts too much emphasis on "regional" interests, which Eliot defines as demands for local political autonomy (his examples are Scotland and Wales), and the second leans too much toward centralization and homogenization in an extension of the "planned economies" of the 1930s:

> At the end of the last war, the idea of peace was associated with the idea of independence and freedom: it was thought that if each nation managed all its own affairs at home, and transacted its foreign political affairs through the League of Nations, peace would be perpetually assured. It was an idea which disregarded the *unity* of European culture. At the end of this war, the idea of peace is more likely to be associated with the idea of *efficiency* – that is, with whatever can be *planned*. This would be to disregard the *diversity* of European culture.[71]

Eliot's ideal "community of European nations" can be created only if no individual nation is completely culturally unified. Homogenization leads at worst to Germany, at best to stagnation. Homogeneous nations will be unable to contribute dynamic elements to the common European culture. He is willing to admit that non-dominant cultures need some degree of political independence to "flourish unimpaired" but wants to ensure this by making each its own nation-state. Responding to Carr's statement in *Conditions of Peace* that "The existence of a more or less homogeneous racial or linguistic group bound together by a common tradition and the cultivation of a common culture must cease to provide a *prima facie* case for setting up or the maintenance of an independent political unit," Eliot writes:

> One cannot say that this statement, as it stands, is unacceptable. But it needs qualification; for, otherwise, one might infer from it that the "culture" of a "more or less homogeneous racial or linguistic group bound together by a common tradition and the cultivation of a common culture" can flourish unimpaired, whatever its degree of political subordination ... though on the other hand I assert that *complete* cultural autarchy is not compatible with the existence of a common European culture. The world's real problems are in practice a complex, usually a confusion, of political, economic, cultural and religious considerations; in one or another situation, one or more of these will be sacrificed to the one which is, in that situation, the most compulsive; but every one of them involves the rest.[72]

It seems contradictory that he believes this, yet also thinks that "the ... man of letters at the present time should be vigilantly watching the conduct of politicians and economists, for the purpose of criticizing and warning, when the decisions and actions of politicians and economists are likely to have cultural consequences."[73] More specifically, Eliot claims, the man of letters is "peculiarly qualified to respect and criticize" "regional stirrings", that is, to understand how to balance political demands from non-dominant cultures against demands for centralization and homogenization.[74] Here the political, economic and cultural are inseparable, yet the man of letters can not only distinguish their separate spheres and refrain from interfering in inappropriate ones (not "precipitate himself into controversy on matters which he does not understand") but also predict how actions in one sphere will affect another. This contradiction seems to me to underscore the degree to which the man of letters' expertise and societal function is founded on the state being the principal form demanded for entrance into the world system.[75] Lisa Lowe and David Lloyd explain that state form itself encompasses the restructuring of civil society along almost precisely the lines Eliot takes for granted here:

[T]he state form ... implies not only an assimilation to a hierarchized system of global power, but compliance with a normative distribution of social spaces within that state's definitions. ... Civil society must be reshaped to produce subjects who might function in terms of modern definitions of social spaces, as the political subject of the state, the economic subject of capitalism, and the cultural subject of the nation, however much the discreteness of these spaces is contradicted by conditions that are lived as racialized and gendered labor stratification, apartheid, and poverty.[76]

Thus, when Eliot warns men of letters to exercise constant surveillance to avoid, among other things, becoming "servants of the State" (writers of cultural propaganda) he notes (literally, as it is a footnote) that the man of letters' relationship with the state once enabled independent authority, but now discourages it:

Formerly, Englishmen of letters often found their livelihood in the Civil Service. But this kind of dependence upon the State enabled them to be all the freer to follow their own aims and observe their consciences as writers. This was a very different thing from serving the State *as men of letters*. In the future it seems likely that Civil Servants will be far too busy to be authors in their spare time, and that the Civil Service will not enlist men of this type.[77]

In marginalizing this discussion but not eliminating it, Eliot simultaneously marks a change in the nature of authority resulting from the new ways state bureaucracies confer subjecthood and denies that it has happened.

We should now understand Eliot's redemption of Kipling as driven by an interest in the cultural authority of the man of letters within the exigencies of state formations, rather than in solely aesthetic terms. Ultimately, Eliot gets around Kipling's lack of poetic "development" by relocating development from the interiors of his poems to the travels that England's imperial history made possible. First, he ties "experimentation" to "development" over a poet's lifetime:

The word "experimentation" may be applied and honorably applied, to the work of many poets who develop and change in maturity. As a man [*sic*] grows older, he may turn to a new subject-matter, or he may treat the same material in a different way; as we age we both live in a different world, and become different men in the same world. The changes may be expressed by a change of rhythm, of imagery, of form: the true experimenter is not impelled by restless curiosity, or by desire for novelty, or the wish to surprise and astonish, but by the compulsion to find, in every new poem as in his earliest, the right form for feelings over the development of which he has, as a poet, no control.[78]

Here Eliot connects experimental development, most literally, to the aging process itself. This seems antithetical to the concept of experimentation as something that a particular poet does to change literary history. If every poet "develops" simply by aging then it can hardly be a standard of judgment. But Eliot's twisting of the definition here, even though he concludes that Kipling does *not* experiment, allows him to shift the grounds of poetic development from form to geopolitics more easily. If development and experiment come simply with the passing of time, Kipling's successive relocations can stand in for the "development" that does not seem to emerge from traditional consideration of his oeuvre. Instead, Eliot finds a pattern that parallels "development" in Kipling's imperial geographies:

The first period is that of India; the second that of travel and of residence in America; the third is that of his settlement in Sussex. These divisions are obvious: what is not so obvious is the development of his view of empire, a view which expands and contracts at the same time. He had always been far from uncritical of the defects and wrongs of the British Empire, but held a firm belief in what it should and might be. In his later phase England, and a particular corner of England, becomes the centre of his vision.[79]

Eliot freely concedes that Kipling has not altered the form of English poetry, but with this passage establishes different parameters for the great artist. Kipling's "foreignness" and his geographical imagination give Kipling special and sharper powers of observation and make him "of" both countries in a way that people actually born and raised there are not:

Kipling is of India in a different way from any other Englishman who has written and in a different way from that of any particular Indian who has a race, a creed, a local habitation, and, if Hindu, a caste. He might almost be called the first citizen of India. ... [U]ndoubtedly the difference of early environment to which Kipling's foreignness is due gave him an understanding of the English countryside different from the understanding of a man born and brought up in it, and provoked in him thoughts about it which the natives would do well to heed.[80]

Eliot reads Kipling's later poetry about the legends and history of Sussex as developing from Kipling's firsthand understanding of the geography of the British Empire. Eliot's interest in Kipling's travels in

India and in his retreat to explore the mythology of Sussex are consistent with his (and other modernists') interest in the primitive, anthropological and regional as provocative routes to articulating the essence of industrial modernity. Eliot understands national identity – "England" and "English culture" – from two opposite perspectives. Because of the economic and cultural relations England has established as an imperial power, some of what is quintessentially English comes from its constant expansion and from incorporating foreign cultures. Yet "England" is also anchored by regionalism – Sussex – a philosophy of culture that paradoxically defines the essence of a national culture as inherent in its most particular and "local" traditions.[81]

The simplest summary of the change in Kipling, in his middle years, is "the development of the imperial imagination into the historical imagination" . . . . Having previously exhibited an imaginative grasp of space, and England in it, he now proceeds to a similar achievement in time.[82]

Kipling, like Eliot's contemporary man of letters, is "peculiarly qualified" to understand and render as poetic the "regional stirrings" that mark England's place in space and time, that is to say, the balancing of the global and local cultures for which the man of letters is responsible. Kipling, in other words, has created a category of aesthetic "development" into which Eliot, also taking up matters of geopolitics as an exile in England, fits. In redeeming Kipling, then, Eliot describes the problem of cultural authority for the artist as geopolitical.

Critical descendants of Eliot have continued to describe the modernist artist in terms of threatened authority and imperial genealogy in the shadow of state formation and language. In the next chapter, I examine how contemporary "modernism and empire" criticism takes up this earlier problem of "the man of letters" in relation to what are vilified as governmental, non-aesthetic discourses. I then consider two cases that challenge this view – novels about empire by Sara Jeannette Duncan and Katherine Mansfield in which these authors, like Kipling as Eliot reads him, find excesses in bureaucratic discourse that generate new kinds of narrative.

CHAPTER 2

Set in authority: white rulers and white settlers

In this chapter I reconsider the possible relationship between modernism as aesthetic project and late nineteenth- and early twentieth-century empire, an immense organizational problem of long-distance state administration. I begin with a more detailed critical backdrop: Louis Menand's and Michael Levenson's modernist genealogical readings of Joseph Conrad's aesthetics in terms of the political economy of empire. In the main section of this chapter, I examine Sara Jeannette Duncan's and Katherine Mansfield's fiction about administering India and colonizing New Zealand as "white settler modernism."[1] I am not trying to demarcate a subset of modernism by using the category "white settler modernism." Nor am I trying to argue that simply writing about empire – regardless of style – is modernist. Rather, I document the ways in which Duncan's and Mansfield's work alerts us to a modernist understanding of realist technique derived from an awareness of the narrative elements of state administrative languages. Thus, these works both have a place in and expose the limits of modernist genealogies which do not aim directly to address the issue of empire's entanglements with modernism, yet nonetheless rely on Joseph Conrad's imperial economies.

"Modernism and empire" criticism exposes the conceptual difficulties of simultaneously defining modernism as a historical and as an aesthetic phenomenon. Critical genealogies of modernism and empire intertwine claims about the relations between economic and political phenomena and literary history with an assumption that "modernist narration" is the conversion of content into style. Critics may understand the turn to formal innovation as political cowardice ("retreat into style") as a deeply, if not obviously, subversive underwriting of Western form with the violence of its imperial acts, or as an imitation of the technological and authoritative imperial move of categorizing and organizing the world. But all of these genealogies present authors such as Kipling, Haggard and Buchan as naïve about the morality, implications or sustainability of empire. Critics depict realist style in their novels as another version of the same naïveté – when confronted by modern empire, these authors believe it can be described using ordinary language. Literary innovation, by contrast, indicates that an author has perceived the structures and consequences wrought by a newly globalizing economic and political system.

Some arguments correlate the peak and others the decline of empire with the birth of modernism. But both sides of this argument agree that the distinguishing feature of imperial modernism is aesthetic innovation. Thus, some critics might link the founding of *Blast* in 1914 with the fact that by that year, Europe held 85 percent (a rapid increase from the 35 percent of 1800) of the earth as "colonies, protectorates, dependencies, dominions and commonwealths."[2] Fredric Jameson argues in "Modernism and Imperialism" that the successful expansion of Europe demanded new formal literary tactics that could map the structure of imperialism.[3]

Michael North, on the other hand, focuses on challenges to empire. For modernist studies, of course, 1922 is the year during which *Ulysses* and *The Waste Land* were published. North points out that it was also the year in which the Irish Free State was born, self-determination was accorded to Egypt, Lord Lugard published *The Dual Mandate* in an attempt to quell rising calls for the end of empire and the Prince of Wales made a markedly unsuccessful colonial tour to assert British good-will and authority.[4] Also arguing against Jameson's link between Western imperial success and modernism, Edward Said writes that narrating empire precipitates the transition from realism to modernism. Authors such as Conrad, Forster and Malraux mark the fall from "the triumphalist experience of imperialism" to "self-consciousness, discontinuity, self-referentiality and corrosive irony, whose formal patterns we have come to recognize as the hallmarks of modernist culture." Modernism is an aesthetic response to the "problem" of no longer being able to "assume that Britannia will rule the waves forever ... as more and more regions ... challenge the classical empires and their cultures."[5] Note here that the authors Said mentions, ones who directly address empire, are "transitional"; that is to say, they can be precursors only to a modernism characterized by particular techniques but that does not directly address imperial events. Similarly, for Jameson, despite his focus on imperial success rather than imperial anxiety, the empire's significant productions are aesthetic; he describes his own argument as drawn from texts that "scarcely evoke imperialism as such at all; that seem to have no specifically political content in the first place; that offer purely stylistic or linguistic particularities for analysis."[6]

Set in authority: white rulers and white settlers

Viewed in these terms, modernism and empire studies exemplify what Astradur Eysteinsson has outlined as a central paradox of modernist studies:

> [I]n writings on modernism the theory of aesthetic autonomy frequently appears to coexist with that of cultural subversion ... we need to ask ourselves how the concept of autonomy, so crucial to many theories of modernism, can possibly coexist with the equally prominent view of modernism as a historically explosive paradigm. This dichotomy, hardly recognized by most critics, is characteristic for the divergent approaches to modernism as, on the one hand, a *cultural force* and on the other as an *aesthetic project*.[7]

Modernism and empire studies incorporate their own version of this paradox. As in many literary histories, modernism supposedly makes realism defunct, even as it (modernism) emerges from imperialism's impact. But if only formally innovative writing generated by veering away from actual events is modernist, this is to invent a paradoxical modernism, both historic and independent of history. Thus, as I discuss in more detail below, Joseph Conrad's *Heart of Darkness* (1902) enters modernist genealogies as an imperial novel that renders empire indescribable (or, as he might put it, ineffable) in order to invent a language that can (not) describe it.

To reject realism here is to reject it for partaking too much and too naïvely of the empire's own languages: enumeration, bureaucracy, categorization, military campaign, survey. But this is also to claim that it can no longer effectively comprehend, let alone articulate, the changes wrought by its own instrumentality! This is an example of the critical paradox Eysteinsson describes here, for it requires "hardly recognizing" that the modernism emerging from the heart of darkness is simultaneously relying upon imperial realism *and* disavowing it.

Eysteinsson explains the implications of recognizing this critical paradox as paradox: "But if we refuse, as I think we must, to acknowledge any strict boundaries between the two [modernist autonomy and modernism as historically explosive paradigm], then the Dedalian view of the work of art as a 'transcendent object' and an isolated aesthetic whole is invalidated as a critical basis for modernist studies."[8]

We should not, in other words, conceive of modernism in terms of the distinction between a deterministic, unimaginative, naïvely reflective, crudely styled and politicized (or "Victorian") realism and a complex, ambivalent, aesthetically sophisticated, detached and ironic modernism.[9]

Such valorizations of modernism's aesthetic program oversimplify realism in the same way that modernism is oversimplified by paradigms that define postmodernism's complexity in terms of modernism's over-ordered (even "totalitarian") narratives and naïve belief in depth. In both of these catalogs, one literary historical category is a complicated and adroitly deployed set of contingent techniques while the other is a simplistic (and incorrect) ideology.

To imagine modernism as a mode distinguished by a commitment to defining language as a set of technologies that produce the possibilities and limits of subjectivity suggests that modernists would also have understood realism as more than a naïve belief in language's ability to represent an obvious "reality." Realism's aesthetics, after all were already engaging so-called "modernist" issues: fragmented realities, the place of narrative in defining the subject's understanding of his/her social functions, and mass cultural forms of representation.[10]

In their discussions of Joseph Conrad as exemplary early modernist, both Louis Menand and Michael Levenson emphasize the way his writings stage problems of literary authority in parallel with problems of political economy. According to Menand, *Heart of Darkness* overlaps the economic history of the capitalist in the world economy ("Marlow's plot") with the literary history of Romanticism's decline into "stock devices" and "decorative embellishments of aestheticism ('Conrad's plot')"[11] to mark a point of occupational crisis – professionalism. Kurtz's methods and aesthetics (the shrunken heads) are "outmoded and slightly absurd"; he is not, Menand argues, a figure for twentieth-century liberal imperialism, but rather "a throwback, the incarnation of an earlier era in the history of capitalist expansion ... a reenactment of the first industrial revolution."[12] Menand historicizes Kurtz as artist: he is not "the artist" but a first-generation Romantic artist. The fatal difference between Kurtz the "genius," the man of "no method" and the Station Manager or Marlow's audience (men at the center of imperial administration) encompasses also the problem of the literary artist at the end of the nineteenth century. If the literary writer was not to become a Kurtz, absurdly out of date, he needed to become a professional. But to garner respectability was to become an accountant or Station Manager, and the literary artist had heretofore prided himself on his difference from such unimaginative work. The solution was to generate aesthetic authority. As Menand sums up: "If aestheticism might be said to belong to the phase of professionalism's first serious challenge to occupational values, modernism belongs to the phase of its successful hegemony over them."[13] The social changes in administration that arise alongside the discourses of vocation and professionalism manifest in Conrad's style, Menand argues, as an early version of an important modernist strategy: "making capital out of the worn-out quality of received literary form."[14]

For Levenson, Conrad's style similarly stages social changes in discourses of authority as a conflict between the artistic and the professional. Like Menand, Levenson identifies in Conrad's work a contest between the claims of "duty, obedience, authority and silence" (Menand's "method," "vocation" and "professionalism") and the claims of "individualism, consciousness, and loquacity" (Menand's "genius," "originality" and inspiration") that will be played out in his work as modernist style.

Where Menand's analysis reminds us that the development of the business of empire is intertwined with the professionalization of the literary artist, tying both to the history of capitalism as a world economy, Levenson points out that *The Nigger of the Narcissus* is a "political meditation ... we ought not to be misled by the fact that in Conrad the *polis* floats."[15] The contest between consciousness and authority (or subjectivity and fact) in *The Nigger of the Narcissus*, he argues, is a dramatization of the same arguments Matthew Arnold ambivalently outlined and Irving Babbit extended to more definitive conclusions about the dangers of ceding authority to the autonomous individual of liberal philosophy.[16] *The Nigger of the Narcissus* thematically comes down on the side of authority; its narrative form makes "an implied commitment to the values of a registering consciousness"; in this, it exemplifies a struggle in modernism that would emerge more forcefully as the movement developed.[17]

To sum up, although neither Levenson nor Menand is trying to link modernism and empire directly, both find modernism's early manifestations in Conrad and implicitly describe them in terms of the problems of rule and of administration. Levenson's descriptions of the contrast between George Eliot's Victorian omniscience and Conrad's first- and third-person strategies, for instance, compare Eliot's "prerogatives" as an "assimilating amalgamating force" which "remorselessly invad[es]" characters' psyches under a convention of "seizing ... privileges for the narrator."[18] He describes Conrad/modernism, on the other hand, as administering the text differently: "Where George Eliot maintains the consistency of a single omniscient voice, Conrad here draws upon distinct voices, distinguishable points of view."[19] Levenson's language practically sums up the (idealized) distinction between sovereign rule and the liberal state.

Note that in both of these arguments the practical, moral and epistemological problems posed by administering empire become significant only if we understand them primarily as attacks on the autonomy and authority of art and artists. The point of formally generated ineffability in these readings, despite Menand's discussion of global economics, is that it triumphs over the crushing materialism of imperial necessity. In his essay on the modernist novel, David Trotter calls this move on the part of a modernist author "will-to-literature." He argues that modernist novelists confront the "perceived impossibility" of the novel as a genre. One response is to stage this impossibility in order to triumph over it, to take up subject matter and techniques that "resist" literature, necessitating the production of "excess literature" or masterful form to allow for the revamped novel's generic restoration.[20] In these critical narratives of modernism and empire studies, then, empire and its discourses (including realist writing) are understood to be aesthetically inert.

For Mansfield and Duncan it is nearly the opposite. The literary challenge – and relevance – of imperial content to artistic form and authority lie in the fact that imperial administration was proliferating its own discourses. These discourses, though strictly speaking "realist," were anything but naïvely representational or instrumental. The works I will discuss here are marked by a consciousness of the ways modern state management generated expanding new modes of authority and subjectivity in excess of strictly representational and organizational ends.

Katherine Mansfield is generally acknowledged as having become a modernist in her mature work, especially for stories such as "The Garden Party," "The Wind Blows," "Prelude" and "At the Bay." Critics usually point to these stories as containing fragmentation, stream-of-consciousness, ironic distance and the spare images characteristic of the "metropolitan modernist" style she is assumed to have developed from being in the literary-intellectual publishing circles of little magazines such as the *New Age* and *Rhythm/Blue Review*. Because Mansfield was born in New Zealand and moved to London, in other words, she has been fit to a theory of modernism that works in terms of imperial economics:[21] Mansfield becomes assimilated to Virginia Woolf and London, sloughing off New Zealand except as local color or autobiographical authenticity.

For instance, although Sydney Janet Kaplan finds prefigurings of modernist technique as early as Mansfield's letters in 1908, she considers the Burnell texts "the true beginning of her *conscious* sense of a new shape for prose fiction."[22] In asserting the significance of "The Woman at the Store" (1911), I am not quibbling about dates, but arguing for the primacy of political structures of empire in defining modernism's emergence. "The Woman at the Store" is not "innovative" in the striking ways that "Prelude" or "At the Bay" are. Mansfield demonstrates interest in the shape of prose fiction by chronicling the pressures of the colonial project on narrative representation rather than on highlighting a breakthrough aesthetic detached from imperial content and polished by the urban metropole. Here I critically restage the emergence of the new from the literature of empire. I draw attention to what Nicholas Thomas has termed "white settler failure" (the inability to imagine one's local career within the narrative of empire projected by state ideologies) as a place to investigate narrative authority's underpinnings in political authority.[23]

In "The Woman at the Store" Mansfield makes (white, British) female bodies the sites where authority and national identity are constructed and destroyed. After traveling for a month in the New Zealand outback, the three main characters, Jim, Jo and the unnamed narrator, ride through particularly hot, dry, desolate and uninhabited territory. Jim is guiding the party to an outpost he knows from before and encourages them with the vision of "a fine store, with a paddock for the horses and a creek running through, owned by a friend of mine who'll give yer a bottle of whiskey before 'e shakes hands with yer . . . there's a woman too, Jo, with blue eyes and yellow hair who'll promise you something else before she shakes hands with you."[24] When they finally reach the store, a woman comes out to greet them but her yellow hair now is described in conjunction with her mangy yellow dog. The narrator congratulates Jim for the joke he has played on Jo, "smiling" at the difference between the women and Jim's description. "Certainly her eyes were blue and what hair she had was yellow, but ugly. She was a figure of fun. Looking at her, you felt there was nothing but sticks and wires under that pinafore – her front teeth were knocked out, she had red pulpy hands, and she wore on her feet a pair of dirty Bluchers." Jim doesn't laugh and instead protests that there really was a beautiful woman here when he last visited his friend. "No – look here. I can't make it out. It's four years since I came past this way. . . . She'd been barmaid down at the Coast – as pretty as a wax doll. . . . Told me once in a confidential moment that she knew one hundred and twenty-five different ways of kissing!"[25] They discover that she is the same woman, no longer beautiful after years of isolation, four miscarriages, a birth and an abusive husband:

"Now listen to me," shouted the woman, banging her fist on the table. "It's six years since I was married, and four miscarriages. I says to 'im, I says, what do you think I'm doin' up 'ere? If you was back at the coast, I'd 'ave you lynched for child murder. Over and over I tells 'im – you've broken my spirit and spoiled my looks, and wot for – that's wot I'm driving at .... I 'ear them two words knockin' inside me all the time."[26]

Jo sums up what the woman is "for": "She'll look better by night light – at any rate, my buck, she's female flesh!" His reduction of the woman to her sexual function is not very different from Jim's and the narrator's characterizations of her as the former "wax doll" or the current "figure of fun." The mother and the kid are something to see and describe, like the landscape. But Mansfield suggests that the narrator's ability to take control of the landscape after the fashion of the traditional Victorian traveler depends on "forgetting" about the local inhabitants, which is equivalent to being able to dispose of them at will:

I went to the end of the paddock where the willows grew and bathed in the creek. The water was clear and soft as oil. Along the edges held by the grass and rushes, white foam tumbled and bubbled. I lay in the water and looked up at the trees that were still a moment, then quivered lightly, and again were still. The air smelt of rain. I forgot about the woman and the kid until I came back to the tent.[27]

Here the narrator claims what Mary Louise Pratt has described as the imperial Victorian traveler's privilege of being "the monarch of all I survey." Imperial travelers created a verbal painting "whose highest calling was to produce for the home audience the peak moments at which geographical 'discoveries' were 'won' for England." This relationship of mastery between the traveler and the landscape is not only imperial, but critical, since the explorer is the only one who can define and judge a "scene" and then explain its significance to the reader.[28] Mansfield's narrator does not here need to claim land for England and thus does not have to "forget" about native inhabitants. However, she must exclude colonists who could challenge her story. In addition to establishing critical mastery over the imperial scene, colonists were responsible for establishing a positive affective relationship to the landscape. Nicholas Thomas describes such an imperial landscape as raw material "fresh and suitable for new endeavors and new families." With her greater rhetorical facility, the narrator establishes a relationship to the landscape that is better than the one the woman at the store and her daughter have been able to establish. Only by excluding the woman and her daughter except as amusing adjuncts to a standard traveler's tale of a visit to the colonies

Set in authority: white rulers and white settlers 63

can the narrator construct a coherent narrative of a settler colony in which "space reserved for a white future and white accomplishments"[29] is successfully used. Mansfield depicts this as a struggle over the literary power to "survey" the colonial landscape.

"The kid" angrily challenges the visitors' condescension by abruptly embodying the narrator as the female object of her own "narrative" gaze. At this point, about three-quarters of the way through the story, the reader realizes that the narrator has been disguising her gender under the generic guise of the male traveler into rough country. Because the narrator has neither been addressed by name nor had any requirements or thoughts which distinguish her from Jo and Jim, she seems to be one of them – a man. Jo's desire for "female flesh" also creates the impression that there is no "female" in the party. There is no indication that the narrator is a woman until the kid uses the pronoun "her." Confronting Jim, who condescends to the six-year-old, the kid defends her claim to adult expression:

"Come over here," said Jim, snapping his fingers at her. She went, the lamp from the inside of the tent cast a bright light over her. A mean, undersized brat, with whitish hair and weak eyes. She stood, legs wide apart and her stomach protruding.
"What do you do all day?" asked Jim.
She scraped out one ear with her little finger, looked at the result and said, "Draw."
"Huh! What do you draw? Leave your ears alone!"
"Pictures."
"What on?"
"Bits of butter paper an' a pencil of my Mumma's."
"Boh! What a lot of words at one time!" Jim rolled his eyes at her. "Baa-lambs and moo-cows?"
"No, everything. I'll draw all of you when you're gone, and your horses and the tent, and that one" – she pointed to me – "with no clothes on in the creek. I looked at her where she couldn't see me from."[30]

Jim treats the child like a specimen (snapping his fingers to call her, putting a bright light on her and forcing her to submit to his examination), and the narrator describes her as one ("a mean undersized brat, with whitish hair, and weak eyes"). Jim also suggests that even if the kid really *can* draw, her ability will be circumscribed by her youth and provinciality ("baa-lambs and moo-cows"). The passage ends with the kid, also female and an artist, competing for the narrator's privileged position of disembodiment and merciless description by threatening to turn the tables on her. Mansfield reimagines the landscape the narrator described earlier. Instead of being alone, "neutrally" gendered and a privileged observer, the narrator was being watched. The kid steals the perspective from the narrator. Now we see a woman's naked body in the creek surrounded by bubbling white foam; the narrator is available as an eroticized and vulnerable object, or simply stripped for the kind of cruel physical description she made of the woman and the kid earlier. The narrator is put off balance. As the kid draws on butter paper while the adults eat dinner, the narrator writes, " I wondered, grimly, if she was attempting the creek episode."[31]

The kid's threatened drawing is an improper colonial narrative of a piece with other deliberate misuses of national imagery in Mansfield's New Zealand stories. Earlier in the story Mansfield has the narrator describe the woman's living quarters with metropolitan condescension. This time it is the Queen of England herself who condescends to her subjects in the outback. Upon being taken into the woman's living areas, the narrator notes that the walls are plastered with "old pages of English periodicals. Queen Victoria's Jubilee appeared to be the most recent number."[32] The Queen's oversight seems to emphasize rather than to relieve the isolation of the store and its desolate surroundings. Mansfield uses a similar strategy in "Millie" (1912). Millie, also a white New Zealand rural colonist, decorates her room with a print called "Garden Party at Windsor Castle."

> In the foreground emerald lawns planted with immense oak trees and in their grateful shade, a muddle of ladies and gentlemen and parasols and little tables. The background was filled with the towers of Windsor Castle, flying three Union Jacks, and in the middle of the picture the old Queen, like a tea cosy with a head on top of it. "I wonder if it really looked like that." Millie stared at the flowery ladies, who simpered back at her. "I wouldn't care for that sort of thing. Too much side. What with the Queen an' one thing an' another."[33]

In both of these scenes, the Queen at the center of the world and the woman at the edge of Victoria's empire show up in stark contrast. The contrast is not merely one of power and material comfort, although Mansfield certainly makes the point that Millie's dismissal of the Queen is futile. Jubilee celebrations and tea parties at Windsor Castle become, when inserted into these women's domestic environments as out-of-date wallpaper and alienating reminders of the home country, examples of the kind of national imperial narrative these colonists cannot produce. The kid's drawings, by contrast, are "extraordinarily and repulsively vulgar ... creations of a lunatic with a lunatic's cleverness" – the product of a "diseased" mind.[34] This description of a six-year-old's drawings makes the narrator's continued breeziness about their "adventure" seem pathetic and inappropriate: "We behaved like two children let loose in the thick of an adventure, laughed and shouted to each other."[35] This line suggests the release available in "new" lands away from the burdens of tradition – a return to childhood and to an innocent relationship to history. But the actual child of this story has made both the idea of childhood and the ideal of colonial potential it underwrites absurd. This is not merely thematic; Mansfield shows their chosen genre breaking down.

Compared with their first conversation with the kid, in this one their mockery (of the idea of colonials having propriety? Of a vast system of colonial commerce reduced to keeping accounts of sales of onions, ham, "Camp Coffee" and tinned meats?) seems uncontrolled, without the objective and merciless description of the earlier moments, and possibly hysterical:

Jim and I sat on two sacks of potatoes. For the life of us we could not stop laughing. Strings of onions and half-hams dangled from the ceiling – wherever we looked there were advertisements for "Camp Coffee" and tinned meats. We pointed at them, tried to read them aloud – overcome with laughter and hic-coughs. The kid in the counter stared at us. She threw off her blanket and scrambled to the floor, where she stood in her grey flannel nightgown, rubbing one leg against the other. We paid no attention to her.
"Wot are you laughing at?" she said, uneasily.
"You!" shouted Jim. "The red tribe of you, my child."
She flew into a rage and beat *herself* with her hands. "I won't be laughed at, you curs – you."[36]

The kid can only turn her anger inwards, and, like the Queen, the metropolitan tourists can "pay no attention" to the settler at the edge of empire except to demand that she submit to being part of a larger "scene" she cannot understand. Jim condescends to the kid again. Ignoring her anger and physically overpowering her without effort, he picks her up and sets her back in the counter. "Go to sleep, Miss Smarty – or make a drawing – here's a pencil – you can use Mumma's account book." The kid settles accounts with her mother and the travelers by drawing "the one she told me I never ought to" – a drawing of her mother killing her father and then burying him. This ends the "hilarity." The kid goes to sleep but "Jim and I sat till dawn with the drawing beside us." At first light, they begin to break camp and leave, without even waiting for Jo.

She describes the landscape one last time: "White clouds floated over a pink sky – a chill wind blew; the air smelled of wet grass. ... A bend in the road, and the whole place disappeared." As with the earlier description of the creek, Mansfield depicts the narrator as attempting to produce a colonial landscape available for white settler conquest. But the story's ending – a hasty abandonment of the outpost, the woman and her daughter – belies the white clouds and pink sky, or at least emphasizes the chill wind instead of the lush wet grass. The narrator's final attempt to return to her position as the metropolitan narrator of a local color narrative falters in the face of the kid's defiant drawing of her family's deterioration. Her access to the imperial traveler's perspective depends on the willingness and ability of the frontier family to create and maintain proper imperial space.

The deterioration of these white settlers radiates in several directions. The woman's move away from the coastal town where she met her husband and her increasing isolation once the store is no longer a regular stop on the coach line index a colonial project unable to maintain its expansion, writing it onto the woman reduced to a stick figure. The mother's deterioration passes to her daughter: "I 'ad a bit of trouble with 'er one way an' another. I 'adn't any milk till a month after she was born and she sickened like a cow." Her child is physically a poor specimen, "weak," "undersized" and unattractive. Family structure, the metaphor for interpellative and literal reproduction of the nation in colonial space, has utterly failed. Instead, the next generation is the product of neglect and violence and "[t]here is no doubt about it, the kid's mind was diseased." The state of childhood, representative of the potential for a higher order of the colonizer's civilization in the new world, has been overturned. Instead, the kid has the same fatal knowledge reformers were trying to root out of the children of England's slums. Finally, in the light of the story's conclusion, the traveling conditions at its outset ("white pumice dust swirled in our faces, settled and sifted over us and was like a dry-skin itching for growth on our bodies") suggests that, like the whiteness of the zombies I discussed in the last chapter, whiteness on this frontier is more like a disease than a privileged and stabilizing categorical and cultural identity.[37]

Even granting the absence and unfitness of the father as important elements in this narrative of social eugenic deterioration, it is significant that the characters who represent these failed modes of authority in the age of empire are all women – the kid, the woman at the store, the narrator and the Queen. As I argued earlier in my discussion of landscape, despite the relative lushness of the land near the store, the woman fails to identify possessively with the land available to her. She cannot imagine "wot for." She also fails to attach herself to the Queen as an extension of the national future in an imperial geography; the Queen herself has failed to provide ways of establishing this attachment. The failure to maintain a properly regulated private life is femininity's as well as whiteness' failure. The narrator as the fourth woman in the story (after the woman at the store, the kid and the Queen) is also uncomfortably close to becoming unanchored in the same way – traveling with two men, comfortable with lack of domesticity, whiteness just barely crawling on her skin.[38] Mansfield challenges state use of the colonies: to provide a practical sink for overpopulation (including the "problem" of "surplus" women) and to provide additional economic opportunities and mobilities for emigrants who, if they remained at home, might destabilize the social structure there.

In reading "The Woman at the Store" as a contest between the kid and the narrator, I do not mean to suggest either that historically speaking, white settlement failed in New Zealand (clearly, it did not) or that the struggle between indigenous peoples and British colonizers is unimportant. Rather, I read Mansfield as intensely interested in the discursive dimension of imperial governance and, thus, in the points where imperial rhetoric failed to produce and support proper imperial subjectivities. Working-class "common colonizers," Thomas writes, are often occluded from studies of colonizing narratives, leading to a radical overstatement of these narratives' coherence. "Even a text such as Conrad's *Heart of Darkness*, famous as an expression of the collapse of colonial reason into murky tropical insanity, nevertheless preserves a point from which this degradation can be narrated and accounted for. What that novel may leave us unprepared for is the extent to which failures of colonialism could also be failures of articulation."[39]

In other words, the problem Mansfield sets for herself in "The Woman at the Store" is to invoke one of these failures of narrative without recuperating it to imperial rhetoric in the very act of describing it. Her point is not to "give voice" to the heretofore ignored; rather it is to explore how authority, in its modern, rational, social and consent-driven form, is constituted as narrative authority to create subjectivity. If *Heart of Darkness* ultimately depends on raising the specter of inarticulateness in order to master it through "will-to-literature," "The Woman at the Store" stops just short of that kind of resolution. Instead, Mansfield leaves the governmental aspects of literary narration (and the discursive aspects of governance) exposed and unresolved. "The Woman at the Store" may not exhibit the "will-to-literature" we expect of modernist texts; this does not mean that Mansfield failed to understand her literary historical moment. Rather, she apprehended that moment's new imbrication with (gendered) modern governance and political economy.

I have been suggesting that understanding empire's intersections with modernism entails reexamining the production of modernist identities with attention to state administration. In the next part of the chapter, I discuss a novel by Sara Jeannette Duncan set in India that depicts colonial administration as a narrative project and writing a novel as an imperial one.

Duncan is usually described as an aspiring Jamesian realist, a novelist detailing the ironic contradictions of Anglo-India, or a failed writer of the modern decadent genre. Though critics often praise her for her "ironic" treatment of the conventions of the Anglo-Indian imperial romance, or for avoiding the lurid quality of the feminine picturesque Sara Suleri describes as a "collaboration between violence and sentimentality,"[40] they have not examined Duncan's literary *strategies* as part of a literary history interarticulated with imperial projects. She is sometimes read as a Canadian author instead of as an Anglo-Indian writer, but rarely as being, like Conrad, a writer generated by the dissolutions and consolidations of imperial claims.

Duncan worked first as a freelance reporter and then as columnist and reporter for the *Toronto Globe*, *The Washington Post* and the *Montreal Star*. In 1888, she began a trip around the world in order to write a travel narrative, *A Social Departure: How Orthodocia and I Went Round the World by Ourselves* (1890). While on this tour she met Everard Cotes, a British entomologist working at the Indian Museum. He proposed to her at the Taj Mahal. She finished her world tour, published her book and returned to India for their wedding. The two settled in Bengal province. She traveled between India and London frequently to write and to arrange for the publishing of her subsequent twenty-two books and other essays.

Set in Authority (1906) revolves around the trials and punishment of a private in the British army, accused of murdering an Indian civilian and sentenced very lightly by an Indian but Oxford-educated judge. The Viceroy of India, Anthony Andover, the fourth Baron Thame, and a Liberal, is outraged at the lightness of the sentence and forces his Chief Commissioner, Eliot Arden, to reopen the case. At the second trial, the jury brings in a guilty verdict and the second judge, who fagged for Andover at Eton when they were boys, sentences the soldier to death.

Andover demands that his regiment attend the execution, risking possible mutiny. To the relief of the Anglo-Indian community, the soldier, "Henry Morgan," commits suicide before he can be executed; he is later revealed to the reader and one other character to be the long-lost Herbert Tring, brother of Victoria Tring, the woman Andover will marry at the end of the novel. After Herbert's death, the man he supposedly murdered turns up alive in Calcutta. Intertwined with this plot is the story of the married Eliot Arden's unconsummated and largely unacknowledged "middle-aged" romance with Dr. Ruth Pearce, one of the "new women" taking to the professions, who provides him with the intellectual life his wife does not. Pearce befriends Herbert Tring (she may have helped him commit suicide) and he gives her a letter to his sister. This letter would reveal to Victoria that her lover killed her brother. When Pearce learns that Victoria and Anthony are engaged, she burns the letter.

Duncan's title, of course, refers to Anthony Andover's appointment as viceroy, a behind-the-scenes event his sisters, mother and Victoria discuss over tea at the novel's opening. Victoria says laughingly to Anthony's family: "Do tell me how it came – the offer. On a gold-emblazoned scroll, I suppose, with the royal arms at the top and the rising sun at the bottom. Carried on a scarlet cushion and escorted by a detachment of Horse Guards." "I can tell you Victoria. Mr. Craybrooke met him somewhere, directly after a Cabinet Council, and offered it to him. 'Anthony, old fellow, how would you like India?' he said."[41] The joke or anxiety here is about (not) being able to trace the origins, sites and limits of state power.[42] Self-consciously and securely "modern," Victoria and the Andovers can laugh at what "everyone" understands to be absurd ways of grounding authority. They know that scarlet cushions and Horse Guards are meaningless, and approve of being irreverent about fetishizing authority. At the same time, Duncan also highlights this historical moment of imperial rule as one in which the imagined authority granted by the imagined community hovered uncomfortably between national imaginary and state bureaucratic procedural. National objects like the gold-emblazoned scroll paradoxically both mystify and make intelligible the relationship between "a people" and their rulers. The elusiveness of the legitimating transfer of authority they purport to capture and represent is a far cry from the informal verbal offer made by a practical bureaucrat, a "Mr." of the civil service. Duncan underscores the parallel change overtaking this generation's aristocratic rulers as they became administrators. The Viceroy is neither Anthony Andover, Liberal, scholar, politician, administrator nor the fourth Baron Thame, "aristocratic scion," and therein, Duncan suggests, lies his historical significance.

The conflict between these two modes of authority and regulation (and the citizen-subjects they constructed) was writ large in British colonial India, and especially with regard to the post of viceroy. The British inscribed two contradictory theories about ruling mandate in the Government of India Act of August 2, 1858 (proclaimed November 8, 1858). Bernard Cohn describes these as the "feudal" and "representational" modes of colonial government:

> If India were to be ruled in a feudal mode, then an Indian aristocracy had to be recognized and/or created, which could play the part of "loyal feudatories" to their British queen. If India were to be ruled by the British in a "modernist" mode, then the principles which looked to a new kind of civic or public order had to be developed. Those adhering to this view desired a representational mode of government based sociologically on communities and interests with individuals representing these entities.[43]

Cohn explains that this proclamation assumes that authority should be grounded in a "usable past." A British past, an Indian past, and the relationship between them had to be codified and represented to both the Indians and the British as part of the post-Mutiny establishment of Indian peoples as subjects with a relationship to the Queen. But this codification did not resolve the feudal versus representational characterization of the imperial subject; it merely contained it in the Viceroy's position:

> The head of the British government in India after 1858 had a dual title and office. As governor general, he was responsible ultimately to the parliament and as "viceroy," he represented the monarch and her relationship to the princes and peoples of India.[44]

Anthony Andover's appointment, and the women's reactions to it, invoke the dual function of this office and the problems with representing this "relationship." He seems determined to get, as the Anglo-Indian community bitterly describes it, "his chance of playing iron arbiter at last. ... That's what he was born for – to hang an Englishman for shooting a native of India, and take the glorious consequences."[45] Anthony's Liberal principles, though endangered by his imperial service (his mother is horrified by his policies and worried that he will not be able to publish his radical book denouncing the idea of holding "lands by the sword" when he returns), are in the Morgan case related to a desire to display England's principle that all subjects can expect equal protection from their sovereign. On the other hand, answering to Parliament in a representative system means that he answers to his party. The Parliamentary Under-Secretary for India, with the support of Lord Akell, another MP, attempts to get Anthony's mother to soften his absolute attitude toward the British soldiers' treatment of natives. "Pride in the principle, in the unquestionably lofty motive, by all means dear Lady Thame. But, also, how much more there is to consider! We politicians have to look at things in the rough, you know – in the block."[46]

Duncan works this problem of representing government (and representative government) into the lineaments of the novel by never directly "representing" Anthony Andover in any scene. He remains behind the scenes – his discussions, actions and appearances either remembered, guessed or done by proxy. This difficulty Duncan creates around representing the Viceroy focuses attention on the process of codification and representation of authority Cohn outlines as part of the Proclamation. Various constituencies produce representations of Anthony's functions as if to embody his authority.

The least convincing of these representations are the ones produced by Ruth Pearce and Eliot Arden, who persistently try to depict him as an individual with a conscience, that is, to bring him into the narrative as a character. Ruth and Eliot, in other words, expect to produce themselves and other people as individualities who transcend their institutional circumstances. Duncan clearly marks this view of subjectivity as outmoded. Their failures function to underscore how Duncan uses Anthony Andover. Significantly, these are the two characters in the novel doomed to an unsuccessful romance, even after Arden's wife dies, because they are incapable of reading each other's expressions of interest or of conveying their own feelings.

Like Conrad, Duncan writes about professional administration. What ultimately causes her work to look less modern than Conrad's is that unlike Conrad, she does not occult her administration onto fetish items of imperial capital: ivory, heads on poles, the perversely decaying body of the white European. One way to read traditional characterizations of Conrad's work as the imperial birth of modernism is to see them as focused on the processes of this fetishization rather than on his interest in its foundation in the transfers of administrative authority which must be made over the distances capital has to travel. This is a critical fetishization of the techniques of the "will-to-literature."

Precisely the things that critics read as modern in *Heart of Darkness* actually re-engage older varieties of imperial fantasy. Though both Conrad and Duncan create their imperial backdrops with an awareness of how "the blank spaces on the map" are overwritten not only with the marks of the national geographer but also with those of the national accountant, it is Conrad who invokes the possibility of escape, up the river or back in time, by going native or in shunning proper "method." Duncan, on the other hand, makes her setting an inescapable chain of command. Nearly impenetrable it may prove, but that is because it bristles with civil and military ranks and responsibilities:

Pilaghur is the capital of the province of Ghoom, which is ruled by a Chief Commissioner, under the Government of India, under the Parliament of Great Britain and Ireland, under the King. Ghoom is, in fact, very far under. The Chief Commissioner has the glory and the responsibility of power ... he administers through his Commissioners, and they through their deputies and assistants, and they through their native clerks, their "baboos," and adjunct to the baboo through the churprassie, the herald and messenger of Government, who is dressed in scarlet and gold, and has often been known to collect taxes which were never imposed. The police aiding all. Down beneath the bare feet of the churprassie and the police we may see dimly the province of Ghoom.[47]

Conrad constructs a fantasy of a place in which colonial travel can be more than simply the "dynamic tendency of capitalism itself,"[48] in which one could eventually see Ghoom clearly, or in which capital's travels are like those of imperial adventurers. Duncan undercuts the idea of empire as white spaces on the map. Herbert Tring/Henry Morgan's family and friends imagine him as having gone to America (to the gold fields) or to South Africa (to the diamond mines); he has actually joined the army in India as a gentleman ranker.[49] But all of these destinations are bounded rather than expanded by international politics and economics. In lieu of Marlow, Duncan offers James Kelly, the man who comes to the Trings claiming to have seen Herbert six months ago in San Francisco (it is more like three years) headed for the Klondike gold fields and offering, if the Trings will pay his expenses, to find Herbert and bring him home. "This Kelly" is a slightly unsavory imperial traveler, "over here on some Irish-American business – he made a secret of that, but one can imagine the sort of thing."[50]

James Kelly was an Irish patriot by one parent only; but he was a man of business in his own right. He could quote the parent – a mother – to explain his connection with the Clan-na-Gael society for reasons of sentiment; and he could point to a considerable account for services rendered to justify it on other grounds. His sympathies, in fact, brought him a handsome turnover. He had pride in them and profit out of them, and did well.

It was like that with regard to his enterprise in commission from Mrs. Tring and Miss Victoria Tring. He had a liking for the job; it had the touch of drama that appealed to him. He often thought of the moment when he should walk up to Tring and clap him on the shoulder and say ... "Young man, I'm here to send you home." Just as he anticipated the telegram which should one day flash Irish-American congratulations to Dublin upon the laying of the foundation-stone of her own House of Parliament. It would be a consummation worth doing something for, at a reasonable figure.[51]

Neither a mercenary nor an idealist, Kelly works in the fissures of national identity, generating money and his own self-conscious sympathies, emotional consummations and pride from imperial conflicts and problems. "The sort of thing" he does is clandestine, possibly violent, and eminently readable as a variety of semi-professional imperial adventuring.

Conrad's Marlow objects to his aunt's belief that he takes his commercial imperial job for idealistic reasons. "She talked about 'weaning those ignorant millions from their horrid ways,' till, upon my word, she made me quite uncomfortable. I ventured to hint that the Company was run for profit."[52] Marlow is not solely motivated by profit. Conrad links dreams of imperial travel and imperial spaces not only with childhood innocence but also with adult psychological development. As a "little chap," Marlow explains, "I had a passion for maps. I would look for hours at South America, or Africa, or Australia, and lose myself in all the glories of exploration. At that time there were many blank spaces on the earth and when I saw one that looked particularly inviting on a map (but they all look that) I would put my finger on it and say, 'When I grow up I will go there.'" By this time, Africa has "ceased to be a blank space of delightful mystery – a white patch for a boy to dream gloriously over." Nonetheless, when Marlow looks at the river on the map, even as an adult, "it fascinated me as a snake would a bird." Marlow's trip into the "blank space" of Africa turns out to be everything he dreamed it would be: "It was the farthest point of navigation and the culminating point of my experience. It seemed somehow to throw a kind of light on everything about me – and into my thoughts."[53]

But where Conrad contrasts the expansiveness of Kurtz's and Marlow's complex psychologies to the task-oriented, utilitarian minds of the bureaucrats and administrators, Duncan emphasizes the ways in which Kelly and Arden are alike. Traditional modernist studies criticism implicitly understands what Conrad has Marlow call the redeeming "idea" of empire ("An idea at the back of it; not a sentimental pretence but an idea") behind the brutish part of empire as precisely this ideal of an expanding modern subjectivity. This is the kind of subjectivity that can see that the "tranquil waterway" of the civilized Thames leads "into the heart of an immense darkness" – without specifying what that darkness is. Marlow, like T. S. Eliot, finds a place to shelter the European man of letters from the state's bureaucratization and managed capitalism. Modernist studies would have it that this retreat is aesthetic; in other words, Duncan's realism is a stolid and naïve acceptance of the accountant and the manager – the men whom Conrad rejects as imperial men who do not, unlike Marlow, allow empire to develop their psyches. But Duncan's decision to work within the boundaries of realist narrative is far from naïve. Rather than dismissing bureaucracy as a strictly utilitarian phenomenon, Duncan evokes the excesses of its discourse. The petty bureaucrat and civil servant's name is almost "ardent." Moreover, James Kelly and Eliot Arden are alike in the fact that each attaches himself to "sentiments" through his imperial work and expands, as it were, the strictly practical aspects of his job – the administrator no less than the adventurer – because they are both discursively produced by the same state-managed systems. Arden is a bureaucrat; the "whole worth of the man" has gone into his job of colonial administrator for eighteen years. Correspondingly, "the chief value of his life [for him] had come out of" performing his job, as with Weber's "official," whose office demands "the full working capacity of the official, irrespective of the fact that his obligatory time in the bureau may be firmly delimited" and who "is chained to his activity by his entire material *and ideal* existence" (italics added).[54] The kind of man who "would have swept a chimney with a thought of the sparks that made his work," Arden is nonetheless valued not entirely for his national sentiments or devotion to the study of Indian culture (which perhaps allows him to be the man who "knows just where and why it [the Act] would pinch") but for his work on the Agricultural Holdings Act and the coal industry in Ghoom. Arden is less crass than Kelly, but like Kelly, Arden can devote himself to the consummation of empire as long as the figure is reasonable.

The viceroy provides a model for consummation. Andover has principles; he writes books on them and takes stands on them as if there are no "figures" at all. In outlining the gradients of imperial self-gratification,

Duncan connects the transfer of authority and the rise of imperial professionalism with a class-marked, racially and nationally closed circuit of subjectivity creation. This passage follows a description of the "more than moral support" Arden draws from Andover. Duncan describes him as standing first with his hat off on the "beflagged" platform to see Andover's ship off, and then driving back to his official residence with "his sowars in blue and khaki cantering and jingling behind":

Whatever happens elsewhere in these days of triumphant democracies, in India the Ruler survives. He is the shadow of the King, but the substance of kingship is curiously and pathetically his; and his sovereignty is most real with those who again represent him. The city and the hamlet stare apathetic; they have always had a conqueror. But in lonely places which the Viceroy's foot never presses and his eye never sees, men of his own race find in his person the authority for the purpose of their whole lives. He is the judge of all they do, and the symbol by which they do it. Reward and censure are in his hand, and he stands for whatever there is in the task of men that is sweeter than praise and more bitter than blame. He stands for the idea, the scheme, and the intention to which they are all pledged; and through the long sacrifice of the arid years something of their loyalty and devotion and submission to the idea gathers in the human way about the sign of it. The Viceroy may be a simple fellow, but his effigy is a wonderful accretion.[55]

Here Duncan reverses Victorian assumptions about the "special susceptibility of the Indian to parade and show" which meant that they could be ruled by "appeal to their Oriental imaginations."[56] As Cohn describes it, the British use of spectacle and display in India, from the flags and the jingling uniforms of Arden's escort to the carefully planned assemblies at which "the Queen," through her representatives, gave out titles and presents to Indian hereditary rulers, represented and thus created acceptable authority for British rule in India. As Duncan reads it, however, the viceroy's spectacles are not a show for the natives, but for the British administrators, effective only on "men of his own race." The transfer of authority is a sterile interaction in which the administrators and the viceroy authorize each other. The only Indian in *Set in Authority* who reacts with this kind of investment is an administrator for the British – Sir Ahmed Hossein, the first sessions judge to sentence Morgan/Tring.

Duncan's imperial geography emphasizes the limits state processes set on identity rather than the vast potential of empire for remaking the self. Herbert/Henry's ultimate disappearance into the empire to remake himself is entirely illusory. His sentence of execution/suicide underscores, rather, the ways in which state narratives such as the "evidence" and the stories of his supposed motives as well as Andover's narrative about British justice keep him from composing his own. As Hiria explains to her mistress Ruth Pearce, a soldier's ability to disappear into the wilderness is easily foiled: "'Surat is the cunning one, miss-sahib. It appears to him that soldier will get away quick. ... So very quick he cuts the belt of the gorah, miss-sahib, thinking he will have something. ... This Surat did not know, but inside is the lumbra, that marks all the gorah-log – ' 'His equipment number – yes.'"[57]

The limitlessness of the empire has been elided in varieties of Conrad criticism with a modern sense of the limitlessness of the human psyche and particularly the essential unknowableness of the (female) native psyche. Kurtz has become a dictator. He has "gone native." He has participated in "unspeakable" ceremonies. Conrad's Marlow, however, claims that the quality of thought his mode of imperial participation produces is vastly superior to that of the Accountant or that of the Manager. Men like those are no more than the discourses they work within: accounting, management, surveillance. The modernism of *Heart of Darkness* emerges from Kurtz. In such readings the contrast between Kurtz's heart of darkness and the account books of the inner station are understood as precisely the contrast between empty naïve realist detail and modernism's complex ineffability. But Conrad's novel can be read as "throwback" rather than "breakthrough" narrative for what can only be called its nostalgia for the individualistic, self-making adventures of colonial violence. The style that Kurtz (and Marlow's) superior minds supposedly allow is based on a failure to see the new developments in the rhetoric of administration at the turn of the century.

My larger point here is that Duncan's colonial fiction demonstrates the inadequacy of the assumption that modernism is a matter of style. Her use of realist techniques, when intertwined with issues of twentieth-century colonial governance, is qualitatively different from the realist novel's traditional investment in what Trotter, paraphrasing Ford Madox Ford, has described as confidence in the ability to create imaginary worlds dispensing "reliable knowledge about the way our fellows live their lives."[58]

The repeated "realistic" descriptions and discussions of British administrative authority in Duncan's Anglo-Indian narrative echo two dynamics of twentieth-century colonial governance in their deviation from the way detail is generally used in the traditional realist novel. First, there is the intentional failure of this descriptive detail to produce the Viceroy as either a physical presence or as a subjectivity to which we have access. This underlines the failure of colonial "details" (in the sense both of military escorts and of the elaborate attention to "representing authority" and incorporation through the use of objects Cohn describes) to inscribe consent and implicit authority in the way that sovereign authority and power could be inscribed in an earlier period. The British look to the Viceroy for a clear mandate, but can never be fully satisfied. Like Mansfield, Duncan does not attempt to transcend this "failure" with "will-to-literature." I take this as a politics of modernism rather than as a failure to practice modernism. The proliferation of realist detail in the twentieth-century colonial context is different from George Eliot's omniscience, in which, as Levenson puts it, the narrator is a confident, "assimilating, amalgamating force who makes transparent the opacities between individuals."[59]

This brings us to another dynamic of twentieth-century governance that becomes more visible to Western elites when it occurs in the context of colonial governance: sociological detail, categorical identity and the invention of group particularity as the levers of administrative power. As Thomas puts it, "rather than there being a savage to be conquered, there [is] ... a variety of native to be documented, enumerated, disciplined and uplifted."[60] While the realist commitment to the novel as an intelligible and useful account of people's lives[61] bears a resemblance to the twentieth-century administrative imperative toward accurately surveying "the social," the former describes norms while the latter creates them; the former amalgamates all into one omniscience while the latter is obsessed with differentiation. In the colonial context, Duncan seems to suggest, it becomes clear that what is administered in the details, conventions and paperwork of empire is consciousness, the administrator's no less than that of his supposed subjects. One of the Viceroy's first appointments is of Arden to the Chief Commissionership of Ghoom. The appointment excites comment because although Arden is qualified for the job, there are several other men in line for promotion who have more practical, tangible and recent accomplishments.

Arden had, of course, the qualifications that had brought him so brilliantly along to the Home Office. Those were understood. But the Viceroy had been known to say of him that he could read as well as write. ... Ghoom was a prize, a plum, a troublesome job and a great compliment; no Viceroy would make the selection in a hurry. That Thame should have given it to Eliot Arden – well, it threw a light on Thame. ... [O]ne man remembered how ... he had come upon the Viceroy and his Home Secretary stretched among the pine needles and arguing like a pair of undergraduates; and another had heard His Excellency say, "For all I know about the Upanishads I am indebted to Arden." There is no recognised official channel for conveying information about the Upanishads to anybody; Arden had not sent it in the files. The uncomfortable hypothesis under it all seemed to be that this, in his Excellency's point of view, was the sort of fellow to give things to, the sort of fellow who could talk and who knew about the Upanishads.[62]

Of course, there certainly were many "channels," official and otherwise, for conveying cultural knowledge, many of them permeable with channels for official police power. Political insurgence and crime were assumed to be intertwined, just as "culture" was often feared to be "nationalist."[63] Duncan mocks the "secretariats" because they look askance at Arden "consoling exile with a pocket Horace" when Arden's reading is what consolidates his power. This is in contrast to readings of realist novels that find in administration, knowledge gathering or institutions something that works against the "true human" consciousness demonstrated by an appreciation of Horace.

Duncan's deployment of "realist" style in the context of twentieth-century colonial administration suggests that defining modernism should not be merely a matter of categorizing a style to which a work seems committed as if the commitment were to the style itself. Duncan's commitment is not to realism but to how realist narrative functions in the discursive aspect of modern governance.

For Mansfield and Duncan, the point of a describable empire is not to generate the ineffable to war against the transparent and pedestrian bureaucratic, but the reverse: describable empire is an attempt to render governmentalization's practical yet stubbornly invisible new *discursive* proliferations. The reason that *Heart of Darkness* and work by these authors do not currently coexist in modernism and empire's genealogies is a critical failure to understand changes in literary authority in terms of the broader cultural and historical changes in the perception and exercise of state authority. In the next chapter, I turn to another instance in which assumptions about the nature of modernism's cultural history – in this case the modernity of "fluid identity" – have, in the absence of attention to the rise of twentieth-century state technologies such as identity documentation, similarly restricted other modernist genealogies.

CHAPTER 3

Soldiers and traitors: Rebecca West, the world wars and the state subject

> When, in 1936, General Emilio Mola announced that he would capture Madrid because he had four columns outside the city and a fifth column within, the world pounced on the phrase with the eagerness of a man who has been groping for an important word. ... In the 20th Century treason became a vocation, whose modern form was specifically the treason of ideas.
>
> *Time*, December 8, 1947

Modernist fictions of identity and subjectivity are often taken as indexing the newly fluid, indeterminate and performative elements of gender, racial and class identities generated by social phenomena such as metropolitan life, consumerist ideology, celebrity and expatriation. Critics often describe a distinctive modernist sense of identity as being without a fixed and authentic core. Modernist writers develop an interest in masquerade, illegibility, personae, artifice, proliferation of surfaces and perspectives, and so on. Against this, I argue that the historical period of modernism is not one in which identities proliferate, but one in which they become increasingly bureaucratically fixed.

The unfixing of identity itself should not be considered specific to the modernist period, or to modernist literature. The nineteenth-century novel, with which modernism's supposedly new sense of modern identity is often contrasted, abounds with changed names, adoptions, faked deaths, and the discovery of blood relations in strangers. While the point of these fictions may seem to be to return people to their proper places, it is nonetheless significant that the possibility of leaving those places lingers.

What *is* specific to the modernist period is the creation of a modern state infrastructure with the bureaucratic and administrative technology to identify, track and regulate its populations while institutionalizing "nationality" as a socially significant and codifiable identity. The use of identification documents, while not new, increased markedly at the end of the nineteenth century, as did all state functions.[1] Liberal ideologies of "freedom of movement" coincided with economic liberalism's demands for mobile and reserve labor forces. European states began to lift restrictions on populations whose internal movements had been restricted by poor relief tied to domicile and other (class-based) regulations, and to centralize benefits such as poor relief. But although states may have allowed more movement, keeping these mobile populations available to the state and distributing entitlements required increased documentation of individual identity.[2] Democratization, as historian John Torpey points out, ties citizens more tightly to the state. This is not to say that states had never taken an interest in documenting their populations. What had been missing was the bureaucratic and other technology for uniform dissemination of identity documents through entire societies.[3]

In what follows, I discuss Rebecca West's work as consistently and intensely engaged with this increasingly close relation between the citizen-subject and the state. I extend my argument about West's work and its history to claim that literary modernism marked not just the apprehension and expression of a new kind of modern subjectivity, but also a specific sense of state infrastructure's role in constructing that subjectivity.

By the age of fourteen, West had begun to participate in suffragist movements and to write about how gender determined the relation of each citizen to the state. In 1918, she cast the World War I soldier as victim of state sovereignty in *Return of the Soldier*. By 1938 she had traveled to Yugoslavia three times; she described her experiences in *Black Lamb and Grey Falcon* (1941), a mixed-genre narrative of over a thousand pages that had the history of Yugoslavia, the sources of World War II and the rise of fascism among its subjects. In 1945, she covered the treason trials of William Joyce and John Amery for *The New Yorker*. She later turned these articles into *The Meaning of Treason* (1947), which she updated and reissued with stories of cold war spies in 1964 and 1981. During the 1950s, she read the House Committee on Un-American Activities (HUAC) reports, asked contacts in Washington to interview FBI agents and couriers for the Communist Party for her, and was friends with CIA director Allen Dulles and with chief of the New York *Herald-Tribune's* Washington Press Bureau, Bert Andrews. Andrews had written a book on Alger Hiss and participated in the investigation under Nixon.[4] She had Admiral Rickover send her copies of the latest U.S. nuclear submarines as they were deployed,[5] compiled her own lists of secret communists and wrote articles discussing forms of government and authority in the wake of the two world wars.

I begin with one of the earliest of West's extraordinary series of engagements of the nation-state's capacity to embrace and create its citizens at length. I read *The Return of the Soldier*, written during World War I, as a product of a time when historical subjectivity was being recast as male, following the suffrage movement's decline, to accommodate the men who returned at the end of the war. West uses a female narrator to tell the soldier's story. This strategy, as well as the centrality of shell shock and amnesia to the novel's plot, is West's way of exposing the gendered stakes various citizens could be granted in the nation, the way nationalism was mobilized as gendered narrative, and the way Freudian psychology had the potential to make even "the unconscious" available to the state for management. The fluidity of identity that Chris Baldry – West's protagonist – tries to produce to escape the war is useless against the efficiency of military conscription.

Where critics such as Bonnie Kime Scott separate West's later explicit interest in the state as an entity from her earlier work ("[a]fter 1940, West did extensive trial and crime reportage, specializing in themes relating to treason that seem very distant from her modernist tendencies and her early socialist feminism"),[6] I will argue that the two are continuous. I conclude this essay by suggesting that my reading of *The Return of the Soldier* connects it to the section on William Joyce in West's later work *The Meaning of Treason* (1947). Joyce was tried for treason because he traveled to Germany and worked as a radio propagandist for the Nazis during World War II. He was found guilty and hanged.[7] As West describes it, Joyce's defense, which was based on the fact that he was not a British citizen (and therefore could not commit treason), reveals the emblematic nature of his position as what Torpey might call the "modern embraced state subject." I read the trajectory from *The Return of the Soldier* to the case of William Joyce as a culmination of the process by which the subject's freedom to have a national (imagined) identity dissolves in the face of state documentation, even as that documentation reinforces particular structures of national identity that are far from imaginary or voluntary.

CHARTING THE ENGLISH (E)STATE

The Return of the Soldier is about Chris Baldry, a young British army officer. Chris's wife, Kitty, and his cousin, Jenny (the narrator), are waiting for him in the family estate, Baldry Court. They are visited by a woman, Margaret, from Wealdstone, a lower-class suburb. Margaret says that Chris has been wounded and is in a hospital in England. Having heard no news from the War Office, the women think she is a con artist. Margaret is telling the truth. Chris wires her from the hospital because he has lost fifteen years of his memory. He has forgotten that he and Margaret, once nearly engaged, had a fight and then lost track of each other. He has also forgotten his father's death, his rescue of the family business, his marriage to Kitty and all the events of the war. He believes that he is twenty-one years old and about to ask Margaret to marry him. The doctors send him home to recover. He insists on spending his days with Margaret, who has married someone else because she thought Chris had left her. Although he does not recognize Kitty and feels betrayed by fifteen years of aging in Jenny, he seems not to notice any change in Margaret or the her cheap, ugly clothing that reveals the way she lives now. Margaret is the one who understands and explains to the doctor that the way to bring Chris's memory back is through the only memory truly important to him – the son who died at the age of two. The doctor tells her she must do it. Although both Margaret and Jenny at first object because Chris will no longer be happy, they eventually agree that they can't leave him the way he is. Chris's memory returns, meaning that he will ultimately have to return to the trenches.

Chris's condition is recognizable as part of the World War I epidemic of shell shock, although his specific symptom, fifteen years missing from his memory, is not an actual symptom. Amnesia in shell-shock cases tended to be more general and to last for shorter periods of time. West's portrayal of a shell-shocked soldier is an interpretation of the cultural meaning of shell shock rather than an attempt to mirror the medical literature or to combine cultural interpretation with imagining, as Woolf does in *Mrs. Dalloway*, the workings of a shell-shocked consciousness. Although it was the problem of shell-shocked soldiers that definitively ended the assumption that neurotic illness could not have a wholly psychological cause and brought Freud (in a much-revised, non-sexual version) into British psychiatry,[8] the turn toward seeing nervous illness as moral weakness and lack of will power had begun at the turn of the century. The war strengthened a tendency to think of male nervous breakdown as unmanly rebellion or cowardice.[9] West's interpretation of shell shock in Chris's case accepts and expands the conventional judgments of this disorder, but her ultimate target is not individual cowardice, but war itself.

Chris's amnesia is, of course, a refusal of the trenches. But he doesn't forget merely the war. Chris's amnesia places him not only in a time before he was a soldier but also in a time before he was a businessman and head of his family and its estate. Thus, his symptoms reject both military and civilian expectations of masculinity. This rejection, as I discuss in detail below, takes the form of blaming Kitty and Jenny for policing male gender roles. West's interpretation, which in part did have contemporary medical advocates, goes beyond an analysis of the demands of male citizenship to examine how rebellion against them is played out over women's bodies and representations of the national body as female.[10]

Chris's amnesia also references traditional meanings of "nostalgia." Again, this is a way for West to expand her account of Chris's symptom into a cultural reading. Although the term "nostalgia" is now popularly understood to refer to positive feelings of remembrance, Fred Davis points out that its original meaning, homesickness so severe that it was a disease, persisted into the twentieth century.[11] Patients were understood to be responding to the trauma caused by the increased dislocation of modern life, as a much greater part of the population no longer lived on its native soil, thus losing an essential continuity with birthplace and history. Doctors considered nostalgia a man's disease because women's attachments to the home supposedly protected them from the dislocations and instability of the modern world. Indeed, women could provide the antidote for nostalgia by providing a source of wholeness for men. "In other words, while women were the classic objects of nostalgic affection in their role as mothers, they were less likely to be subjects of it ... the female body signifies the originary birthplace, the familiar yet enigmatic homeland from which the male subject has been irrevocably exiled."[12]

Margaret, Baldry Court and the Harroweald countryside are the things that Chris attempts to return to from this particularly male exile. Both his family and Margaret are tremendously burdened with Chris's expectations of "home." Jenny is forced to reconsider both in the light of Chris's need for them to be what they were and his seeming disregard for the changes the past fifteen years have made to Margaret.

Baldry Court, like Margaret, is paradoxically the site of tremendous change – Chris hates the inside of the house because he was expecting it to be as it was fifteen years earlier, forcing Jenny to think about exactly how many changes have been made to its space – and a fixed center for an existence that would belie anything happening in the outside world. West wrote this novel during the war, and interpretations of "home" and the "insolent" privacy of Baldry Court must be understood in this political context. The resonance of the (oft-repeated) phrases about the "green pleasantness" of the Harroweald countryside comes from the way they are counterposed to the desolate trenches, the "brown rottenness" that haunts Jenny's nightmares about Chris running from shelling at the front. Home is a respite from fighting, even as, frighteningly, it is also a place under siege because of the threat of German invasion. Thus, "Home" is also "England" and Margaret's body is also a nurturing motherland. The two ("home" and "Margaret") come together in Chris's nostalgia for the time of his first love to produce a pastoral ideal of his nation as his mother. He is only happy when he can be outside the house yet still on the grounds of the estate with Margaret. Margaret is depicted as understanding sensuality and sexuality in ways that neither Kitty nor Jenny can. While her relationship with Chris encompasses sexual desire, it is also true that Jenny describes her as a transfiguring maternal figure. Watching from the window as the two former lovers meet again, she sees Margaret as strengthening and saving Chris:

How her near presence had been known by Chris I do not understand, but there he was, running across the lawn as night after night I had seen him in my dreams running across No Man's Land. I knew that so he would close his eyes as he ran; I knew that so he would pitch on his knees when he reached safety. I assumed that at Margaret's feet lay safety, even before I saw her arms brace him under the armpits with a gesture that was not passionate, but rather the movement of one carrying a wounded man from under fire. But even when she had raised his head to the level of her lips, the central issue was not decided. I covered my eyes and said aloud, "In a minute he will see her face, her hands." But although it was a long time before I looked again they were still clinging breast to breast. It was as though her embrace fed him, he looked so strong as he broke away.[13]

The picture Jenny has is of Chris being carried "home," away from the war. Margaret is more than a former lover or a symbol of childhood. She is also a place. Contrasted to "No Man's Land," she is safe, familiar and claimable – the homeland of the mother's body – and she feeds him from her breast.

Jenny sees that Chris's illness temporarily exempts him from experiencing a modern state that "has" its citizens as both responsibilities and resources. The same bureaucracy both provides for the entitled poor and keeps track of draft-age men. "While her spell endured they could not send him back into the hell of war. This wonderful kind woman held his body as safely as she held his soul."[14] The reality of Chris's situation, shared with many European men on both sides of the war, is that he stands under the jurisdiction of a state's prerogative power to act arbitrarily as a state in the domain of international relations. Far from being a nurturing motherland, state domination, which is always based on a territorial monopoly, leads to the rooting of state power in "the state's pursuit of values other than the welfare of its citizenry; its aim is self-affirmation through displays of power and prestige and not in protection or sustenance of mortal life."[15] Chris's amnesia highlights a disjuncture between things the state would like to depict as seamlessly attached: the ideal nurturing motherland one fights to protect and which protects its subjects, and the state's prerogative right to labor, military service and other resources that can be drawn from its subjects' bodies. Ironically, Chris has deprived the state of his fighting powers because he believes too strongly in exactly the structures of national identity that would ordinarily facilitate his participation in the military.

If we read his amnesia as rebellion, or treason, against the state, it falls into the class of treasons that only became possible with the advent of a modern sense of national identity. Citizens, whatever the official words of their national oaths, can now imagine that actions taken in opposition to official government policy or even to direct orders of the head of state are not necessarily morally treasonous (though they may be legally treasonous) because loyalty is not clearly understood or articulated in terms of a monarch or person. Instead, loyalty is understood in terms of the will of a people or of a written constitution. Even a head of state can commit treason. The legally treasonous subject can envision him or herself as holding a country or a leader to "true" national obligations or ideals.

But Chris's rejection of state demands in favor of a national fantasy is complexly gendered. Chris cannot be held responsible for the things he forgets, so Jenny, Kitty and Margaret must accept those burdens. To Chris, Margaret has no age and he does not see the marks poverty has made on her body. While Jenny finds this "beautiful," partly because she so desperately wants to bring Chris the world as he sees it, it is also horrifying. Because Jenny sees through her own eyes rather than through Chris's, we know that there are two Margarets. The one Chris sees is Margaret "transfigured by eternity." But, as Jenny sees when she goes to Wealdstone to ask Margaret to come to Chris, this glowing Margaret mixes painfully with details of fifteen years of poverty and suffering that have transfigured her body not into eternity but from the beauty of youth in the country to the "ugliness" of middle age and lower classness on an allotment:

It would have been such agony to the finger tips to touch any part of her apparel ... I perceived clearly that that ecstatic woman lifting her eyes and her hands to the benediction of love was Margaret as she existed in eternity; but this was Margaret as she existed in time, as the fifteen years between Monkey Island and this damp day in Ladysmith Road had irreparably made her.[16]

In contrast to the rural countryside where Chris once courted her, Margaret's present garden is corrupted by industry. It is "imperfectly reclaimed from the greasy field," the grass is "rank" and the soil is "clay mould blackened by coal dust from the railway line and the adjacent goods yard."[17] But Jenny's real consternation is that "not only did Margaret live in this place; she belonged to it"(91) and "belonging" is certified by the ugliness of lower-class tastes and necessities. Poor enough to live in Wealdstone, Margaret also has to do her own baking and hasn't had the luxury of protecting her hands and face from the marks of aging and work.

When she opened the door she gazed at me with watering eyes and in perplexity stroked her disordered hair with a floury hand. Her face was sallow with heat, and beads of perspiration glittered in the deep dragging line between her nostrils and the corners of her mouth. ... as I spoke of his [Chris's] longing I turned my eyes away from her, because she was sitting on a sofa, upholstered in velveteen of a sickish green, which was so low that her knees stuck up in front of her and she had to clasp them with her seamed floury hands; and I could see that the skin of her face was damp.[18]

Jenny goes on to chronicle other furnishings in the room that are as repulsive as the sofa, and cannot seem to stop noticing Margaret's "dreadful" hands and the unprepossessing appearance of Margaret's husband, who "lacks mastery" in the garden, wheezes and has unbuckled straps at his waistcoat, a "prominent Adam's apple" and "curly grey hairs growing from every place where it is unadvisable that hairs should grow."[19] Unlike Chris, Mr. Grey was never fit for the military and does not have the aura surrounding the young subalterns protecting the country. It is too simple to say that Jenny and Kitty represent the worst features of upper-class snobbery and to look at West's politics or personal life for the reasons. West also uses Jenny's narration to emphasize the most disturbing aspect of Chris's amnesia – the way it empties of meaning and obliterates the very real suffering Margaret has gone through in the past fifteen years. Chris ignores what (partly because of him) has happened to her and uses her as an icon of his unclouded youth. She stands for his rejections of the war, the business life he had to lead and the kind of marriage he made. She becomes symbolic of a place out of time and history, and her actual relations to these are rendered irrelevant. Moreover, Chris, because he is ill, does not have to take responsibility for the choices he made and forced onto other people. It is Jenny's narrative and vision, then, that do what Chris cannot. Because of the war, he needs to see Margaret, Harroweald and the motherland in this way. But Jenny, "exiled"[20] from Chris's life and also from, as I will argue, a particular kind of stake in the nation, must look not only at the realities of Margaret's history but also at the estate's relation to national history.

First, she remembers that the moment when Chris saved the family business – and its holdings in Harroweald – came at the time he took a trip to Mexico during the revolution there. Jenny does not know exactly what Chris did, but suggests that the family business has been benefiting from Mexican labor in the mines and that Chris forced the workers to continue working instead of joining the revolution:

That night he talked till late with his father and in the morning he had started for Mexico, to keep the mines going through the revolution, to keep the firm's head above water and Baldry Court sleek and hospitable, to keep everything bright and splendid save only his youth .... [21]

The brightness and splendor of Baldry Court, up until this point, have revolved around its isolation, not its connections with international trade. Jenny describes how she and Kitty maintain Baldry Court, despite the war, as "the splendid house which was not so much a house as a vast piece of space partitioned off from the universe and decorated partly for beauty and partly to make our privacy more insolent."[22] Jenny's memory of Chris's coming-of-age interrupts the fantasy of Baldry Court's gracious living as purely English and isolated from the power relations of the international economy. The land expropriation taking place in Mexico stands in contrast to the vast acreage of Baldry Court and its inhabitants' ability to partition it off.

As Jenny reflects on the estate itself, West considers imperialism's role in the current conflict:

Why had modern life brought forth these horrors that make the old tragedies seem no more than nursery shows? Perhaps it is that adventurous men have too greatly changed the outward world which is life's engenderment. There are towns now, and even the trees and flowers are not as they were; the crocuses on the lawn, whose blades showed white in the wide beam let out by the window Chris had opened, should have pierced turf on Mediterranean cliffs; the golden larch beyond should have cast its long shadows on little yellow men as they crossed a Chinese plain. And the sky also is different. Behind Chris's head, as he halted at the open window, a searchlight turned all ways in the night like a sword brandished among the stars.[23]

In this distorted pastoral vision of England, the mercantile-imperial adventures of men, which make foreign plants available for English estate landscaping, cause the "horrors" of modern life that Chris has retreated from. Moreover, relating these changes in the landscape to the presence of a wartime searchlight links these same "adventurous men" and imperialism to the current war. Jenny seems a traitor here as she betrays all national memory and propaganda to insist on the impure and imperial construction of England. Chris and his peers, like Baldry Court and England, do not stand apart from nationalist systems as innocent victims of world politics.

Margaret's first reaction to seeing Baldry Court is to say, "It's a big place. How poor Chris must have worked to keep it up." Jenny understands how absurd this idea is. No one at Baldry Court works as Margaret and her husband work in their garden or as she and her father worked at the inn on Monkey Island, but the very absurdity of Margaret's words forces Jenny to drop the pretense that the life they lead is work. It also underscores the way she and Kitty consistently shift moral responsibility away from Chris:

The pity of this woman was like a flaming sword. No one had ever before pitied Chris for the magnificence of Baldry Court. It had been our pretence that by wearing costly clothes and organizing a costly life we had been the servants of his desire. But she revealed the truth that although he did indeed desire a magnificent house, it was a house not built with hands.[24]

Because Chris's nostalgia produces an ideal nation iconized as Margaret rather than an imperial state, and his condition evokes pity for the price young men are paying in the war, he effectively escapes from comprehending his life in relation to the national history. Chris prefers to see Margaret as she used to be: young and beautiful against the backdrop of her former home – a rural inn on an island in the middle of the Thames. We should not miss the significance of the fact that, like England, it is an island.

His memories of their courtship include quintessential features of the English landscape: chestnut, walnut, willow trees, swans, cow-parsley, rabbits. He "forgets" that part of their fight was over the fact that he did not treat Margaret with the same respect he would have given to a woman of his own class. Chris's amnesia, then, allows him to place himself in innocent relation to the English rural landscape and the ideal of the English estate. It also places England in innocent relation to him; that is to say, he turns away from the government to the iconic "green England" that Margaret represents and renegotiates his own participation in the war. Chris's defection from historical knowledge and his accompanying valorization of Margaret leave Jenny and Kitty historically and institutionally responsible for the war and for the way he is expected to perform as a man. It turns out that the "vast piece of space" they have "partitioned off from the universe" and maintained for him is not partitioned off from No Man's Land at all. He rejects it because of its decadent impurity and imperial connections to the war he has been caught up in. But this takes the form of rejecting Kitty and Jenny. His condition as the wounded national subject leaves him irreproachable, even though he has certainly benefited the most from the class and gender systems which produced Baldry Court. This is perhaps most apparent in the fact that Chris is angry about changes made to Baldry Court when it was he who rebuilt it after his marriage, handing "it over to architects who had not so much the wild eye of the artist as the knowing wink of the manicurist."[25] Unlike Chris, Jenny cannot dissociate herself from her part in the war or in the international power relations constructing Baldry Court by pleading amnesia. She admits they are there but she spares "our soldier" by feminizing the sources of and accepting responsibility for his wounds.

Jenny's narrative compares Chris's nostalgia and amnesia very unfavorably to Kitty's lack of sentiment. Jenny sees Chris's loss of memory as an "adroit recovery of the dropped pearl of beauty"[26] in its rejection of modern warfare and as an explicit statement about the lack of adventure and fulfillment in his life as laid out for him by his family and class. Jenny explains Chris's entrapment in stifling bourgeois structures as the fault of women such as Kitty and herself.

[H]e was not like other city men. When we had played together as children in that wood he had always shown great faith in the imminence of the improbable. ... I was aware that this faith had persisted into his adult life. ... It was his hopeless hope that ... he would have an experience that would act on his life like alchemy. ... There had been, of course, no chance of his ever getting it ... there wasn't room to swing a revelation in his crowded life ... at his father's death, he had been obliged to take over a business that was weighted by the needs of a mob of female relatives who were all useless either in the old way with antimacassars or in the new way with golf clubs. Then Kitty had come along and picked up his conception of normal expenditure and carelessly stretched it as a woman stretches a new glove on her hand.[27]

Here Jenny describes Chris as having his spiritual potential arrested, tied down to a dull life by a "mob" of needy women. Her metaphor for the obligations conferred on men upon marriage – Kitty stretching the glove – is a continuation and development of the way Kitty's participation in the life she and Chris *share* is portrayed as evidence only of Kitty's shallowness, materiality and inhuman lack of sentiment.

Jenny's narrative establishes Kitty, and by association feminine consumption, as the enforcer of conventional bourgeois obligation, as if Chris and his father had no personal stake in the maintenance of Baldry Court. At the very opening of the novel, Jenny finds that Kitty is not mourning when she goes to the old nursery, but drying her hair. Moreover, this opening places Kitty quite clearly in the realm of the feminized consumer as Jenny links her with a cover girl on a woman's magazine.

I had not meant to enter it again after the child's death but I had come suddenly on Kitty as she slipped the key into the lock. . . . I turned away so that I might not spy on Kitty revisiting her dead. But she called after me: "Come here Jenny. I'm going to dry my hair." And when I looked again I saw that her golden hair was all about her shoulders and that she wore over her frock a little silken jacket trimmed with rosebuds. She looked so like a girl on a magazine cover that one expected to find a large "7d" somewhere attached to her person. . . . "I always come in here when Emery has washed my hair. It's the sunniest room in the house. I wish Chris wouldn't have kept it as a nursery when there's no chance – . . . ."[28]

While Chris's amnesia inspires Jenny with awe and pity, she treats Kitty's "forgetting" with contempt. Here, for instance, Kitty is despicable because she doesn't want to maintain the nursery as a shrine. Because she is a woman this is doubly shocking.

Where Chris's memories are sublime expressions of an "act of genius" (130), Jenny renders Kitty's pathetic attempts to mobilize memory on her own behalf as superficial, materialistic and crassly manipulative. Kitty tries to reclaim Chris and remind him of their marriage with her dress and jewelry. She dresses in a dress nearly identical to her wedding gown and puts on every piece of jewelry Chris has ever given her. She carefully plots where she will sit in the room so that the light will reflect off the dress and beautify her expression:

She frowned to see that the high lights on the satin shone scarlet from the fire, that her flesh glowed like a rose, and she changed her seat. . . . she was

controlling her face into harmony with the appearance of serene virginity upon
which his eyes would light when he entered the room. . . . "It seems so strange
that you should not remember me," she said. "You gave me all these."[29]

Despite Chris's polite reply to this woman he cannot really remember, it
becomes apparent that he is thinking about Margaret. The fact that
"Kitty put up her hands as if to defend her jewels"[30] underlines the idea
that Kitty is so devoid of feeling that she literally cannot be hurt. Similarly, as Jenny and Margaret consider letting Chris remain as he is, Kitty
passes the nursery:

Why she had come up I do not know, nor why her face puckered with tears as
she looked in on us. It was not that she had the slightest intimation of our
decision, for she could not have conceived that we could follow any course but
that which was obviously to her advantage. It was simply that she hated to see
this strange, ugly woman [Margaret] moving about among her things.[31]

Jenny consistently links Kitty's femininity, as we have seen, with her
relationship to "things." This association is paradigmatic of a conception
of modernity embodied as the voracious female consumer who is both a
victim in the face of and dangerously released by capitalist commodity
culture. Indexing modernity using the concept of consumption, Felski
argues, puts femininity at the heart of the modern in a way that focusing
on models of production and rationalization does not. Consumption cuts
across the public/private divide and women are no longer "premodern"
but modernity itself.[32] It is because of women's "voraciousness" for things
that Chris had to give up a life of revelation. It is this same voraciousness
that seems to have destroyed the possibility that Chris could find shelter
in the space of Baldry Court from the horrors of war – even though
the adventures (and imperial consumption) of men have deformed the
English landscape, it is as if the women charged with maintaining the
estate have failed. For while Margaret's purity and openness to being
the object of nostalgia are certainly due to her connections with Chris's
adolescence I think it is just as important that she is explicitly disconnected from the kind of capitalist consumption practiced by Kitty on
behalf of the estate. Margaret is not just poor but premodern. While she
doesn't have consumer goods, this is because she doesn't want them.
Unlike Kitty, she is above desire. In this configuration, wealth functions
as a marker of the capitalist modernity that forced Chris to give up his
dreams and on an international scale sent the country to its first modern

war.[33] Jenny presents Kitty as an enticement to participation in capital that crosses even class lines:

> Beautiful women of her type lose, in this matter of [getting] admiration [from men] alone, their otherwise tremendous sense of class distinction; they are obscurely aware that it is their civilizing mission to flash the jewel of their beauty before all men, so that they shall desire it and work to get the wealth to buy it, and thus be seduced by a present appetite to a tilling of the earth that serves the future.[34]

The difference between Margaret and Kitty is really the difference between the nation and the state. Kitty's interest in Chris is like a state's interest – he must be properly productive and what his body produces, indeed, his body itself, should be her prerogative.

West's narrative strategy draws our attention to the inconsistencies and struggles required to keep "our soldier" free of guilt and responsibility. Jenny, as we have seen, is a reliable narrator of sorts, but only because she so obviously either refuses to interpret the things she sees correctly or falsely contextualizes them. Her depiction of Kitty as feminine enforcer of masculinity would be one example of this. In this, West wrestles with what I discussed earlier as the centrality of the idea of the soldier as the national subject. Rather than focusing on a "new woman" as she would later in her career, or even the war nurses, cooks and Voluntary Aid Detachment (VAD) volunteers, making Jenny the narrator confronts the problem of a returned soldier in a way that links what this return entailed for women politically with what it might mean for women as creative subjects.

Discussions of the suffrage movement have focused on how it established women as historical subjects and political agents of change. But this moment coincided with the circumstances of World War I, when the subject of history seemed to be not a British woman but a British soldier. While women authors of this period may have been philosophically and rhetorically repositioning themselves in relation to theories of citizenship, politics and nationality, they nonetheless also had to confront the model of the historical citizen–subject as a draftable male who would die for his country or be responsible for saving it. Sandra M. Gilbert and Susan Gubar have argued that the "good dead soldier" is central to modernist women writers' liberation. They read, for instance, the end of *Jacob's Room* (the question of what to do with the dead Jacob's shoes after the war) as a suggestion that women will now be able to claim Jacob's patriarchal rights to authorship.[35]

This argument proffers a historical explanation for what some critics have described as a marked divergence in the subjectivities crafted by male and female modernists: male artists built the alienated modern subject from returned soldiers bearing wounds of impotence, battle trauma, loss of authority and feminization; female artists built a newly liberated modern subject from women who had worked in the factories, driven ambulances, managed homes and businesses the men left behind, and now occupied public spaces in which they outnumbered the men of their generation. But before taking the soldier's sacrifice as liberatory for women's art and politics, we should consider the history of the postwar weakening of the British women's movement.

England's entrance into the war in August 1914 ended the militant and constitutional suffragist activities which had become a mass movement during the previous decade. In many cases, suffragists became war workers. Militant activists were even released from prison on the somewhat ironic condition that they pledge not to use violent activities during the war. The majority of feminist organizations, including the Women's Social and Political Union (WSPU), were dissolved.[36] Organized feminism never regained its momentum as a mass movement. Historian Susan Kingsley Kent argues that the war led many feminists to modify their earlier demands for the elimination of separate spheres and equality based on rights. They switched instead to a rhetoric that emphasized women's special needs based on marriage and motherhood. This emphasized essential sexual difference, assumed both that all women married and had children and that only those women who performed these services had a claim on the state. This shift was neither sudden nor endorsed by all feminists, but it was firmly in place by the 1920s.

The returning soldier is as significant as the dead soldier. Prewar egalitarian feminism and its focus on the sex war became associated with the recently ended war, while "the new feminism" became associated with a return to peace.[37] Moreover, the frustration and rage of the front soldier who had fought a confining and defensive trench war were often directed at a feminized "home," acted out on the bodies of women (both literally and figuratively), and found expression in a society-wide backlash against feminism.[38] New feminists cited a fear of men's violence as a reason to relinquish positions in the public sphere to returning men and argued for accepting a limited suffrage bill (women who were householders or the wives of householders and who were at least thirty years old) instead of continuing to demand that votes be granted on the same bases as they were to men. While parliamentary debate shows that limited suffrage was granted partially out of fear that militant suffragist activities would be renewed otherwise, it was generally understood as a reward for the war work, lauded by the press and government, that women had done.[39] The idea of national citizenship both within feminism and in the country as a whole had been redefined to accommodate the returning British soldier. The age requirement on women's suffrage, for instance, was set to guarantee that women would not have a voting majority over a male population decimated by the war.[40] The issue of suffrage now "over," the country directed its hostility toward women who continued to work after the war – by 1921 fewer women were working than in 1911.[41]

This history demands that we reconsider the significance of modernist women's novels about the "men of 1914" (*Jacob's Room*, to which I turn shortly, was published just four years after *The Return of the Soldier*). In balancing Jenny's narrative power against the fact that her narrative is the soldier's story rather than her own, West lays bare the way modern subjectivity is created and gendered by the nation-state.

The strength and knowledge contained in Jenny's narrative may seem to exist in inverse relation to Chris's incapacitation. He is unfit to participate in either the war (the national) or the private domestic life of Baldry Court, leaving Jenny as the historical custodian of both. She remembers his childhood, when and how the house was altered, the history of the family business and his old dreams and plans. She remembers his departure for the war, and, on finding out about Margaret, is able to place her in Chris's history. Chris goes to her for confirmation that "all this" – the changes he finds but cannot comprehend, the things he reads about the Germans in Belgium – are true. But while these are knowledges Jenny alone has, the character who has amnesia ironically emerges as the most powerful precisely because of what he has forgotten.

Jenny might get a new voice but it speaks from a soldier-identified standpoint. She is at first glance a power broker in the war and postwar era – a young single woman, undraftable and able to take the place of incapacitated men who have lost their ability to comprehend their lives in relation to national events or "the national" itself. But she is absent from her own first-person narration. Moreover, Jenny's sense of time must submit to Chris's. His return to Baldry Court fifteen years out of synch exposes the fact that it is male time that becomes historic. The women, including Margaret (who now has a life of her own), must act as though it is actually fifteen years ago. The urgency Kitty and Jenny feel is not only because of their love for Chris, but also because without him they cannot exist – "nothing could ever really become a part of our life until it had been referred to Chris's attention."[42] Kitty almost literally does not exist if Chris cannot remember her. She becomes a "broken doll, face downward on a sofa, with one limp arm dangling to the floor, or protruding stiff feet in fantastic slippers from the end of her curtained bed."[43] In a parody of Chris's status as a soldier and of the woman's war work she does not participate in, she fills the time by "holding a review of her underclothing."[44] After Margaret restores Chris's memory, she vanishes from the text.

Karen Lawrence has argued that Woolf's narration in *Jacob's Room* may be understood as feminine not because of its sense of women's power in the wake of the war, but because what the narrator cannot know and where she cannot venture correspond to spaces in England women could not venture into and publics in which they could not participate.[45] The narrator of *Jacob's Room*, while seeming to hold the power of narrative authority over Jacob, is actually restricted by her inability to penetrate male spaces like Jacob's college rooms. Like this narrator, who follows Jacob from place to place only to be stymied by what a woman has never seen and who is best represented in the text by women whom Jacob doesn't really see, Jenny's story is made up largely of what she can see from the windows of the house or glimpse across the lawns. In the process of telling a story she is peripheral to, she realizes that she has known since she came of age that Chris "had never seen me at all save in the most cursory fashion. On the eye of his mind ... I had hardly impinged."[46]

Jenny may be a narrator as the result of a soldier's sacrifice, but just as her "war work" is to maintain Baldry Court, her narrative's work is to maintain a place for the soldier. Her subjective existence in the narrative is justified only by what has happened to Chris. Analogously, as we have seen, women workers could justify their participation in the public sphere only in terms of war work.

But if Jenny's narrative is not a guiltily elated elegy for passing male political, economic and aesthetic power, neither does it capitulate to the male-heroic national subjectivity it depicts. West creates a situation in which a woman's narrative exposes the national-statist grounds upon which modern subject(ivity) for both men and women is created by moving the soldier's story from No Man's Land to the estate. It is only by questioning the "grounds" upon which Chris chooses to locate his subjectivity that Jenny can truly engage the war. When she connects the estate to the empire, she undercuts Chris's nostalgia by revealing the impure England underneath.

It is Chris's passion for the estate that in the end most clearly exposes the gendering of national nostalgia. Jenny and Kitty have always "lost" the estate. Kitty and Chris have lost their son and cannot have another one. Jenny is Chris's female cousin and therefore has no claim to Baldry Court. Many upper-class women lost their family property upon the deaths of men in the war, either because of the rising death taxes or because estates were entailed to be inherited only by males. Masami Usui cites this history in her analysis of Woolf's *Mrs. Dalloway*, arguing that one of the more significant lines of the novel is: "The War was over, except for some one like Mrs. Foxcroft at the Embassy last night eating her heart out because that nice boy was killed and now the old Manor House must go to a cousin."[47] West's Jenny is always once removed from the grounds of Chris's nostalgic national attachment. If the war means that women like Kitty and Jenny lose "their" estates, then their nostalgia can only be for a patriarchal inheritance system in which the men who attach them to "England" are still alive. For women like Margaret, "England" is the pathetic ugly house and bit of land that looks like an "allotment."

This should remind us that West opened *The Return of the Soldier* by suggesting that, as in classic civic republican theory, women can only have secondary national attachments:

[L]ike most Englishwomen of my time, I was wishing for the return of a soldier. Disregarding the national interest and everything else except the keen prehensile gesture of our hearts towards him, I wanted to snatch my cousin Christopher from the wars and seal him in this green pleasantness his wife and I now looked upon.[48]

Declaring her feelings as at least partly national-collective – she is an "Englishwoman" – we might read the novel as Jenny's modernist mapping of the grounds she cannot fully enter and for which she cannot be truly nostalgic. Modernist form, as Jameson has famously argued, comes out of the need to "epistemologically map" the "radical otherness" which one knows exists in the overseas empire, a part of one's system that is invisible. It therefore emerges with the rise rather than the breakdown of empire.[49] West and Woolf, by contrast, imagine narrators who draw maps from the perspective of someone who cannot get into, rather than someone who cannot see out of, the metropole.

But by describing Chris's patriotism as a nostalgic amnesia, as a weakening of the mind, as an incapacitation, West challenges not only the model of the male relationship to the state but also the literary bounds thrown up by the so-called "men of 1914." Unable to have the place Chris can have in England, Jenny struggles to complete a map of national subjectivity that depends on one's place in the nation. Woolf similarly connected literary technique with this kind of political consciousness in *A Room of One's Own*:

[I]f one is a woman one is often surprised by a sudden splitting off of consciousness, say in walking down Whitehall, when from being the natural inheritor of that civilisation, she becomes, on the contrary, outside of it, alien and critical. Clearly the mind is always altering its focus, and bringing the world into different perspectives. But some of these states of mind seem, even if adopted spontaneously, to be less comfortable than others. In order to keep oneself continuing in them one is unconsciously holding something back, and gradually the repression becomes an effort.[50]

In this passage Woolf describes a woman's mind departing from a narrative of her national identity when confronted with a system of government in which she is not permitted to participate. Woolf acknowledges here the nature of cultural narratives and their attraction. Because of their familiarity they may be "adopted spontaneously" and there is pleasure in continuing them. Disruption of expected narrative is, of course, often cited as a (sometimes the) characteristic of modernist form. Most significantly, the model of psychoanalysis Woolf uses carries the idea of repression from the realm of the private sexual into that of the public national.

Chris returns to the twin horrors of the trenches and the bourgeois home. There is no escape from the state, even in one's own mind, because the state is revealed to have unlimited access, through its adoption of psychoanalysis, to the very minds of its subjects. In *The Return of the Soldier*, West marks not the modernist comprehension and description of a new kind of subjectivity, but rather the historical development of increasing state access to that subjectivity. The war, Harold Perkin argues in his study of post-1880 England, "proved the enormous power of the modern state, when roused to accept the responsibility, to control almost every aspect of the life of society."[51] Thus, psychoanalysis, commonly understood as a marker of modernist techniques and themes, appears ominous rather than liberatory in *The Return of the Soldier*, particularly given the context of its entrance into British psychiatry as a solution to the problem of getting shell-shocked men back to the front. The doctor in *The Return of the Soldier* will cure Chris by getting him not to repress his memory of his son and his marriage. But in the description of the physical change that accompanies his cure, West suggests that the point of breaking through one repression is only to create another one:

With his back turned on this fading happiness Chris walked across the lawn. He was looking up under his brows at the overarching house as though it were a hated place to which, against all his hopes, business had forced him to return. ... He wore a dreadful decent smile; I knew how his voice would resolutely lift in greeting us. He walked not loose-limbed like a boy ... but with a soldier's hard tread upon the heel. It recalled to me that, bad as we were, we were not yet the worst circumstance of his return. When we had lifted the yoke of our embraces from his shoulders he would go back to that flooded trench in Flanders under that sky, more full of flying death than clouds, to that No Man's Land where bullets fall like rain on the rotting faces of the dead .... "Jenny, Jenny! How does he look?" "Oh ... " How could I say it? "Every inch a soldier." She crept behind me to the window, peered over my shoulder and saw. I heard her suck her breath with satisfaction. "He's cured!" she whispered slowly. "He's cured!"

The smile he has to produce, the voice he will modulate and the hard tread he will adopt all mark the ways in which knowledge of the unconscious facilitates state control over bodies. The doctor himself is a similar victim. While he waits for Jenny to bring Chris in from the garden he begins playing with a ball left in the yard. Caught in the act and embarrassed, he retreats into authoritarian demeanor and excuses himself by saying " 'Nobody about in there – we professional men get so little fresh air – .' "[52] As an arm of the state charged with putting men back on the front lines, he himself denies his own "loose limbs." In this concluding passage, Jenny fully accepts their position – women who embrace and live in Baldry Court – as co-conspirators with the state. The first horror of Chris's "return" is that he will have to accept the "yoke" of their embraces – it takes her a minute to recall that the other part of his return is to the trenches. Jenny's narrative is revealed here not as a seizure of power in the wake of the soldier's sacrifice. Rather, it is a capitulation to the forms of civil society through which the modern state demands we understand ourselves: we must be cured. While Jenny focuses mainly on Chris's pain, her narrative nonetheless provokes our sense of what it costs her to see herself as a yoke and to commit herself to reproducing in Baldry Court the England that considers Chris's body its own to sacrifice.

To understand West's analysis of the gendered unevenness with which political subjectivity is granted to male and female citizens of the modern state, it is helpful to consider Lisa Lowe and David Lloyd's assertions about the state's role in creating and maintaining gender. They argue that whether the political subject of modernity is understood as the citizen of the nation or the proletarian class subject, "Both forms of political subjectivity depend on a gendered ideology of separate spheres; the political and economic subject is presumed to be male and must be differentiated from the realms cast as 'feminine': the domestic sphere of the 'home,' the 'spiritual' cultural antecedents of modernity, and labors situated as 'reproductive.' The counterspheres marked 'feminine' are seen as sites of *reproduction* rather than *production* and in that respect correspond to sites of culture."[53]

The gendered split Lowe and Lloyd describe, which sets the masculine and productive subjectivity of the political and economic subject against the feminine and reproductive subject of the various sites marked as "counterspheres" shapes West's representation of gendered subjectivity as intertwined with state needs. Margaret and Jenny come to believe that they must restore Chris's memory, or he will "not be quite a man," and in this they accept their job as reproducing culture. Clearly, Jenny is not meant to be read as selfish in the way Kitty is, but she must also play the same role Kitty does and force Chris to become "every inch a soldier" despite the cost to him and to herself. West does not see the return of the soldier as the beginning of a battle between women and soldiers for national subjectivity but rather, and more ominously, as heralding demands on women to reproduce, both literally and culturally, as they were interpellated as modern political subjects.

West's insights about how the significance of the state recast the gendered conflicts within modernism critics often describe as emerging most succinctly in Wyndham Lewis's now infamous notice to the suffragettes. Both Lewis, in whose *Blast* the phrase "men of 1914" first linked the modern artist with the modern soldier as similar historic subjects, and contemporary critics, who attribute Lewis's response to the suffragettes to misogyny, fail to recognize that the modernist sex wars were rooted in the experience of state subjection, miscast as feminization.

Lewis's notice to suffragettes reads:

TO SUFFRAGETTES.
A WORD OF ADVICE.
IN DESTRUCTION, AS IN OTHER THINGS,
stick to what you understand.
WE MAKE YOU A PRESENT OF OUR VOTES.
ONLY LEAVE WORKS OF ART ALONE.
YOU MIGHT SOME DAY DESTROY A
GOOD PICTURE BY ACCIDENT.
THEN! –
MAIS SOYEZ BONNES FILLES!
NOUS VOUS AIMONS!
WE ADMIRE YOUR ENERGY. YOU AND ARTISTS

ARE THE ONLY THINGS (YOU DON'T MIND BEING
CALLED THINGS?) LEFT IN ENGLAND
WITH A LITTLE LIFE IN THEM.
IF YOU DESTROY A GREAT WORK OF ART you
are destroying a greater soul than if you annihilated a whole district of London.
LEAVE ART ALONE, BRAVE COMRADES![54]

Lewis on the one hand seems to treat the suffragettes with respect. When the government and police responded to suffragette civil disobedience with increasing violence on the streets and in the prisons (suffragettes were classified as criminal, not political, prisoners) some groups turned to letter-box bombings, arson, golf course vandalism, window smashing and direct assaults on policemen and politicians. But Lewis refers, of course, also to tactics inaugurated by artist and suffragette Mary Richardson, who slashed the National Gallery's *Rokeby Venus* (Velázquez) four times with an axe, leading to temporary museum closings.

Janet Lyon argues that militant suffrage discourse and early modernist polemics and manifestoes share anti-bourgeois and anti-government discourse, to the point where suffragette "artist-arsonists" caught by police with bombs, paraffin, wire cutters and hatchets in their studios should be read as "making literal ... to an astonishing degree the metaphors and metalepses of iconoclasm used by the English avant-garde."[55] Her point is that suffragism has gone unrecognized as an authentic avant-garde. Thus, Lyon reads Lewis's "word of advice" to the suffragettes as a strategy to "enhance his own group's artistic claims to anti-bourgeois autonomy." Lewis establishes suffragettes as bent on obtaining, with great energy and artistic ignorance, something that Lewis and his avant-gardes are willing simply to give them, because real artists and rebels don't care about having votes. The suffragettes, as Lewis constructs them in this notice, are actually quite bourgeois and so their "energy" accrues to the avant-garde. The alliance between artist and suffragette he imagines is not between peers; rather, the superior artist fondly notes the ways in which suffragettes have some of the characteristics real artists do, and aspire to some avant-garde principles.[56]

Readings like Lyon's and James Longenbach's demand reassessment of an arbitrary divide the *Blast* avant-gardes set between themselves and the British women's movements. Both critics argue that the suffragettes were the "real" avant-gardes – more anti-bourgeois than the men. They might further point out that Scotland Yard set up a special department to handle suffragettes,[57] not avant-garde modernists. Like Lewis, they argue, modernist criticism has refused to recognize suffragism as avant-garde because it was a women's movement.

It is by now a commonplace that much of high and avant-garde modernism's self-construction took the form of setting modernism against feminized aspects of mass and women's culture. This has variously been attributed to "misogyny," "snobbery" or a reaction to the increased access to public space/media and legitimacy women and mass culture were acquiring as the authority of "literature" seemed to dissolve. Another historical context for male modernists' rejection of (their construction of) the (middle-class) feminine is that it stood in for a particular kind of management of state subjects.

Suffragettes fail to measure up as true avant-gardes, according to Lewis, because of their association with the state. Theorists of "the social" and of civil society have described the development of reform movements (largely administered and staffed by women, and often with women as their object) as crucial to subsequent developments of liberal governance and conceptions of political power in the twentieth century. In the nineteenth century the autonomy of civil society from political society was theorized such that "society" became not only the site of liberal government but the limit of state intervention. Barbara Cruikshank, following Denise Riley, argues that the problem of developing the techniques for action on this site was solved by associations of reforming women. "It took a regiment of women ... to transform those principles [of indirect administration] into techniques of government."[58] The act of seizing and developing the field of "indirect government" though social work made reform workers and the working-class, Indian or other Other women who tended to be their objects into newly political subjects.

When women express their desire to expand their attachments to the state (as institutionalized voters), they invoke the ways in which modern personhood is administered – conceived in terms of state recognition, categorization and manipulation of social life. Lewis explains the difference between avant-gardes and suffragettes in terms of the choice between annihilating a district of London and destroying a great work of art. Suffragettes choose to sacrifice the great work of art because they, like the state, depend on ministering to the social realm in order to have authority. Similarly, Eliot writes sarcastically to Pound that American universities teach "how to appreciate the Hundred Best Paintings, the Maiden Aunt, and the Social Worker. Something might be said ... about the Evil Influence of Virginity on American Civilization ... literature has rights of its own which extend beyond Uplift and Recreation."[59] Eliot describes institutionalized education as devaluing literature as a realm of authority and terms this "feminization." In condescendingly offering to "make ... a present of our votes" if the suffragettes will "leave art alone," Lewis similarly imagines the aesthetic as a (male) realm in danger from an administrative power that is female and feminizing.

Belittling suffragism and its connection with women's reform work is a reaction to the significance of bureaucratization as "*the* distinct and ubiquitous domination of our age."[60] But Lewis and Eliot confuse bureaucratization or institutionalization with feminization. Both bureaucratization and feminization create subordinates, but as Wendy Brown explains, engenderment and bureaucracy (the modern proliferation of institutions characterized by hierarchicalism, proceduralism and the cult of expertise) are "specifiable kinds of power."[61]

I am not making a claim that women's participation in new techniques of state management was "empowering" in contrast to the experience of men. One of the most obvious consequences of bureaucratization is that the state defines itself as having an interest in and a right to regulate traditionally "private" aspects of life often associated with women and women's bodies. Women have often seen state regulation as a domination that at least offers protection from male domination. Thus, women's relationships to the state, particularly because their status as citizens is not ideologically naturalized in the way male citizenship is, can become flashpoints for thinking about state subjection generally. In this case, I argue, Lewis's miscasting of state power as "feminization" leads him to describe the experience of lacking political agency using a vocabulary of (male) high aesthetic defended against (women) practical artists who do not understand that "art" is separate from governance.

West, by contrast, describes masculinity in terms of modern agency. In considering the possibility of not restoring Chris's memory, Jenny finds that "being a man" means being a historical agent. Chris cannot fight unless his memory is restored:

We had been utterly negligent of his future, blasphemely careless of the divine essential of his soul. For if we left him in his magic circle there would come a time when his delusion turned to idiocy; when his joy at the sight of Margaret disgusted the flesh because his smiling mouth was slack with age; when one's eyes no longer followed him caressingly ... but flitted here and there defensively to see that nobody was noticing the doddering old man. . . . He who was as a flag flying from our tower would become a queer-shaped patch of eccentricity on the country-side. . . . He would not be quite a man.[62]

The "divine essential of the soul" is now the property of the state. Jenny chooses here between options that echo the images which compose national myth – the flag flying from the tower and the countryside. "To be a man" Chris must reenter history by complying with the modern model of citizenship. He must have the subjective commitment to identity made meaningful by state categories. West focuses on the way the ideal of national fantasy is rendered irrelevant for Jenny and Chris. Both will continue to participate in the same activities they always have, but with the full knowledge that no one but Kitty wants Baldry Court. Its national symbolism is dead; it is a façade for state management.

The Return of the Soldier in this regard explores the death of a particular kind of national narrative. West conceptualizes the end of this narrative in terms of an outmoded narrative convention – omniscience. Jenny gets to narrate the story of the war, but the hero and subject of history must be a soldier. Chris is the center of the story, but must forget so much that he is incapable of a narration that is not a retreat into the purely personal – his affair with Margaret. With this move, West characterizes modernist style as historical practice, and links authority within the text to agency in relation to the state.

THE MAKING OF THE MEANING OF TREASON

In her account of the radio traitor William Joyce, West describes Chris's inevitable counterpart, another "queer-shaped patch of eccentricity on the landscape" who desired to be, but never was, "a flag flying from our tower." West describes Joyce's story in terms of the way it encapsulates the difficulty of defining the British subject specifically and the interwar and immediate post-World War II era generally, as national definitions were fitted to the needs of the bureaucratic welfare state. She frames his treason as being the result of a great and unfulfilled desire for a reciprocal relationship with a national state. Unlike Chris, Joyce wishes desperately to be an officer, and to, as he put it in a youthful application to the Officers' Training Corps, "draw the sword in British interests." Unlike Chris, Joyce's aspirations toward military service are thwarted by his Irishness, his lower-class background and the way these are written onto his body. But as with Chris, West sees Joyce as threatened with "not being quite a man" when he is unable to reconcile what the nation promises with what the state will grant.

To be a man, then, is to be a proper figure in the composition of the estate or battlefield rather than to be "a queer-shaped patch of eccentricity on the landscape." Rather than reading court reporting and the close analysis of the legal and cultural constitution of the treasonous subject as a retreat from the aesthetic concerns of modernism, I understand West's focus on trials and on allegiances to political systems as an interest in twentieth-century forms. To do this is not to aestheticize in the sense of "reduce and distance." Stephen Kern argues that Gertrude Stein's description of World War I as a "Cubist war" is not flippant but a way of comprehending the simultaneity and interrelatedness of the technological and cultural transformations of the war: dramatically increased scales of modern mobilization, the new perspectives derived from aerial views and aerial bombardment, the destruction and creation of landscapes, the flattening out of conventional "lines" with camouflage and unmarked uniforms.[63] If, as Lowe and Lloyd suggest, we can similarly view the state as the form in which the West is instantiated[64] we might also see the trial as a form in which particular states are instantiated and the subject(s) participating in trials as acting according to the limits of particularly twentieth-century forms. As I have argued above, West explores in *The Return of the Soldier* how modern war highlights the disjuncture between national symbolism and state prerogativity by treating the English estate as a formal composition. She demystifies composition to show that it is political while at the same time pointedly recreating the national nostalgic aesthetic of the estate's beauty as the novel. Similarly, her political journalism makes its arguments with attention to composition, medium and form.

At the time West was writing, accusations and instances of treachery had become much more common. The act of treason became associated with groups and ideologies rather than with individuals. The importance of the phrase "fifth column," taken up in mainstream usage and characterized by *Time* as providing a term for an already existing concept, points to some of these perceived differences: first (aside from mercenaries), treason had become a matter of loyalty to the nation as a set of political ideas rather than to a specific sovereign. It was less obvious who or what one betrayed, or even whether one did morally commit treason, when acting contrary to official national policy. It was possible to claim that treasonous actions were for the national good. Second, the numbers, efficacy and professionalism of hidden actual or potential traitors within a larger community had increased dramatically enough to constitute a danger which merited professional-national uses of propaganda, counter-propaganda and increased suspicion and surveillance of citizens. One might make a claim about "big brother" in subsequent years similar to *Time*'s about the phrase "fifth column". This points to the ways in which treason increasingly shaped everyday life and defined political subjectivity. The idea of using a bureaucratic apparatus to counter treason on a large scale and the acceptance of this as necessary marks a specific and significant point in the more general "rise of white-collar bureaucracy" most often associated with how postwar capitalism affected social life. Here we see a starker manifestation of the nation-state split West describes in *The Return of the Soldier*. The idea that lack of civilian commitment might cause countries to fall was both Britain's hope for its aerial and propaganda bombardment of Germany and its fear that a similar loss of morale would happen within its own non-elite population.[65] The new presumptions about efficacy of propaganda, when coupled with such a need for citizen acquiescence, made the citizen's political subjectivity and his or her national identification a field for state intervention in new ways.

Radio made the modern field of propaganda possible. Radio waves could cross national borders easily into the "heart" of enemy territory – people's homes. Radio as a medium challenges the very idea of national boundaries; its use by traitors for propaganda underlines this contradiction and may be one of the reasons West was so interested in Joyce. In an essay on German radio as a "technology of collective fantasy," Brian Currid writes that radio has a history of being in "incongruent" relationship to the national because it is a technology that allows one to receive foreign stations even as it promises to unify listeners in a national community.[66] Francis Selwyn argues that Joyce's crime points to the ways new mediums call political concepts of national states into question. Only the technical breakthrough of radio could have gotten Joyce hanged for treason. Joyce wrote a book while he was in Germany, *Twilight over England*, but its distribution was so limited that only a "handful" of people in Britain would have heard of him if that had been all he had done. If he had stayed in England and made speeches or printed his fascist opinions any paper he published would likely have been shut down, as the *Daily Worker* was after declaring solidarity with all the world's workers, but he would not have been arrested or tried for treason.[67] The issue of Joyce's broadcasts in particular and "radio treason" in general is also confused by the question of audience, in terms of both whether they are complicit and whether the traitor's propaganda is actually effective. Joyce's show was popular before the blitz, it was not illegal to listen to it and it was considered humorous by many people – even inspiring a variety show in London called "Haw-Haw!" – but there were some prosecutions against those who repeated what they had heard (many overturned on appeal). For West, radio's characteristics establish modern treason's characteristics:

> The idea of a traitor first became real to the British of our time when they heard the voice of William Joyce on the radio during the war. The conception of treachery first became real to them when he was brought to trial as a radio traitor. For he was something new in the history of the world. Never before have people known the voice of one they had never seen as well as if he had been a husband or a brother or a close friend; and had they foreseen such a miracle they could not have imagined that this familiar unknown would speak to them only to prophesy their death and ruin.[68]

To experience Joyce's broadcasts was to be introduced not only to modern treason but also to modern political community as technological, disembodied, intimate and indeterminate. Treason no longer highlights individual defection from a community but the indeterminate character of that community. Further, as West tells it, treason arises from not being allowed to determine what citizenship will mean. When Joyce is brought before the judge, the aldermen and the Mayor of London, his body is shockingly pathetic compared with his voice:

> it could be seen that not in any sane community would William Joyce have had the ghost of a chance of holding such offices as these. This was tragic, as appeared when he was asked to plead and he said "Not guilty." Those two words were the most impressive uttered during the trial. The famous voice was let loose. ... It was as it had sounded for six years, reverberating with the desire for power. ... Given this passionate ambition to exercise authority, which as this scene showed could not be gratified, what could he ever have done but use his trick of gathering together other poor fellows luckless in the same way, so that they might overturn the sane community that was bound to reject them and substitute a mad one what would regard them kindly? That was the reason why he was in the dock; that, and Irish history.[69]

Here West uses treason as an index of the difficulty of defining both the British subject and British subjectivity, adding that this trial "started on the other side of the St. George's Channel."[70] Irish, his family pro-British supporters of the Black and Tans, Joyce's national desire is to wield

British authority but his body betrays him. As in *The Return of the Soldier*, West highlights the way in which the imperial state mystifies itself behind the promise of the nation. The bodily betrayal West notes in this passage happens consistently to Joyce and the fascists who attend his trial. The men try to mimic British military bearing or upper-class formalities but fail miserably – they execute the moves, but their bodies make them seem absurd. When Joyce has "dignity," it is clearly not authoritative dignity.

[Joyce] held his chin high and picked his feet up, as the sergeant-majors say ... he held his chin up so very high that his face was where the top of his head ought to have been ... his feet flapped on weak ankles. ... It appeared that there could be such a thing as undignified dignity. Yet in that moment when he compelled respect, it became quite clear that he could never have been one of our governors.[71]

Waiting after Joyce's execution, West reports, "at that moment [his friends] made a shy manifestation of respect. Their bodies betrayed that they had had no military training and they wore the queer and showy sports clothes affected by Fascists, but they attempted the salute which looks plausible only when performed by soldiers in uniform."[72] The significance of the body, which Joyce could discard only temporarily on the radio, is its irreducibility. We know that the kind of transcendent national love Chris tries to achieve by imagining the nation through Margaret's body is already doomed precisely because of the awfulness of Margaret's body. That Jenny dreams that she hears one man in the trenches without legs begging for help from another who has no hands underscores the simultaneous irrelevance and significance of the body to the state. Similarly, the state both claims Joyce's body with its "real Donnybrook air"[73] and ersatz upper-class gestures and uses that body to deny Joyce authoritative political subjectivity in every other way. West juxtaposes the "real" feeling Joyce has for the nation with the purely procedural actions of the British government and its agents:

Here was the palace of Westminster, built to house and glorify a system which he would have liked to adorn. Every morning he was taken into court by his guard ... and on all four days he owned to his warders ... how much he enjoyed making this ceremonial entrance into the Mother of Parliaments. Had he been able to range freely round the pompous halls and corridors, he would have seen the reason for the pomp far better than most visitors. With real reverence he would have bent over the glass-covered display table and looked at the book inscribed with the names of the peers and their sons who had fallen in the First World War; the procession of the Mace into the House of Lords would have been recognized by him as having a meaning. His relationship with the State might have been perfect, had it not been that he had made one stipulation which could not be fulfilled. He wanted to govern, not to be governed; and that, for reasons which were not fair, was quite impossible.[74]

Joyce's real reverence in this passage is for literal and figurative bodies unlike his own. He must agree that the peers and their sons deserve to have the fact that they had bodies and that he does not enshrined permanently behind glass. In order to reverence the "Mother of Parliaments" Joyce, like Chris with Baldry Court, must forget the imperial conditions of Ireland's and India's parliamentary "births." Joyce's relationship to the state can be perfected, like Chris's, only through nationalist amnesia. West notes that the MPs don't share Joyce's real reverence. They were "much less respectful to the ceremonies of the place than the Press and the Fascists had been. They had to be pushed off the carpet by the attendants when the Mace and the Lord Chancellor went by."[75] It is not the case, then, that national affect has a necessary connection to the state or one's relationship with it – there is no reciprocity with the state. Joyce dies because of his national affect. "[H]e would die the most completely unnecessary death that any criminal has ever died on the gallows. He was the victim of his own and his father's life-long determination to lie about their nationality. For had he not renewed his English passport, and had he left England for Germany on the American passport which was rightfully his, no power on earth could have touched him."[76] Pleasure in a national connection with Britain kills Joyce; this is akin to the pleasure he takes in the entrance into a national procession which is a "mnemonic guide" to the "legislative and judicical activities of Parliament" that outline the proper procedure to execute him.[77]

West understands Joyce's treason, which she labels among the last of the classic treasons, as a rejection of an order of the state "contrived by the consultative system known as democracy."[78] There is a way in which, in the narrative, Joyce's treason is also an accession to manhood that revolves around the need to be historically serious. Paradoxically, this passage into manhood can happen for Joyce only as he is executed for his male adolescent treason. Under Mosley,

> He experienced the sharp joys of public speaking and street fighting nearly every night, and every month or so the more prolonged orgy of the great London or provincial meetings. Moreover, the routine of Fascism freshened and liberated the child in its followers. Mosley had taken a black old building in King's Road,

Chelsea, formerly a Teacher's Training College, where he housed his private army of the whole-time members of the British Union of Fascists; and there life was a boy's dream. Uniforms were worn that were not really uniforms, that at once claimed and flouted authority, as adolescence does; there was discipline, savage (and therefore sadistically sweet) while it lasted, but perfectly eluctable, not clamped down on a definite period of time by the King's Regulations; corridors were patrolled by sentries beetling their brows at nothing, executive officers sat a desks laden with papers alluding to mischief as yet too unimportant to justify authority in taking steps to check it. ... His family have denied that he ever went to Germany before 1939. But others believed that he made the journey more than once and shared in the long sterile orgasm of the Nuremberg Rally ... where crowds, drunken with the great heat, entered into union with a man who was pure nihilism, who offered militarism and defeat, regulation and anarchy, power and ruin, the cancellation of all.[79]

Since, as she admits, she doesn't know whether Joyce actually went to the Nuremberg Rally or not, this is an exercise in imagining his entrance into fascism as male adolescent sexualities ("sharp joy," "orgy," "sadistically sweet," "long sterile orgasm," "entered into union"). In these passages, she characterizes fascist politics as irrational subject formation. Political allegiance is not something men make but rather something that makes men. This view of fascism and of Joyce at the close of her narrative is marked by the same elegaic despair that characterizes Chris's options in *The Return of the Soldier*. To be a man, a "flag flying from our tower," is to return to the trenches and sacrifice his body to the state with full knowledge of the nation's betrayal.

But there remains a mystery about William Joyce and all his kind of Fascist leaders. Why is it so important to them that they should stand on the political platform, hold office, give commands with their own voices, and be personally feared? A man who is not acceptable as a national leader is given by our system the opportunity to exercise as much political power as is necessary for his self-respect and the protection of his rights. He can vote in parliamentary and local elections; and he can serve his country as a private Member of Parliament or a member of a local authority or as a member of a special committee. Why should William Joyce and his kind howl after impossible eminence when in the common run they have no occasion for humiliation? ... he hungered for mere audience, for the wordless cheering, the executive power which, if it be not refined to nothing by restraint, is less than nothing.[80]

Both men must give up an adolescent politics that is morally corrupt and inaccurate but contains elements without which the system they eventually subject themselves to is also morally inadequate. For Chris, this is naïve nationalism that West claims is amnesiac; for Joyce it is a fascism that promises political agency to categories of men who have no authority under the current system. West contrasts the exercise of political power in a representative democracy (the power given to "a man") to the adolescent fascist desire for executive power that is poorly comprehended, inarticulate and directed only at self-gratification. The exercise of political power functions as much to produce "self-respect" as it does to protect individual rights, but legitimate subject formation comes through the acceptance of "being represented." The "man" accepts a mediated relation to power; he does not expect to give commands "with his own voice." Joyce does not renounce fascism. Indeed, one might argue that Chris does not voluntarily relinquish amnesiac nationalism – women give it up for him. Joyce must accept, even embrace (like Chris's becoming "every inch the soldier") his conviction. "He maintained that he was not a vile man, but thought England was right in hanging him. He would have taken it as proof of our national decadence that since the year he died no spies have been sentenced to death."[81] She maintains, however, that Joyce's defiance of a system in which he must learn to be represented has legitimacy:

victims of historical predicaments are tempted to pretend that they sacrificed themselves for an eternal principle which their contemporaries had forgotten. ... William Joyce pretended nothing at his trials. ... He did not defend the faith which he had held, for he had not doubted it; he did not attack it, for he had believed in it. It is possible that in these last days Fascism had passed out of the field of his close attention, that what absorbed him was the satisfaction he felt at being, for the first time in his life, taken seriously. It had at last been conceded that what he was and what he did were matters of supreme importance. ... It was an end to mediocrity. ... He sat in the dock, quietly wondering at time as it streamed away from him; and his silence had the terrible petitioning quality we had heard in his voice over the air. He had wanted glory; now his trial gave him the chance to wrestle with reality, to argue with the universe, to defend the revelations which he had believed had been made to him; and that is about as much glory as comes to any man.[82]

Striking about these passages is their generosity to Joyce when compared with passages in which West directly addresses fascism. The trial is not now a site for attacking fascism but for questioning the political autonomy available to an Irish, lower-class man in the system of British representative democracy. In framing this question in terms of whether it makes Joyce not "quite a man," West accepts the idea of political subjectivity as masculine. But this usage, whatever its problems, also allows her to emphasize her claim that the meaning of treason involves the cultural foundations of political systems, that is to say, the creation of state subjects. In these last passages on Joyce, West shifts her focus from fascism to the question of the state's investment in particular modes of manhood. Joyce has impossibly poor taste and cannot learn proper class codes, or look as educated as he is. His lack of proper aesthetics can be read not only as related to his exclusion from legitimate politics but as defiance of representative democracy itself. That is to say, Joyce indexes the history of "representative culture" – what David Lloyd and Paul Thomas describe as the convergence of theories of culture and of the state between the end of the eighteenth and the end of the nineteenth centuries.

A pedagogy based on aesthetic judgement furnishes, as it were, an ethical training devoted to the "educing" of the citizen from the human being. Aesthetic culture represents, therefore, the very form of bourgeois ideology, proffering on the one hand a purely formal space of reconciliation through identification while on the other containing, in transmuted forms, the constant deferral of autonomy that is the inevitable consequence of a substitution of political for human emancipation. For this reason, the aesthetic provides the theoretical rather than the instrumental articulation of the citizen-subject.[83]

West's interest in this juncture of the aesthetic-pedagogical and the political enters her analysis of treason and traitors via considerations of twentieth-century form. Her analysis of the beginning of Joyce's lifelong inability to be successfully political is that he lacks aesthetic astuteness about form rather than that he chose the wrong content:

there is no sight more touching than a boy who intends to conquer the world, though there is that within himself which means he is more likely to be its slave. Young William Joyce was such a boy, and took the first step to conquest. . . . Perhaps he really lay deep in the heather so that he might tell the Black and Tans whether the three men they were looking for were still in the farmhouse. . . . But he did go through the forms of attachment to a dangerous cause because he was ready to die if death was nobler than life . . . behind his political folly was a grain of wisdom. He liked the scarlet coats of the English garrisons . . . and all scarlet coats take up a common argument. They dissent from the dark earth and the grey sky, they insist that the bodies that wear them are upright, they are for discipline, either of drill or the minuet. It was not to be held against the boy that he preferred the straight-backed aliens in scarlet coats to his compatriots who slouched with hats crushed down on cowlicks and collars turned up round unshaven jaws, as they went about their performance of menial toil or inglorious assassination. . . . That the smart soldiers created the slouching assassins he could hardly have been expected to figure out for himself at that age.[84]

My point here is not so much the paradox that West faintly (and illogically) damns him for not having supported the Irish revolutionaries – he was already a traitor even then – but rather that she begins by imagining that the subject becomes political by discerning and choosing pattern and coherence. The issue here is not belief or unbelief in the Black and Tans' agenda but that there are proper "forms of attachment" to political causes. The parallel between the drill and the minuet is not incongruous, but rather marks an appeal made effective by a kind of aesthetic political training. The forms of government produce the modern subject not through indoctrination of content but by being comprehensible, predictable and patterned. Legitimate government is formally attractive. Treason is a crime that violates form in that it refuses the established "forms of attachment" to the state. Treason trials (for a trial itself is a state form), at least in West's hands, force the consideration of what the crime is in terms of form, rather than content, while simultaneously exposing the kinds of subjectivities demanded by those forms.

What makes William Joyce particularly significant to West, and links her work on his crime with *The Return of the Soldier*, is the way his trial depended on defining what it meant to hold and use a passport. It was against British law for British subjects to become the naturalized citizens of a country at war with Britain, so Joyce's naturalization as a German citizen in 1940 was charged as high treason. But Joyce had been born in America after his father had become a naturalized American citizen and was thus legally an American citizen himself. He did not owe allegiance to England, and since Germany did not declare war on America until December 11, 1941, he had not committed treason against the United States either. This argument is based on an idea of allegiance West defines as the "natural kind of allegiance which springs from ... birth."[85] Against this the prosecution argued that Joyce owed a different kind of acquired allegiance, that is, the allegiance traditionally owed by a subject who has taken "the King's protection." Joyce had taken the King's protection not only by declaring himself a British subject for some thirty years, but also by renewing his passport, and then traveling on it to Germany. This, the prosecution claimed, put him under British protection and he owed allegiance until the passport expired. Thus, his broadcasts for Germany during the time his passport was valid were illegal. As West put it, "Much depended on the nature of a passport, and this had never been defined by the law, for a passport has been different things at different times and has never been merely one thing at a time."[86]

West is irritated by people who think Joyce should have been freed because of a technicality. Those who thought of his conviction as a miscarriage of justice are ignorant. Others she categorizes as taking pleasure in the idea that Joyce had "out-maneuvered the law and ... [was] deserving of safety in recompense for having worsted that decrepit enemy."[87] These people, she writes, have lost the (proper) conception of the law as "the recognition of an eternal truth and the solution by a community of one of its temporal problems."[88] That is to say, they fail to recognize that passport law is only secondarily invested in the rights travel documents extend to the individual. The "temporal problem" passport law solves is how states are to identify and protect only their own citizens and others they wish to, while accepting back any citizens other countries do not want.

The state constitutes itself by embracing Joyce as citizen even if the purpose of claiming him is only to denounce his way of being a citizen, and then kill him. This is why West's painstaking creation of Joyce's subjectivity begins with his trial, conviction and execution, for it is, in essence, the story of a how even bad subjects must nonetheless *be* subjects. Passports and other identity documents function to construct and enforce fixed identities. West refers to Joyce's voice as imprisoned by his body now that he is in the dock. This is in stark contrast to Joyce's former ability as "radio traitor" to throw his voice anywhere, to cross the border back into England with impunity, to make his voice as familiar as a family member's, to nearly compel people to listen to him by having his voice broadcast on a strong signal almost everywhere in England. The radio allows free movement of this sort but the passport fixes national boundaries and national identities. It is absolutely necessary to the state's monopolization of legitimate movement, a characteristic of, as Torpey puts it, "the state-ness of states."[89]

The power of the state to "discourage people from choosing identities inconsistent with those validated by the state"[90] is at the core of West's thinking in these two works. Both *The Return of the Soldier* and *The Meaning of Treason* are stories of men who proliferate imaginative identities in order to change their relations to history, yet are grasped by a state that imposes "durable" identities amenable to state administration. The assumption that fluidity inevitably accompanies modernity underlies a claim that avant-garde and high modernism are of their time in a way that West's work on the state is not. Both seem glib in light of the history of the development of twentieth-century state powers.

In the next chapter, I take up the question of durable administrative identities and modernist narrative strategy from a slightly different angle. In examining how Ellen Glasgow sets a traditional-seeming story of a jilted heroine alongside her transformation into one of the nationalized "agriculturalists" the United States needed to participate in the world economy, I show that Glasgow explains modernization in terms of the state's annexation of affective identities such as "bride" no less than through obviously modern identities such as "agriculturalist."

CHAPTER 4

White turkeys, white weddings: the state and the south

> All the articles bear in the same sense upon the book's title subject: all tend to support a Southern way of life against what might be called the American or prevailing way; and all as much agree that the best terms in which to represent the distinction are contained in the phrase, Agrarian vs. Industrial.
>
> Twelve Southerners, *I'll Take My Stand* (1930)

Most analyses of modernity assume that marriage is socially atavistic, that is to say, that it exists *despite* modernity. Thus, feminists might theorize that women continue to marry because the promises of modern liberatory fields of subjectivity and economic agency have not been kept, or because marriage's structures remain hidden by ideology. One argument attributes marriage's persistence to its derivation from male exchange of women and a system of private property; marriage continues to exist because it is interarticulated with capitalism. In other conceptions of the relationship between heterosexual marriage and modernity, marriage provides, both ideologically and materially, an alternative to or refuge from the unrelenting alienation and economic pressure of industrial modernity.

Modernist literary criticism generally characterizes the whole complex of narrative structures and styles organized around institutional marriage as something that modernism eschews. Sentimental style is the most obvious of this collection of elements; though its excesses may be exchanged for those of "écriture feminine," these are nonetheless imagined to run counter to a marriage *plot*, with its teleological, conventional, calculable and realistic social infrastructures. Marital form, in this view, is as outmoded in literature as it has presumably become with the advent of twentieth-century modernity. It becomes by definition a form outside modernism – indeed, a form that can only negatively define modernist form.

I argue instead that as an arena where private affect and governmental administration of social structure came prominently together, marriage was far from outmoded as a literary and philosophical motif. Modernism confronts new technologies of state power that are formal, procedural, and administrative. Overdetermined redeployments of marriage and of weddings reveal modernism's visceral engagement with modern governance and regulation.

The wedding has traditionally functioned to assuage anxiety about individual agency and authentic desire by highlighting, through repetition and symbolism, the participants' considered and public acceptance of marriage's terms. But repetition and symbolism are necessary precisely because the mechanism of consent is inherently subordinating. As Wendy Brown puts it, "Insofar as consent involves agreeing to something the terms of which one does not determine, consent marks the subordinate status of the consenting party. Consent in this way functions as a sign of legitimate subordination."[1] Marriage *formally* folds anxiety and reassurance together. The anxiety is that liberal subjects (subjects with agency and power freely to consent) might in consenting actually be coerced into having intimate relations with institutional structures. The assurance is that legitimate consent to authority is possible, recognizable and an expression of the participants' unique, individual and immutable subjective desires and agency.

Marriage's legal and cultural histories made it available as a paradigm for understanding private feelings and individual agency as products of state management. Early twentieth-century legal, legislative and popular contention about the definition and purposes of institutionalized marriage signals marriage's compatibility with administrative modernity rather than, as is often assumed, its death throes as an outmoded social form eking out an existence on the privatized margins of American life. As I discuss in more detail below, accounts of this historical shift describe it as a change from understanding marriage as a *contract* to understanding it as a *status*. In the former, individuals have obligations to one another, even if those obligations are part of common law. In the latter, individuals consent to a set of privileges and responsibilities determined by the state and marriage changes their relationship to the state. In other words, examining modern marriage highlights state investment in the bureaucratic and legal administration of supposedly private and subjective relationships. Indeed, marriage has a long history of functioning as a metaphor for American citizenship. It gave sentimental or patriarchal social form to a list of the citizen's legal privileges and obligations. As

Nancy Cott puts it, "As a freely chosen structure of authority and obligation, it [marriage] was an irresistible model."[2]

Marriage becomes an irresistible literary model for describing modernization because it is recognized as a state form itself, rather than because it explains state form in other terms. As I argued in Chapter 1, in *White Zombie* our ability to recognize Madeline's consent to institutionalized heterosexuality is the centerpiece of the film's resolution of the anxieties it raises about the structural similarities between subjects of American empire abroad and elite Western citizens at home. Along a different north–south axis of modernization, in her novel *Barren Ground* (1925), Ellen Glasgow creates a heroine who is both one of the "new [white] men" of U.S. agricultural business who are being integrated from the southern regional economy into an (inter)nationalized federal economy and a woman who suffers that stock tragedy of the sentimental genres – she is jilted.

White Zombie and *Barren Ground* produce accounts of material and political modernization that also address modernization in the literary and visual arts. Earlier, I read Halperin's use of sentimental and melodramatic conventions of silent film in a modern production as indexing early cinematic theory on the camera's mechanical relation to sentiment even as it relies on the authenticity of sentiment we can *see*. Glasgow similarly uses the seemingly retrograde marriage plot of the novel to set herself at odds with two conventional mappings of modernism: first, a masculine, agrarian and "high" or New Critical modernism and, second, a metropolitan feminist modernism.

Up to this point I have been addressing the geographical axis of this book that runs along the global "north–south" divide in order to emphasize the ways in which the nature of "modernity" – the new administrative capacities of states to define and manage their subjects – that grounds "modernism" becomes evident when we consider points of imperial governance. As with readings along the global north–south axis, uneven modernity invites consideration of modernization and the state's role in the material and cultural experiences of modernity. The American south is not an imperial location in the same way that Haiti is, but, significantly, its intellectuals often presented it as a valiant province colonized by federal power. The U.S. government's drive toward integrating the south into a centralized market economy emerged from its growing international power, which was certainly imperialist. This "anticolonial" regionalist rhetoric had both literary and historical significance. As Paul Bové reminds us, the agrarians who fought the economic and cultural integration of the south into a centralized market economy were the same men who professionalized U.S. academic literary study and institutionalized New Critical modernism.[3]

Glasgow's most intense engagement with modernism takes the form of a trope usually associated with sentimental or realist genres. Dorinda's fiancé Jason jilts her in the first third of the novel; she runs away to New York City to return with northern capital, metropolitan sophistication and agricultural know-how. But Glasgow does not describe marriage as something Dorinda leaves behind in order to become modern. Dorinda, after all, marries another man later on different aesthetic and thematic terms. Rather, Glasgow produces an account of modernization, modernism and regionalism in which marriage, far from being an obsolete, gruesomely popular and transparent narrative, serves as a paradigm for modern subjectivity. As in *White Zombie*, marriage in *Barren Ground* is not meant to invoke narrative or social traditions as alternatives to modernization but rather to highlight the significance of modern administration to imagining identity, relationships and agency in the twentieth century.

BARREN GROUNDS

Like the agrarians, Glasgow links the cultural politics of producing modern, "dispassionate" writing with the national geopolitics of the period: the time when professional agriculture, as administered by the federal government through market controls and state university training programs, replaced the agrarian ideal of farming. In her preface to *Barren Ground*, Glasgow writes that the novel is the product of a resolve to treat "the South not sentimentally, as a conquered province, but dispassionately, as part of a larger world."[4] We might understand Glasgow's use of "dispassion" in light of T. E. Hulme's call (later echoed and answered by Eliot and the New Critics) for a new classicism of dryness, hardness, precision and definite description as against sentiment, infinity, vagueness and dampness.[5] She here categorically associates different narrative styles with different views of the American south's negotiations of modernization and industrialization, while setting herself the task of imagining a modern novel that was also a regionalist one.

As Bové has described it, the agrarians cast their resistance to northern/federal culture and economic incorporation in aesthetic and cultural terms. An economy grounded in farming by small landholders independent of a centralized money economy managed by the state produces a political and cultural economy with a role for traditional intellectuals. This role, under northern incorporation, would pass to the bureaucrats, scientists and technicians of intensive capital agriculture.

This is Bové's description of the agrarians' own characterization of their position. His own argument is that an understanding of the Gramscian extended state allows us to see that while the interwar workings of state power did in fact displace southern intellectuals and create a new sociopolitical environment in which men became connected to the state in new ways, southern intellectuals also became part of this hegemony:

With Gramsci's concept in mind we can see ... that [while] the rapid deployment of state institutions in "agriculture" both displaced traditional intellectuals ... and developed new men, "scientific farmers," powerfully linked to the state ... [that] the state ... met some of the real needs of ... [the] intellectuals by allowing them to carry on their struggles in the international cultural arena ... the cumulative resistance of the literary intellectual caste to their progressive displacement by the "new men" of the extended state earned them, in turn, a new place to speak and new functions to provide ... they ... became and produced other "new men," new "types": the academic critic and intellectual professionalized, specialized, and sometimes still politically oppositional.[6]

Agrarian cultural projects such as retelling southern history and supporting and publicizing southern writing that met contemporary international aesthetic standards were meant to challenge not only northern representations of the south but also to "restore the aesthetic critical intellectual to a position of leadership within the South by assigning its strengths to virtues far from from the technical, abstract civilization offered by an imperial Northern hegemony."[7] For the agrarians, canonical modernism's aesthetic will-to-knowledge, disinterested impersonality, mythic projection and "successful deployment of visionary power upon the external world" (characteristics critics would consolidate later in phrases such as Robert Langbaum's "modern traditionalism")[8] were akin to virtues held by the great antebellum men who fashioned and were fashioned by southern civilization. Bové argues that Allen Tate's Stonewall Jackson "resembles no one more than Hart Crane as that poet appears in Tate's criticism."[9]

But Glasgow does not offer *Barren Ground* as a part of the agrarian economic or aesthetic high modernist program. Instead, she thematizes critical conceptions of that modernist aesthetic project and its relationship to modernization. Her barren ground is the site of a challenge to the agrarian characterization of the relationship between modernism and modernity as male nationalist property holding against the state. Gender figures prominently here insofar as agrarian paradigms of state-free productivity metaphorize women *as* land, or cast the state as a set of institutions feminizing men.[10] We can see much of this in her near-explicit references to T. S. Eliot's *The Waste Land*.

The agrarian canonization of *The Waste Land*, a text about agriculture and modernity, should not surprise us. Glasgow invokes Eliot's poem in order to reject its historical and aesthetic premises. Beginning with her title, Glasgow counterposes her land to Eliot's. She takes up his high modernist cultural concerns and metaphors but renders them in terms of material and historical concepts. Both authors envision landscapes of sterility and impotence. For Eliot, the waste follows from World War I; for Glasgow, it stems from the Civil War. Both authors open with spring as a month of illusory burgeoning. In *The Waste Land*, even though lilacs come out of the dead land, this serves only to accentuate the emotional, spiritual and intellectual vitiation of twentieth-century Western civilization. Dorinda experiences seeing Jason for the first time as the coming of spring. It is "as if an April flush had passed over the waste places" of the futile, fallow farms of Pedlar's Mill and Dorinda's impoverished, tedious life.[11] Jason will jilt Dorinda, setting in motion the events that will lead to her miscarriage, and, as I discuss below, he represents a reproductively exhausted family line.

When Dorinda awakens in the hospital after her accident, her emotional capacity, like that of Eliot's characters, is gone. Even things that are "bright, gay and beautiful" look as if they "might have been made of glass in the windy hollow of the universe." She tells herself she must pretend to be alive like other people even though "she felt nothing; she expected nothing; she desired nothing" and has the sensation, like J. Alfred Prufrock, who "has known the eyes already, known them all," that "she has seen everything and everybody before. . . . There might have been a general disintegration and reassembling of personalities since she had gone to the hospital, and she felt that she had seen them all before in other circumstances and other periods."[12]

For both Eliot and Glasgow, infertile ground hides corpses and rattling bones beneath the lilacs. Glasgow's allusions to the images Eliot uses throughout *The Waste Land* are apparent in the following passage about the woman Jason jilts Dorinda to marry:

[H]er face in its masklike immobility resembled the face of a dead woman. . . . [She was] so thin that her bones seemed to rattle as she moved . . . with hollows in her chest and between her shoulder blades. ... "I had a baby and Jason killed it. He killed it as soon as it was born and buried it in the garden. He doesn't know that I saw him. He thinks that I was asleep, but I found the grave under the lilac bushes at the end of the garden path."[13]

But Glasgow establishes significant critical distance between herself and Eliot. She reworks the gendering of such tropes as sterility and fertility. What so many critics have noticed about *The Waste Land* is the extent to which a poem commonly described as being about "the emotional and spiritual sterility of Western man"[14] describes this problem in terms of the biological sterility of Western women. Despite the centrality of the king's impotence in *The Golden Bough*, Eliot's symbolic system guides our understanding of Lil, who refuses to have any more children, as the appropriate metaphor for modernity. Donna Haraway has described this paradigm in reproductive politics as the way that reproduction provides "the figure for the possibility and nature of a future in multinational capitalist and nuclear society." This, she continues, conflates production with reproduction.[15] Despite Eliot's possible putative sympathy for Lil, the fertility metaphors of *The Waste Land* obscure and naturalize both the labor that goes into reclaiming fallow land and the female labor that goes into bearing children. By contrast, in *Barren Ground*, Glasgow specifies the labor that goes into making Old Farm fertile again. She breaks the mystified link between production and reproduction by making Dorinda's miscarriage productive. It is only because Dorinda does not remain pregnant that she can be caught up in the events that allow her to return from New York with the capital and training to install her father's farm into the national economy.

Glasgow also disrupts Eliot's metaphor by marking the cost of romantic relationships to women. Love seems only to restore the waste places. Real restoration of the land requires hard labor. The fertile world of Dorinda's romance turns out to be illusory; its disappearance permits her to produce "other things":

The world in which she had surrendered her being to love – that world of spring meadows and pure skies – had receded from her so utterly that she could barely remember its outlines. ... Never would it come back again. The area of feeling within her soul was parched and blackened, like an abandoned field after the broomsedge is destroyed. Other things might put forth; but never again that wild beauty. Around this barren region, within the dim border of consciousness, there were innumerable surface impressions, like the tiny tracks that birds make in the snow. She could still think, she could even remember; but her thoughts, her memories, were no deeper than the light tracks of birds.[16]

This passage also reveals the gendered aesthetics of modernist criticism buried in Eliot's fertility metaphor. Eliot's typist says, "Well now that's done: and I'm glad its over."[17] Dorinda, too, says repeatedly of love, "I'm finished with all that." But where Eliot describes modern civilization's failure in terms of a sex act that makes no impression on the modern woman, Glasgow does not define the refusal of physical fertility as a deplorable inability to have impressions made on one. Dorinda's "land" registers impressions more clearly after she is jilted. When she surrendered to love, she thought in terms of vague meadows and skies. In the dispassionate aftermath there are numerous clear impressions of the sharpness and coldness of Imagist work.

In *The Waste Land*, as for the agrarians who canonized Eliot's work, mythic and metaphoric processes of modernist writing and criticism productively circumscribe the historical processes of production. Eliot hailed Joyce's "mythical method" in *Ulysses* as "making the modern world possible for art." The artist gives "shape and significance" to history; the novel form is inadequate to the "immense panorama of futility and anarchy which is contemporary history." Eliot writes that Joyce (and earlier, Yeats) has by "manipulating a continuous parallel between contemporaneity and antiquity" discovered a new method to replace the narrative method of the novel. Here Eliot seems almost to say that the modern artist must find a way to declare modernization itself irrelevant.[18] Like agrarian economic and cultural arguments that represented farming as outside of the modern state-directed economy, *The Waste Land* presents production in the industrialized, capital-intensive twentieth-century West from within a mythical narrative of biological reproductive capacity. But for Glasgow, modern fertility, like the modern aesthetic, emerges historically, rather than mythically or morally. She revises the sexual agriculture of the high modernist mythos.

Despite this rejection of a significant thematic strand of agrarian high modernism, one remembers from Glasgow's preface that the point of *Barren Ground* is nonetheless to inaugurate a new regional yet modern aesthetic ("write of the South not sentimentally, as a conquered province, but dispassionately, as part of the larger world"). Glasgow's characterization of nationalistic regionalism as "sentimental" reminds us of criticism that reads her as a herald, but not successful practitioner, of Faulkner's later strategies of radical desentimentalization in novels such as

The Sound and the Fury or *As I Lay Dying*. Seen in this way, *Barren Ground* is simply not a modern text because of its conventional language and tropes. This literary historical mode of understanding Glasgow exists partly as a result of the wedge Faulkner's work puts between provincial regionalism and new southern modernism. This wedge depends upon conflating "regional" with "feminine," and "non-innovative" and then "metropolitan" with "avant-garde" and "masculine." Unlike Glasgow, Faulkner would have the option of becoming modern while remaining southern by making a claim to excise the feminine from regionalism.

Faulkner clearly, for instance, sets his text *Absalom, Absalom!* against the kinds of writing women do about the south. Rosa writes a thousand odes to Confederate soldiers after her father nails himself into their attic,[19] and she thinks that the story she is telling Quentin, the backbone of *Absalom, Absalom!*, will be a simple magazine story fueling female consumption. "You will be married then I expect and perhaps your wife will want a new gown or a new chair for the house and you can write this and submit it to the magazines."[20] Faulkner here encapsulates nearly every cutting comment ever made by writers and critics delineating serious modern literature as a masculine provenance. Even women with important stories can imagine them only in terms of market commodities; women understand publishing in terms of the culture of popular magazines; women fail to see the significance of *Absalom, Absalom!*, that is, of modernism itself. Told by Rosa, the story is a quaint relic of literary history. Told by Faulkner, it is a masterpiece of modernity.

Rosa characterizes the south as a place for women and men of Mr. Compson's generation. Faulkner depicts her as having a pathetically limited vision of the south as a feminized place while his own *tour de force* proves the opposite. Even more damning is the way Rosa imagines Quentin as assimilating to northern commercialism. His regional ties, she thinks, will be something he can sell as he assimilates to a northern lifestyle. "I dont imagine you will ever come back here and settle down as a country lawyer in a little town like Jefferson since Northern people have already seen to it that there is little left in the South for a young man."[21] Faulkner himself, of course, renders Rosa's declaration laughable.

Like Faulkner, Glasgow wants to write as a modernist and as a regionalist. But for her, writing "dispassionately" takes the form of analyzing how so-called "feminine" local color and sentiment might be interarticulated with their supposed opposites, the allegedly more complicated modern metropolitan genres. The self-consciousness about language we are accustomed to associate with modernism plays out not in technical innovation itself but in her thematization of the implications of such innovation.

Local color genres set the traditional and non-technological against the homogenizing techniques of the industrialized city. The wholeness and naturalness of realistic regional narrative seemed to oppose the interruptive, fragmentary quick-cutting of city consciousness. Metropolitan styles were characterized as faster, more varied and more complicated than styles practiced in the provinces. One of the impulses behind local color was recording unique ways of life before industrialization homogenized the entire country; another was to provide an alternative (sometimes nostalgic, sometimes programmatic, always political) to a harsh and fast-paced life driven by industrial capitalism's needs. Technically, of course, modernist literary criticism makes the opposite claim: cosmopolitan life provokes unique aesthetics while traditional narrative styles become the medium for conserving traditional folkways.

Glasgow makes a point about the way "color" functions in both kinds of texts at the beginning of the twentieth century. Far from experiencing rural life as a refuge for colorful particularity as against industrialized sameness, Dorinda acknowledges that in leaving the city to return and run the farm, "[c]olor, diversity, animation, all these were part of the world she had relinquished."[22] Pedlar's Mill literally pales in comparison with what she could see and experience in the city:

Beyond the fields and the road the sun was sinking lower, and the western sky was stained with the color of autumn fruits. While she watched the clouds, Dorinda remembered the heart of a pomegranate that she had seen in a window in New York; and immediately she was swept by a longing for the sights and sounds of the city. "There's no use thinking of that now," she said to herself. . . . "Like so many other things it is only when you look back on it that you seem to want it. While I was in New York I was longing to be away. There comes Nimrod with the cows, and Fluvanna bringing the milk-pails."[23]

In this passage Dorinda gazes at a pastoral scene whose colors make her homesick for the sights of the city and then recovers from that emotion by appreciating local color – her African American workers. Note here how the pomegranate represents the diverse and colorful things one can find in the city. The window, though transparent, is a barrier that makes the pomegranate into a "sight," an object that encapsulates the "sights and sounds of the city." This tightly crystallized image seems especially taut next to the more vaguely drawn sunset, supporting the idea that modernist (metropolitan) imagery and language is both more dynamic and more compressed. The passage ends in the present as Dorinda reminds herself that when she was in New York Nimrod and Fluvanna could be recalled only as sights but now they are present. In marking their presence and appearance, Dorinda attempts to encapsulate what she has received in exchange for the city: the authenticity of local color. There is nothing – no glass – mediating between the object and the viewer. Things behind glass in the city are also (although not entirely) things to be purchased. Part of the allure of the pomegranate is the way it balances between inaccessibility and accessibility on the edge of the glass.[24] Dorinda consoles herself for the loss of one kind of color with another.

With these two kinds of color – racialized unmediated authenticity in the region and eclectic collections of items behind glass in the city – Glasgow sets production in the region against consumption in the city. The point is not that Nimrod and Fluvanna are turned into objects of desire but that they are her laborers. They appear performing actions that make her farm profitable. I return to this discussion of racialized modern labor below to argue that one of the things that distinguishes modern regionalist narrative from its literary predecessors is that labor is no longer owned and must narratively be incorporated into the production process without losing its putative non-industrialized and non-alienated nature.

The point I want to draw out for the moment is that Glasgow's play with "color" challenges the way modernist criticism pitted (feminine) sentimentality and other transparent genres against modernist difficulty, opacity and intellectual substance. Twentieth-century "color" (including race) is the product of uneven modernity, itself intrinsic to modernity and modernization. "Metropolitan" aesthetics, then, are such only in conjunction with their alleged opposites, just as the seeming liquidity of consumer culture is possible only because of the rationality and bureaucracy of centralized systems of production and delivery.

And, indeed, Glasgow directly addresses the question of hardness and difficulty as part of the aesthetic of *Barren Ground*. The "hardness" of *Barren Ground* is the difficulty of reading Dorinda once Glasgow removes her capacity for emotion. Dorinda exults that she is "through with soft things" when she rejects Jason's overtures at her father's funeral. Jason's pathetic refrain in the latter chapters of the novel is "you're hard, Dorinda." From the time she wakes up in the hospital in New York, she suffers "a nervous inability to express any emotion" and feels herself separated from the rest of the world by a "fantastic humor" that is ironic, "cool and detached." She is "emotionally ... unequal to the supreme occasions of her life." Glasgow replicates this as a quality of her narrative. Dorinda is pointedly misplaced in a novel whose setting and structure evoke sentimental narrative. Moreover, her hardness coexists with and draws its significance from a genre that historically fostered opposite effects. In short, Glasgow challenges a characterization of herself as Rosa Coldfield, even as she makes it impossible to consider her either a proto- or failed William Faulkner.

My point in situating Glasgow in relation to Faulkner and to the agrarians' Eliot is to demonstrate that she engages similar literary concerns from a different perspective on material and literary modernization. Glasgow's importance to my project's larger argument is that her work resists another common critical move: reading women writers who do not exhibit high modernist strategies through the lens of a feminism privileging consumer culture and the public spaces of the metropolis. Critics have often described the difference between male and female modernists as a male pejorative feminization of the fantasies of mass commercial culture versus a female recognition of the possibilities for women in the fluidity of identity and access to public space enabled by consumer culture. Glasgow's engagement with the region and its history of modernization, however, reveals the ways in which this critical turn to consumption at the metropole to theorize women's modernism elides the state's significance.

A DRESS, A COW OR A BEAU IN THE CITY?

Glasgow does not depict Dorinda's transition from a family economy of rural subsistence to one of independent modern urban consumption as liberating. She also pointedly refrains from making Dorinda a New Woman, someone who finds an alternative to marriage in the metropolitan economy. Dorinda returns to the Pedlar's Mill economy to practice capital investment in agribusiness and she eventually marries another farmer. The trains she watches yearningly at the novel's opening as "a part of that expected miracle, the something different in the future ... glamour ... adventure" become a way for her to move her products to the city for sale. Rather than promising an alternative to routine, the train schedule relentlessly determines work on the farm. "Chores were done not by necessity, as in the old days without system, but by the stroke of the clock."[25] Adventure and "audacity" come from borrowing money to create a large-scale farm that produces surplus – profit with which to pay off the mortgage and then expand. "Without borrowed money, without the courage to borrow money, she could never have made the farm even a moderate success. This had required not only perseverance but audacity ... and it had required audacity again to permeate the methodical science of farming with the spirit of adventure."[26] Adventure and innovation do not come solely from the metropole.

Dorinda's first purchase in response to consumer culture's promise of self-fashioning leads her out of the family farm economy. Home from the city only to care for his abusive, alcoholic doctor father and to help with his medical practice, Jason is unhappily waiting for his father to die so he can leave and go back to the city. When Dorinda says she would do anything to help him, he tells her to wear a dress the color of her eyes. Dorinda has been saving money she earns as clerk in a country store to buy a cow from Jason's father. Since her own family's cow died, they have gone without milk and butter. But Jason's courtship suggests that the family economy might be broken. Dorinda now sees that there is a choice between the red cow and the blue dress.

In order to buy the dress that would give her a way of possessing her own eyes, Dorinda must take her thirty dollars and outshop Geneva Ellgood, her competitor for Jason. Geneva's father is the richest man in Pedlar's Mill. Old Matthew, the town gossip, teases her: "Geneva would take him in a minute, I reckon, an' her Pa is rich enough to buy her a beau in the city if she wants one, hee-hee! ... "[27] Dorinda must fetch and wrap items for Geneva that the Oakleys can't afford. When Dorinda decides to sacrifice the red cow to buy the blue dress, she has a heady sense of the same power. Upon hearing that Geneva has ordered a new dress for Easter with "yards and yards" of figured challis and a pattern from a fashion newspaper in New York, plus a new hat with a high bandeau and a wreath of wheat and poppies, Dorinda buys even more than she had planned:

A primitive impulse struggled like some fierce invader in her mind, among the orderly instincts and inherited habits of thought. She was startled; she was frightened; but she was defiant. ... Beyond the beaten road in which her ideas and inclinations had moved, she had discovered a virgin wilderness of mystery and terror. "I want a hat too, Miss Seena," she said quickly. "A white straw hat with a wreath of blue flowers round the crown."[28]

Dorinda doesn't just make a decision to buy a new outfit; she practically has a paradigm shift. Admitting the possibility of buying clothing instead of cows is like opening the frontier. In the context of how carefully Glasgow describes the agricultural economic history of Pedlar's Mill, the metaphor of new land is especially powerful. Although the opening of the American frontier is long past, the fantasy of new land still circulates in Pedlar's Mill in the form of reclaiming the acres lost to broomsedge post-Civil War.[29] Dorinda's consumer-culture-driven fantasy about what new clothes will do for her both replaces and repeats this fantasy about agricultural production. Both are capitalist fantasies. The frontier confers property and therefore civic identity and individuality on formerly undifferentiated, landless and powerless men. Fashion as the new fantasy similarly associates Dorinda's choice with participation in a self-individuating economy (urban public space, women's wage labor) at the expense of the family and farm economies.

But Glasgow reminds us that Dorinda doesn't imagine her first new dress, Jason does. That Jason forgets he told her to wear a blue dress – "How did you know that you ought to wear blue?" – underscores the way his decisions are naturalized even in a system supposedly driven by women's self-fashioning. Dorinda has to agonize over the cow and the mortgage and the "careful cutting"; Jason has a woman magically appear before him just the way he wants to see her.

When Dorinda finally gets to the city, someone else picks her second new dress. The doctor who operates on Dorinda after her accident in New York arranges for her to work in his office and care for his children after she leaves the hospital. His wife visits Dorinda in the hospital to discuss her move to their house. Dorinda asks whether she ought to get a dress. Mrs. Faraday begins by saying it doesn't matter what kind of dress she wears so long as it is plain and simple, then, in the same sentence very specifically requests a particular dress design. "Oh any plain simple dress will do. Navy blue poplin with white linen collar and cuffs would be nice . . . ."[30]

One of the claims feminist modernist criticism has made is that women's involvement in consumer culture is significant because consumer culture makes female identity more performative and builds communities among women. "Shared female play with commodities" offers an alternative to identification with "traditional masculine identities."[31] Unlike Jason, Mrs. Faraday participates in fashion herself. Dorinda notices at their first meeting that Mrs. Faraday is suffering because her figure does not "conform to the wasp-waist of the period," and her gloves are too tight. Crimping her hair and wearing it with a small hat – a trend Dorinda notes earlier as the current style in

New York – makes her temples "look skinned." The clothes and hairstyle have the effect of making her look "astonished" while her "wrists bulge in infantile creases." This belies her actual manner, which is "sprightly" and "happy," as well as her "fresh, sweet" voice and complexion. She is at the mercy of rather than in control of her appearance and "panting a little from her tight stays and her unnatural elegance." Dorinda distinguishes between the surface of fashion and the woman underneath when Mrs. Faraday shakes her hand goodbye. Dorinda can "feel the soft flesh beneath the deeply embedded buttons."[32]

Women can use dress to manipulate but ultimately do not control their public identities. The "plain, simple" dress is a necessary sign of Dorinda's virtue and of the Faradays' ability to detect it. It will also indicate her status as their employee. As her doctor, Dr. Faraday knows that Dorinda came to the city unmarried and pregnant. "I've talked to my wife about you. ... I believe you are a good girl, and we both wish to help you to lead a good life."[33] What, one might wonder, makes them so sure? Is it really the case that her "absurd and countrified" clothes so clearly distinguish her from the girls who are unmarried, pregnant and not good? After all, when she first came to New York, a madame offered her a job as a prostitute and men occasionally assumed she was one.[34] Dorinda realizes that she needs new clothes because she doesn't measure up to the fashion standards of New York. But to measure up to these standards – to look more metropolitan – might mean to look less "good." Mrs. Faraday intervenes to make sure a girl working for her will produce the metropolitan version of respectability. Dorinda doesn't have free play to recreate herself nor will Mrs. Faraday tell her to get a dress like the one she, the wife of a wealthy doctor, wears.

Glasgow emphasizes the limits of metropolitan femininity when Dorinda brings her new dress back to Pedlar's Mill. The dress allows her to make a triumphant return when she steps off the train, but this will be meaningless unless she can back it up with a successful farm. When she goes to buy her first herd of dairy cows from Bob Ellgood with money borrowed from the Faradays, the dress allows her to pretend she is not intimidated by their successful farm. Then, because Bob finds her attractive, she drives a better bargain:

It gave her pleasure to feel that she was more distinguished, if less desirable, than she had been two years ago; but her pleasure was as impersonal as her errand. She had no wish to attract this heavy, masterful farmer, who reminded her of a sleek, mild-mannered Jersey bull; no wish, at least, to attract him beyond the point where his admiration might help her to drive a bargain in cows ... the Jerseys were standing in a row, satin-coated, fawn-eyed, with breath like new-mown hay. What beauties they were, thought Dorinda, swept away in spite of her determination to bargain ... "Rose. Sweetbriar. Hollyhock. Pansy. Daisy. Violet. Verbena." To think that she, who had never owned anything, should actually possess these adorable creatures![35]

The focus shifts rapidly here from "pleasure" at being attractive because of a dress to the "blissful" delights of shopping for cows. These cows have a solidity that renders the dress insubstantial. Even the man present who might find her attractive turns into a bull. Suddenly the dresses it has meant so much to her to own (remember that originally a blue dress was far more alluring than a red dairy cow) seem not even to count as possessions. When Bob shows her the Ellgoods' prize bull she has a similar reaction: "'I wonder if I shall ever own a creature like that?' she thought. 'He looks as if he owned everything and yet despised it,' she said aloud."[36] Dorinda wants to own real substantial things. She describes the Ellgoods' bull's desirability in terms of its insusceptibility to consumer desire – it already owns everything and despises it. To imagine owning the bull is to imagine having something so solid that it has no element of performance about it. This is a fantasy about being invulnerable to shifts in meaning as well as to having more things become desirable. To put this another way, she gives up property for capital. Once she has the cows, Dorinda dons a pair of her brother's overalls and works in them for ten years.

THE JILT

> They will have told you how I came back home. Oh yes, I know: "Rosie Coldfield, lose him, weep him; caught a man but couldn't keep him."
>
> William Faulkner, *Absalom, Absalom!* (1936)

One way to characterize the metropolitan modernist New Woman narrative is in terms of its commitment to representing new subject positions available to women with the emergence of alternatives to marital economies. As with canonical modernism, these works were often critically valued when they depicted social change in terms of modern aesthetic innovation. Where the sentimental nineteenth-century women's novel represented for such critics the dovetailing of (feminized) generic style and conventional women's roles, the modernist feminist metropolitan novel connected radical aesthetics with radical modernization. Jane Tompkins has (non-derogatorily) described the structure and style of nineteenth-century sentimental American novels as responsive to the authors' desire to "state and propose solutions for social and political predicaments." To this end they privilege stereotypes, forceful expressions of emotion, spiritual and religious idiom, sensation, clarity, repetition and improbable plots. Modern criticism's privileging, in contrast, of "psychological complexity, moral ambiguity, epistemological sophistication, stylistic density [and] formal economy"[37] led, as Suzanne Clark puts it, to a gendered view of the sentimental as "a past to be outgrown and a present tendency to be despised."[38] According to these definitions, *Barren Ground*, too, falls structurally and stylistically short. The trope of the jilted heroine is too transparent and conventional. It does not challenge narrative expectations. Certainly this is the way Faulkner told the story of telling the story of the jilt in *Absalom, Absalom!*

In addition to being a bad poet and poor literary critic, Faulkner's Miss Rosa Coldfield is a jilted bride. She and Sutpen get engaged when he returns from the war; he later makes his infamous proposal that he get her pregnant and marry her only if the child turns out to be a son. She immediately storms away from his property and returns to her family's house in town, where she will tell her story to Quentin some four decades later. For Faulkner, these two tropes – the jilted spinster and the deluded "poetess laureate" of the county – reinforce each other along the gendered barricades dividing the new production of modern southern literature from its regional antecedents. Miss Rosa is permanently "outraged" by being jilted and because of that mired in the "mausoleum air" of her own narrative account of Sutpen. Her narrative appeals to conventional understandings of social order; the outrage in it is both for (southern) womanhood insulted and for the Confederate way of life destroyed. She mixes these so thoroughly it seems as if God himself jilted the south in letting the Confederacy lose. Rosa returns to the same points repeatedly because she wants the narrative to be completed differently. Her way of telling the story represents literary archaism itself. As Mr. Compson tells Quentin, "Years ago we in the South made our women into ladies. Then the War came and made the ladies into ghosts. So what else can we do, being gentlemen, but listen to them being ghosts?" Elizabeth Freeman has described *Absalom, Absalom!* as "the U.S. novel that most dramatically deconstructs the marriage plot."[39] The marriage plot is outmoded, a ghost haunting modern narrative and modern life; Freeman's use of the term "deconstruct" here should remind us of the ways in which many modernist paradigms require a degraded conventional narrative against which to establish their literary modernity.

Glasgow describes Dorinda's modernization in terms quite different from metropolitan women's modernism. She emphasizes production and capital investment in the new rural economy rather than consumption at the metropolitan center. One might measure Glasgow's rejection of this line of modern literary thought by noting the play on words in Rose Emily's, Geneva Ellgood's and Jason Greylock's deaths by consumption, suggesting that she did not imagine women's entrance into modernity as that simple a turn in the century.

Dorinda depends on consumer culture in the city for her profits, but thinks of its excess as something she rationalizes and sells. She explains to her mother that selling to the customers in the city means setting a higher price: "Some people are always ready to pay a high price, and they value a thing more if they pay too much for it." Her dairy is "*as* well managed, her butter *as* good, as any that could be found in the country" but her products "with the name Old Farm stamped under the device of the harp-shaped pine, were bringing the *highest* prices in the market."[40] The brand is a "device"; the price is not based on the products themselves.

The narrative structure of *Barren Ground* parallels Dorinda's modernization of the farm with her interrupted yet ultimately completed entrance into marriage. With this coupling, Glasgow suggests that Dorinda's public identity and function – one of the "new men" of agriculture the state created – can be described in terms of her marital trajectory, and vice versa. Glasgow's heroine marries not because Glasgow fails to understand that sentimental narrative is outmoded but because she understands that marriage is a modern schematic relationship subject to the same kinds of social management as agriculture.

Indeed, although much has been made of the problem of keeping the boys on the farm post-World War I, the U.S. government busied itself with putting and keeping women in the domestic farmhouse as early as 1908. Theodore Roosevelt convened the Roosevelt Commission on Country Life (1908) to improve the quality of rural life when it became clear that the country would be depending on a proportionately shrinking rural population to feed a rapidly rising number of city dwellers. If the quality of rural life improved and agriculture became more profitable, farmers would stay on the land and mass produce lower-priced food. The Commission focused on rural women, as would Woodrow Wilson's Secretary of Agriculture in 1913. The Smith–Lever Act of 1914 established agricultural extension services for rural women that included teaching and encouraging farm women to use more technology for household work. These initiatives and others of the same period focused on the association between women and consumer goods. Some encouraged purchasing appliances for mechanizing women's work in the farmhouse at the same rate that men's field work was being mechanized. The explicit standard here may have been rural men, but the implicit standard was the urban middle-class housewife who created the domestic sphere with her purchases. At the same time, the consumer goods and conveniences of city living posed a danger to rural life – women were lured to the city by its modern conveniences. This assumption, Katherine Jellison points out, ignored the fact that sons normally inherited family farms. While the earliest of these initiatives recognized the lack of clear lines between rural women's house and field work and acknowledged their complaints about patriarchal work and family arrangements, postwar USDA policy on modernizing farm life sought to establish and reinforce "separate spheres." These policies assumed that nuclear families were necessary to stabilize American agricultural production[41] and divided rural modernization into male production and female commodity culture.

This history of federal modernization allows us to understand how Glasgow's evocation of the jilt and the heroine of sentimental fiction is just that – an evocation, not an imitation. Glasgow's marriage plot emphasizes the degree to which the modernist "crisis of the subject," in which modernization provokes a reassessment of the formerly transparent relation of the individual to the outside world,[42] is a crisis of the citizen-subject. The individual farmer becomes, as Dorinda does in contrast to her father, the intensive credit agricultural capitalist with a social significance and identity assured by the USDA; the lover becomes a similarly assured marital subject.

The legal history of jilt (breach of marital contract) suits reveals a link between private feeling and the regulatory state forged at the site of modern marriage. In the turn-of-the-century tug of war between the judiciary and the legislatures over whether a jilt constituted grounds for either legal or moral damages, one of the contentions was that forcing adherence to a contract treated marriage as a matter of public business rather than as a private and sacred realm of feeling. This argument ironically dovetailed with other contemporary arguments that the state could act in the public interest with regard to feelings in the private family because of the family's effects on social life. Although the judiciary kept jilt suits from being outlawed despite shifting public attitudes and rising state activism, these suits lost their legal and social significance, becoming "marginal suit[s] for marginal women"[43] – and, one might add here, material for marginalized narratives.

Without using the term, Simmel describes economic and contract-based liberalism as the force behind sociological and psychological life at the turn of the century:

> Through the calculative nature of money a new precision, a certainty in the definition of identities and differences, an unambiguousness in agreements and arrangements has been brought about in the relations of life elements – just as externally this precision has been effected by the universal diffusion of pocket watches. However, the conditions of metropolitan life are at once cause and effect of this trait. The relationships and affairs of the typical metropolitan usually are so varied and complex that without the strictest punctuality in promises and services the whole structure would break down into an inextricable chaos.[44]

Metropolitan life forces people to schematize their relationships, purge them of the imprecise and subjective, and establish exact equivalents. Modern relationships must be administered – organized and coordinated – to be compatible with maintaining a stable money economy. The buried metaphor for tailoring individual life to market logic at this time is the reciprocal relationship of promise and performance: the engagement and wedding.

Glasgow uses a similar paradigm. Dorinda must "translate" her success as a farmer for her neighbors. Their persistent recurrence to her history with Jason has always bothered her; ten years after returning from New York she realizes also that

> there were no spectators of her triumph. She had kept so close to the farm that her neighbors knew her only as a dim figure against the horizon, a moving shape among corn-shocks and hay-ricks in the flat landscape, an image that vanished with these inanimate objects in the lengthening perspective.[45]

Glasgow describes Dorinda's problem as compositional obscurity, and one remembers here how Glasgow earlier differentiates her barren ground from the wasteland Eliot metaphorizes as a woman's body. To distinguish Dorinda from the landscape is, for Glasgow, to challenge the gendered agrarian high modernist account of modernity and literary modernization.

Dorinda rises out of the landscape by buying a new dress:

> [W]hile she walked slowly up the aisle [in her new dress] in church, she felt rather than saw that the congregation, forgetting to stand up to sing, sat

motionless and stared at her from the pews. For the first time in her life she tasted the intoxicating flavor of power. On the farm, success was translated into well-tilled acres or golden pounds of butter; but here, with these astonished eyes on her, she discovered that it contained a quality more satisfying than any material fact. What it measured was the difference between the past which Jason had ruined and the present which she had triumphantly built on the ruins he had left.[46]

This scene resembles a wedding in its ritual transformation of the economics of private property exchange into a personal odyssey. Nathan begins repeated proposals of marriage a week later and Glasgow describes Dorinda's "dispassionate" reconsideration of whether they might marry in terms of its "expediency" in managing their farms. They marry about a month after she buys the dress, and Glasgow describes all of these events (realizing that she must translate herself, buying the black dress, returning to church and accepting Nathan's proposal) in rapid succession. And yet Dorinda's actual wedding is characterized by lack of self-knowledge and lack of recognition from others. "The exact moment of her yielding was so vague that she could never remember it," she hears the refrain "How did I ever come to do such a thing?" in her head, there is no walk down the aisle, Fluvanna compares baking the wedding cake to "baking a cake for a corpse" and Glasgow suggests that the marriage is never consummated. As a married woman, however, Dorinda mysteriously passes from this state to standing in a "secure place" which is independent of any man, yet somehow reliant on marriage:

Her happiness was independent, she felt, of the admiration of men, and her value as a human being was founded upon a durable, if an intangible, basis. Since she had proved she that she could farm as well as a man there was less need for her to fascinate as a woman. ... Looking back from the secure place where she stood, she could afford to smile at the perturbation of spirit which had attended her wedding.[47]

Dorinda's marriage is much like her participation in modern production. Simmel writes that the economy of modern life promotes a new kind of "equation" between "the individual and the supra-individual contents of life." Colin Gordon describes this, following Foucault, as "a mechanism at once of individualization and totalization" in which governance consists of maintaining and managing the link between the conduct of individual citizens and the regulation of the population as a whole.[48] Marriage as the supreme expression of individuality, in terms of its assertion of the singularity of the participants and their feelings, is not Glasgow's objective here. Rather, Dorinda's "individualization" comes in the way that her development as a farmer did – she achieves a stable *civic* identity. Marriage as a status rather than a contract means that her security comes from a new relation to the state rather than to a person. Marriage is not a sign of a failure of Glasgow's literary modernity so much as it is proof of her comprehension of administrative modernity's incorporation of earlier narratives of self-making.

WHITE TURKEYS, BLACK LABOR

> Dan: Those silly women arguing feminism. Here's what I should have said to them. "It should be clear to you women, that the proposition must be stated thus:
> Me, horizontally above her.
> Action: Perfect strokes downward oblique.
> Hence, man dominates because of limitation.
> Or, so it shall be until women learn their stuff."
> So framed, the proposition is a mental-filler, Dentist, I want gold teeth. It should become cherished of the technical intellect. I hereby offer it to posterity as one of the important machine-age designs. P. S. It should be noted, that because it is an achievement of this age, its growth and hence its causes, up to the point of maturity antedate machinery.
>
> Jean Toomer, *Cane* (1923)

Above, I wrote that one of the things that distinguishes ("dispassionate") modernist regional/southern narrative from its ("sentimental") predecessors is that though not free, black labor was no longer literally capitalist property. We might understand this as a literary move away from an American sentimentalism whose commitments would mean emphasizing how (or that) labor felt (asserting, for instance, that slaves were either happy or unhappy in the plantation system) or exploring what it meant socially and politically to own feeling property. If, as Jane Tompkins has described it, the sentimental American novel embraced a "sensational design," American regional modernism rejected sentiment by embracing good design and regional planning paradigms. Thus, Glasgow's manifesto-like resolve to write about the south "not sentimentally, as a conquered province, but dispassionately, as part of a larger world," is one of literary critical political economy.

American modernism and modernist literary criticism have been significantly shaped by the centrality of the modernizing region as a model for American political life, cultural subjectivity and aesthetic design. At the turn of the century and with an accelerating pace during the interwar years, the American population shifted from the country to the city rather than out into a frontier. Urban life – understood as industrialized, mechanized, standardized, centralized, socially isolated and consumerist – seemed to have become American life. The end of freeholder self-sufficiency in rural America seemed emblematic of a general trend in Americans' economic and political lives.

Describing the "Americanization" of the south – the shift from traditional, small-scale local production to capital-intensive and mechanized agricultural business that could be incorporated into an international cash-crop economy – became a way for even non-rural Americans to map the contours of what it meant to be a citizen in the modernizing American political economy. The modernization of the south encapsulated the losses, gains and contradictions of American modernization. The "southern question" became the American question.

Regionalist ideas not only were interesting to intellectuals and artists, but were also a significant part of American interwar understandings of American industrialization, urbanization and the development of consumer culture. Sociologists, urban planners and architects – remember that Glasgow has Dorinda characterize Central Park as "an imitation of the country" – also incorporated regionalist thinking into their responses to the social problems raised by industrialized modernity.[49]

Dorman notes that in his essay "The Aesthetic of Regionalism," John Crowe Ransom admired the Pueblo tribes' folk culture, which he described as a "regionalism" originating in their economic and political life: "as economic patterns become perfected and easy, they cease to be merely economic and become gradually aesthetic." The things people manufactured, such as tools, became "ornamental." Ransom's earlier work on white southern folk culture argued that similarly, southern regional culture had become a whole and modern aesthetic.[50] Glasgow builds a regional economic way of life for Dorinda that, like interwar regionalism, was neither "anti-modern" nor industrialist, but which modernized established hierarchies by taking them under the aegis of regional planning and design.

If economic patterns eventually become so "perfected" as to become aesthetic (or if an aesthetic results from the refinement of an economic system), then the modernist rejection of sentiment and other ideologies of the social may not be the story of the rise of the avant-garde in opposition to femininity, social realism and mass culture. It may instead be the story of how elements of a widespread interwar regionalist paradigm added the vocabulary of "design" and "program" to modernist "style." Some regionalists responded to the socioeconomic changes of modernization in kind. They began to describe possible responses in terms of problem solving and balancing modern and traditional cultures. Instead of maintaining utopian myths of the frontier, the farmer and their communitarian civic virtues, they turned to modern social programming and political reform – "the compelling if elusive programmatic ground of regional-social planning."[51]

Recognizing the regionalism of American modernism in these terms should allow us to see the ways in which, though Jean Toomer's *Cane* is stylistically different from Glasgow's novel, it and *Barren Ground* illuminate each other's "modernism."

From the time of its publication, Toomer's stylized and meticulously structured novel was readily recognizable as having adopted "modern" style. It is one of the texts cited to define the Harlem Renaissance as "modernist." But to consider Toomer's aesthetic as a singular revolt against realism invokes the paradigm of the genius rather than the historical practitioner. Instead, we might read Toomer's style as, like Glasgow's, a historical aesthetic that considers the contrast between realism and modernism itself a feature of twentieth-century culture rather than imagining that modern writing renders older styles obsolete and irrelevant. As with the Department of Agriculture's policies directed at farm families, planned gender hierarchies constituted "modernity" because they were planned. Glasgow's black laborers are more than literary throwbacks to the local-color regional narrative; their dialect, appearance and colorful comments are modern functions. Balancing black manual labor against white capitalist investment as mechanized farms rise from the newly regreened acres of Pedlar's Mill does not repeat the pre-Civil War economy. Rather, it modernizes racial hierarchy and economics.

Like *White Zombie*, *Barren Ground* invokes popular assumptions about miscegenation and race only to redefine the "problem" of genetic *race* as one of modern *labor*. Jason is an example of the deterioration of the family line. He is prone to nerves and weak, almost destined to jilt Dorinda because his father is a drunkard and his family have shown themselves incapable of maintaining their bloodlines or their estate. Jason's family owns the white turkeys of my chapter title, but, like the rest of Five Oaks, they have deteriorated: "Dirt, mildew, decay everywhere! White turkeys that were discolored by mould. Chips, trash, broken bottles littering the yard and the back steps, which were rotting to pieces. Windows so darkened by dust and cobwebs that they were like eyes blurred by cataract. Several mulatto babies crawling, like small, sly animals, over the logs at the woodpile."[52] The whiteness of the turkeys, like the whiteness of Jason's family (his father has a mulatto mistress), collapses, carrying Five Oaks with it. Dorinda's family, the Oakleys, in contrast, keep their lines pure. Glasgow emphasizes that Dorinda's family, at the end of the novel, has white cats, white dogs and white chickens – leghorns most decidedly not discolored – descended from animals introduced at the beginning of the novel. Dorinda's success as a dairy farmer depends not only on the genealogies of her cows but also on the genealogies of her workers. She chooses her black workers from the "colored aristocracy" of Pedlar's Mill, people descended from Aunt Mehitable Green, a friend of the family and former slave to a family with good slave "stock."

But Glasgow dismisses the specter of miscegenation as an archaic mode of racial anxiety. Dorinda miscarries; she never bears Jason's child; in fact, she never bears any children. The (non-)white turkeys do indicate a problem with Jason's "line" but it comes from the same sort of postbirth "deterioration" that we see happen to white people in *White Zombie* and in Mansfield's "The Woman at the Store." Dorinda maintains racial lines through labor management, not marriage. In the early days of restoring the farm, Dorinda is indistinguishable from Fluvanna, her black worker, with regard to how hard they work. But Glasgow later distinguishes the modes in which Dorinda and her other black workers work. Aunt Mehitable's descendants are good workers despite having been modernized. "I never saw a darkey that had as much vim as Fluvanna [Mehitable Green's granddaughter]. And she belongs to the new order too. I always thought it spoiled them to learn to read and write until I hired her."[53]

What does it mean to say that African Americans are "spoiled" by modernity? Dorinda encounters the limits of electrification and industrialization even after twenty-five years, when, after World War I, the farm has become mechanized and electrified. Although she has installed machinery to milk the cows, only the new cows will accept it, and in a conversation between Dorinda and her stepson about the new work available to African American labor, we read Glasgow's racialized mapping of modern production. Where laborers work well, it is from the tradition of slavery, not an understanding of modern economic forces:

Cows must be milked twice a day, and no darkey wants to work more than three times a week.

"They're still living on their war wages. ... Perhaps," she suggested hopefully, "when the negroes have spent all they've saved up, they'll begin to feel like working."

"Perhaps. But it takes a long time to starve a darkey."

"Well, I'll see what Fluvanna can do about it," Dorinda retorted.

The problem, she felt, was a serious one. The negro, who was by temperament a happiness-hunter, could pursue the small game of amusement, she was aware, with an unflagging pace. Without laborers, the farms she had reclaimed with incalculable effort would sink again into waste land. ... In the end, it was Fluvanna who, with the assistance of the patriarchs among the Moodys, the Greens, and the Plumtrees [families descended from Aunt Mehitable], drove the inveterate pleasure-seekers back to the plough.[54]

Like the old cows, black people will not accept new systems of industrialization. And yet the racialized labor of Pedlar's Mill and the south must not be modernized, else there will be no labor for Dorinda's farm. In her narrative, consumption for black people is only a throwback to premodern subsistence rather than a participation in national change and industrialization. Fluvanna and the patriarchs who respect the Oakleys and understand work and obligation in the tradition of stereotypical "good slaves" are what Dorinda and the country need. Thus, modernity is by definition uneven – "Machinery could not work alone, and even tractor-ploughs were obliged to be guided."[55] Dorinda may not be in a reproductive marriage, but she makes a contribution similar to her mother's strict genealogical monitoring of their white leghorns by maintaining a system in which black labor gets "driven back to the plough" to support Dorinda's (and the nation's) large-scale mechanized agricultural transformation.

In the epigraph I take from *Cane*, Toomer's character Dan Moore describes clichéd heterosexual sexual positions and their parallel in social positioning not as archaism or tradition but as related to the modern machine. These are positions that are not unique and crafted, but rather infinitely reproducible, and that make practical sense. Here the machine age, far from equalizing all in a wave of homogenizing, liberating and inexorable modernization, is itself the source of differentiation. The experience of modernization envisioned here is that of being processed into politically institutionalized unequal relations. The "women arguing feminism" are presumably animated by arguments about which theories best account for, and thus suggest remedies that will end, women's subordination. This debate would be cast within a moral framework. Those making a "normative commitment to women's emancipation" would not consider theoretical "analyses that sustain the systematic or structural privilege of men."[56] But Dan Moore describes dispassionate standards of good design as underlying male domination. That is to say, positions should be decided by what objectively "works" rather than according to such moral commitments. How he sees is less important than that his eyes "BURN CLEAN!"[57]

This passage demands a rereading of the usual male–female pairing in *Cane* criticism: that women like Karintha and Avey bear feminized burdens of sensuous fertility, inscrutability and trauma while modernized men watch them from trains and leave them for cities. "Karintha is a woman. Young men run stills to make her money. Young men go to the big cities and run on the road. Young men go away to college. They all want to bring her money."[58] As many critics have noted, the first part of *Cane*, associated with the rural south, focuses on stories of women (Karintha, Becky, Carma, Fern, Esther), while the middle section follows African American migration to urban areas and focuses more on men's stories. Toomer supposedly tracks this movement in his prose style, setting cyclic natural time marked by the sun and the growing seasons against the urban, modern "syncopations of jazz."[59] In the final section, the first two parts come full circle, as a male African American urban intellectual goes to rural Georgia to work as a teacher. Certainly, the way *Cane* seems to (flexibly but recognizably) gender the binaries rural/urban, organic/mechanized, lyric/syncopated, and traditional/modernized as female/male could reasonably result in describing its central preoccupation as how narratives gendered as "women's" sustain men's modernization.

Dan Moore's ranting, however, suggests a different notion of design in *Cane*. Toomer's use of a circular graphic to structure the collection suggests the possibility of entering the text at any point, rather than following a historically linear migration narrative. Male and female do not represent modern and traditional so much as they indicate gendered entrances into the same modernity. Dan Moore's "technical intellect" is one that grasps, above all things, that there are no categorical refuges from modernity, whether in sex or in pastoral life.

The "perfect strokes downward oblique" are both naturalized and machine-like. Likewise, the death of the field rat in "Reapers" comes from a perfect downward stroke dealt by farmers using a mix of manual and horse-drawn equipment:

Black reapers with the sound of steel on stones
Are sharpening scythes. I see them place the hones

In their hip-pockets as a thing that's done,
And start their silent swinging, one by one.
Black horses drive a mower through the weeds,
And there, a field rat, startled, squealing bleeds.
His belly close to ground. I see the blade,
Blood-stained, continue cutting weeds and shade.[60]

This alliterative, symmetrical and tightly encapsulated account of rural farming aesthetically evokes mechanization alongside images more commonly associated with the aestheticization of agrarian life as representing work in harmony with nature. The men work together with shared, almost essential motions and gestures – "things that are done." These lines echo the violence that saturates the rest of *Cane*, drawing attention to the violence of good technical design and its foundation in *designation*, that is, the planned categorical unevenness and inequalities of modernity.

Throughout *Cane*, Toomer displays interest in the implications of the "design" paradigm, extending it to an analyis similar to (though ultimately, perhaps, more critical than) Glasgow's insights into uneven modernity as designed (and racially designated) rather than incidental or prepatory to full modernity. Aesthetics and politics shared a vocabulary of design. The twentieth century was an era not merely of machine-age design but of "good design" as the exercise of political power. As Kirstie McClure explains, twentieth-century political power after the Progressive era was grounded by the assumption that "'politics' is strongly identified with problem-solving activities within a bounded social system" so that the "privileged form of political knowledge is cast as the diagnosis of social problems, the isolation of their underlying causes, and the recommendation of specific sorts of practical interventions in system dynamics as their appropriate 'solution.'"[61] Du Bois's famous formulation of what it feels like to be a problem of this politicized social type reveals that how "good" the design seems may depend on who falls into the category of the social problem and who falls into the category of the problem solver. Thus, good "machine-age" design could encompass the organization of segregation and the construction of voting districts – state-enforced design to which race is integral and in which "the machine" refers not only to abstract modernity but also to how political power is distributed.

Many critics have read *Cane*'s oppositions of rural landscape and its activities with urban modernity as both critical of modernity as destructive of the utopic potential of rural life and an attempt to "spiritualize machinery and absorb its sublime power" as in sections such as "Her Lips Are Copper Wire."[62] Another set of readings debates Toomer's construction of racial identity, citing his essays or comments on his own racial identity as indeterminate. Werner Sollors, for instance, notes that *Cane* works against a trend in American racial thought demonstrated by the removal of the category for mixed race from the post-1920 U.S. census.[63] Ross Posnock argues that Toomer tries to write about the color line without accepting racial binaries. Without rejecting these readings' insights into Toomer's interest in indeterminate categories, I see his point as rather designation, or the way that racial categories continue to be information-bearing as part of machine-age social design. That is, I would emphasize his interest in the census and court decision rather than his personal philosophy about "race." The paradox of machine-age design as Toomer has Dan Moore describe it is that although "it is an achievement of this age, its growth and hence its causes, up to the point of maturity, *antedate* machinery."[64] And indeed, although *Cane* is described as an aesthetic breakthrough in modern African American writing, "Blood-Burning Moon" bears strong resemblance to Du Bois's "Of the Coming of John" in *The Souls of Black Folk*.

My intent here is not to offer a comprehensive reading of *Cane* so much as it is to suggest that a theory of American modernism focused on the significance of increasing state involvement in the political, economic and social arenas of modernization draws *Cane* into a modernist ambit that could also include texts such as *White Zombie* and *Barren Ground*.

That American modernism and modernist literary criticism were shaped by regionalist ideologies responding to interwar modernization seems clear; less obvious is how that should matter. These texts all recognize rigidly maintained unevenness as a particular and foundational condition of modernity. Marriage highlights the kind of public, national consent that founds modern subjectivity. Modernity is not simply homogenization and/or "progress," but mass differentiation and division: of labor, of access to authority, of the production of "culture(s)" and of market identities. The American south reads during this period as the model for maintained uneven modernity where the management of racialized national subjects and the labor and agricultural markets was at once a local way of understanding the United States as a world power and a way of delineating the boundaries of national subjectivity and citizenship holding. It is this mode of understanding the south, rather than technologizing its depiction in opposition to earlier "sentimental" portrayals, that should define the southern modernist text.

In my concluding chapter I give a final example of the difference considering this politics of modernization might make. If the modernization of "natives" consisted of pacifying them into behaving as voluntarily good governmental subjects, what did it mean that Western peoples were the most modernized of the world's peoples? I argue that modernist desire for the primitive was a political fantasy, not a psycho-sexual one.

CHAPTER 5

Modernist (pre)occupations: Haiti, primitivism and anti-colonial nationalism

Critics traditionally define the "primitivism" of the 1920s and 1930s as a psychoanalytically influenced Western elite practice in which artists treated "natives" and native cultures as sources of rejuvenation in a rapidly modernizing world. Primitivists assumed that modernization and its accompanying social norms separated modern Western people from their authentic impulses: sexuality, physicality, violence and play. Rather than considering natives as simply deficient in "civilization," primitivists saw them as conduits to the unconscious or as alternatives to Western civilization's rationality, bureaucracy and mechanization. Paradoxically, primitivist representations of natives were, as Elazar Barkan and Ronald Bush maintain, "a highly charged signal of otherness... that came to signify modernity."[1] Thus, primitivists see natives as unaware of the significance of modernization or their relationship to it, but primitivists themselves, as rebellious cultural relativists, can understand both modern and primitive modes of thought.

Perceiving the native as the leading edge of modernity allows us to understand modernists' affiliations with the primitive as stemming from political rather than metaphysical concerns. Modernists may have used "natives" or "primitive art" to invoke tangible remnants of "pre-history" – fragments to make modernity and modernization visible – but their materials always emerged as by-products of Western exploration, conquest and territorial organization. In this chapter, I emphasize the geopolitical aspects of modernism's natives and primitives.

Elite Westerners could see that the technological modernization of occupied territory – roads, schools, sanitation, commerce – had to be accompanied by governmental or administrative modernization. Britain and the United States offered to replace the "feudal" or "tribal" hierarchies of indigenous peoples with centralized representative government structures and national identities. This involved, as many critics have documented, information gathering, policing, categorization and the regulation of social life.

Consider, for instance, the U.S. government's Philippines census of 1903–5. Conducted shortly after the U.S. Congress had forbidden a census unless the islands were completely pacified, the act of beginning the census declared victory for the United States. The census was conducted despite the fact that nationalist guerilla resistance continued and the constabulary had to secure some areas of the country before census takers could enter. The census established the conditions for national elections of a U.S.-approved colonial legislature, which would further consolidate the counterrevolutionary nationalism (Benedict Anderson's "official nationalism") the United States wanted to establish. The U.S. government and U.S. corporations also needed the data to guide their capital investments in the islands. But, Vicente Rafael argues, this census did not merely enumerate but also created governable citizens. The U.S. government used 7,502 Filipinos in its corps of census workers. Allegedly exemplifying the Filipinos' potential for eventual self-government, these workers demonstrated their ability to work as disciplined subjects within a state apparatus *and* their acceptance of the categories that modern states establish for the purpose of creating a proper national population out of heterogeneous colonial subjects.[2]

This process had a popular audience in the United States. Far from burying the Philippines census results in a government archive, William Howard Taft, U.S. Secretary of War and former Governor General of the Philippines, personally informed Gilbert Grosvenor, the editor of *National Geographic*, of its release. *National Geographic*'s issue of April 1905, only the third to contain photographs, covered the census and brought in so many new subscribers that the publisher had to put it back on the press to meet the demand.[3] Founded in 1888, *National Geographic* was the most widely read source of general science information in America.[4] By 1920, it was the publishing industry's major success story, having increased its circulation during the war to 650,000 (while other publications failed) and then to over 750,000 within the next two years.[5]

National Geographic's use of the Philippines census material indicates the social forces behind these numbers. The Spanish-American War spurred an interest in geography and *Our New Possessions* (as an early *National Geographic* book put it). *National Geographic* may have begun using photographs as a marketing tool, but the adoption of conventions of photographic realism quickly established the magazine as a reliable, objective and current source for information about American empire.

In the Philippines census issue, *National Geographic* converted a government document into a mass cultural one in order to position readers so that they could enjoy pleasurable positions as surveyors of "the world and all that is in it," the theme of the magazine as described in 1900 by Alexander Graham Bell, the society's second president.[6] But this position obviously depended on appreciating power as embedded in surveillance, enumeration and social control, even if *National Geographic* consistently emphasized the ultimate benefits of U.S. colonization.[7]

If the imperial arena displayed the exertion of state power more starkly, it also provided the backdrop for imagining anti-state activity. Epstein's lines on modernity should also remind us of C. L. R. James's claim in *The Black Jacobins* that the conditions of plantation production in the Caribbean produced proletarianized revolutionaries ahead of the rest of the world.[8] I argue that modernist primitivists construct "natives"/nationalists[9] as enviable for their "fortunate" *political* position: able to see and thus actively fight subjection by the state. In making this argument, I am outlining a new critical understanding of primitivists' objects of desire, not realigning their cultural politics. In fact, criticisms of primitivists as innaccurate, appropriative, manipulative and indifferent to the political and psychological price of their discourse for "natives" and racialized others still apply. The primitivism I describe involves envy of an imagined ability to rebel projected onto a racial other. Primitivists were not necessarily anti-imperialists.[10] To understand primitivism as grounded in imperial governance rather than psycho-sexual repression is to recognize one of the ways in which modernists engaged with state formations as they constructed their definitions of modernity and of themselves as "revolutionary" subjects of modernity.

Modernism's arena, then, is not merely the battlefields of Europe and the "men of 1914" but also the imperial land grabs of the 1880s and 1890s, the countries of the Monroe Doctrine, the great powers' remapping of the world post-World War I and American areas of "intervention." When Woodrow Wilson adopted the ideal of "national self-determination," it circulated popularly in the context of a war framed as the battle between free (national) peoples and illegitimate (state/imperial) conquest.[11] Many critics have discussed the inconsistencies of its application after the war; I will not attempt to summarize their work here. What I find significant about the popularization of "national self-determination" and its associated ideologies with regard to modernism is its contribution to defining the modern self as a national subject potentially at odds with a state. Benedict Anderson describes the end of World War I as the historical moment when the "legitimate international norm" became the *nation-state* "so that in the League [of Nations] even the surviving imperial powers came dressed in national costume rather than in imperial uniform."[12] Centralized state authority can legitimate itself by appearing national.

A uniform signals the wearer's contemporary agreement to mask difference in subordination to centralized authority; a costume invokes a standard of historically grounded, affective identity that governing authorities must acknowledge. Governance will now be judged on whether it has truly converted national desire into state policy. As I discussed in Chapter 1, the United States, although it violently occupied Haiti, actively worked to maintain an appearance of Haitian independent agency. Wilson unwittingly outlined the paradoxes of imperial democracy when questioned by the British Foreign Office about his imperial policies in 1914: "I am going to teach the South American republics to elect good men."[13] Wilson uses the *National Geographic* version of the United States as a world power. As with the Philippines census, Wilson's words underscore representative democracy's entanglements with domination. The deployment of U.S. imperial power raised questions about how the state acquired and managed subjects at home and abroad and of how "freedom" in a state modernizing into a newly internationalized context might be imagined. Occupations, interventions, spheres of influence and the oppositions mobilized against them threw the condition of being subject to a state apparatus into sharp relief. Subjection took on the rhetoric of empowerment – the Filipinos prepare for independent nationhood by surveying their own country for U.S. occupation.

One gets a sense of U.S. popular unease about this aspect of modern U.S. empire from debates about the government's censorship of American news coverage of the Philippines War and about restrictions placed on mail addressed to U.S. soldiers in the Philippines. The government refused to deliver a telegram from an organized group of families and friends to the men of the Nebraska regiment that read: "Boys, don't reenlist; insist upon immediate discharge."[14] Edward Atkinson, a well-known political speaker, decided to make a test case of his anti-imperial pamphlets and sent copies to military and civilian officials in the Philippines. The Postmaster General ordered them removed from mails going to Manila. Some public criticism took the line that government control of the information U.S. soldiers were allowed to have demonstrated that the kinds of authority and categorization colonial rule supposedly necessitated for colonial subjects would be applied to citizens at home. Other writers claimed that voters on U.S. soil had been treated like Russian, German, Turkish and Papal subjects when denied information. The president had acted as if he had "carte blanche authority to conduct the affairs of the nation."[15] The government had adopted a category of "incendiary literature" of the type that all conquerors must have and which southern postmasters had used during the Civil War.[16]

This debate focused on whether the men's status as soldiers in time of war superseded their standing as voters entitled to full access to national debates. The May 18, 1899, issue of *The Nation* published a letter from a Civil War (Union) veteran who wrote that during the 1864 presidential campaign "Nothing was withheld from the soldiers of that most bitter and critical period. ... When our lines were near together and there were periods of lull in the firing ... we exchanged our [news]papers ... for the [news]papers of rebeldom. We were men who had minds of our own ... and could draw our own conclusions."[17] The Philppines colonial context triggered discussions about state power rather than national identity. The ideal these writers articulate is that of an informed voting public – the stuff of a representative democracy. And yet the anxiety is that it is precisely their status as individual voters that allowed and encouraged the state to train them to elect good men rather than to think for themselves. Some newspapers asserted that the censorship order had originated not from General Otis, but from McKinley's administration.

The shift Anderson describes from imperial "uniform" to national "costume" also highlights another element crucial to my analysis: how the world powers justified their decisions with regard to the numerous sovereignty cases presented after the war. The Wilson administration's group "The Inquiry," for instance, was charged with gathering geographical, historical, economic and legal data to support Wilson's recommendations during the post-World War I settlements.[18] Wilson's elaborations of what constituted a nation as a proper "self" were imprecise and often contradictory. He claimed to give the most weight to what he considered "organic" characteristics: commonality of language, long-standing borders, shared historical consciousness and "ethnographic affinities."[19] The Filipino people did not qualify for national self-determination because they were too "diverse and heterogeneous," and Wilson did not insist that national self-determination required breaking up the Hapsburg Empire or freedom for Ireland, Egypt or India.[20] On March 1, 1919, unarmed citizens in Korea, partly inspired by a speech in which Wilson vowed the support of the United States for the self-determination of small nations, rose against Japanese colonization. Support from the

United States never came and the Japanese killed and imprisoned tens of thousands. Despite these inconsistencies, and regardless of the reasons behind them, "national self-determination" became an important part of the vocabulary anchoring an aspect of modern political identity in anthropology's redefinition of "culture" and in an ideal of cultural authenticity.

When I examine the importance of U.S. imperial action to modernist thought, I focus on the significance of governance, rather than on individual artists' views on imperialism. My interest is in how primitivists derived their "natives" out of a sense of the interrelatedness of the U.S. colonial "regime" abroad and its domestic metropolitan "administration." The primitivist fantasy is to understand how one is being ruled.

Matthew G. Hannah writes that on the "epistemological register" the two are nearly identical, for state power in both places requires surveying and classifying territory, people and resources as well as imposing inventories to get this knowledge without consent. And in both the colonial and the metropolitan settings the state uses this knowledge for social control.[21] Wilson's rhetoric about American domination in the Caribbean differed markedly from Roosevelt's or Taft's. He argued that domination was necessary in order to bring other countries constitutional democracy.[22]

In his infamous film *The Birth of a Nation* (1915),[23] D.W. Griffith confronts this concept of "democratic occupancy," creating a narrative in which white men must free themselves from the forms of U.S. representative democracy, while black men have pathetically succumbed to the false agency of voting. Written nearly twenty years after *The Birth of a Nation*, in another medium and, most people would assume, out of a different politic, Zora Neale Hurston's *Tell My Horse: Voodoo and Life in Haiti and Jamaica* (1938) is surprisingly and significantly shaped by the same discourse: the relation of cultural nationalism to modern forms of government in a newly postcolonial world. In both these works, modernism's investment in primitivism emerges as an engagement with a modern, centralizing, imperialist governance that is racially stratified. Griffith's films are notable for, among other things, their "run to the rescue" sequences that exemplify the move from a "cinema of attractions" to one based on narrative integration. Tom Gunning explains that chase films introduce the idea of focusing on how individual shots are linked. As a result, "[t]he process of following a continuous action through a series of shots created new relations to the spectator, new approaches to space and time."[24] Griffith also contributed to the development of parallel and contrast editing, which allowed audiences to see simultaneous reactions to the same occurrence, to "stop" time, to show one event from several perspectives or unexpectedly and rapidly to juxtapose different places and times. Although critics have not described "run to the rescue" sequences as themselves aesthetically "modernist," the editing techniques that create them are, of course, classic descriptions of how modernism altered not only perceptions of space and time but also understandings of the relationship between past and present. But as Michael Rogin and Walter Benn Michaels have demonstrated, Griffith's greatest "run to the rescue" does not take place in abstract space and time but in the space and time of America's empire.

Thomas Dixon's Klan trilogy (especially the second volume, *The Clansman* [1905]), can be read either, as Walter Benn Michaels has argued, as "anti-imperialist" with a critical vocabulary mobilized against McKinley's exercise of arbitrary powers in the Philippines or, as Michael Rogin argues, as anti-Populist novels that take the Spanish-American War and the suppression of the Philippine independence movement as a model for a united Anglo-Saxon race which would revitalize the United States. I will not try to produce a resolution to these characterizations here; suffice it for my purposes to say that between the two of them, they establish Dixon's novel, and by extension Griffith's film, as very much of their time in their engagement of the nature of American empire. To this, Amy Kaplan adds that the Dixon novels reference the Spanish-American War and that both fictional and documentary footage of American troops in that war influenced Griffith's depiction of African Americans in federal uniform as dangerous as well as his understanding of the international significance of American whiteness.[25]

The nineteenth-century white supremacist solution to the end of slavery – violent social and economic subordination and political disenfranchisement – worked.[26] But although Griffith casts political power based in representative government as effective enough to drive a plot necessitating violence against black men when they vote, he also characterizes the vote itself as pathetically inadequate – something only black men would be foolish enough to want. Following the titles "Enrolling the Negro vote" and "The franchise for all blacks," an elderly black man refuses to register for the vote when he finds out that "franchise" is not something the Bureau is handing out: "Ef I doan' get 'nuf franchise to fill mah bucket, I doan' want it nohow."[27]

The Birth of a Nation's deliberate use of racist myths of Reconstruction by now needs no introduction. What I wish to discuss here is how a narrative of an uncertain white masculinity that must be transformed and shored up by a massed Klan and its rituals intertwines with a narrative about a different kind of white power: electoral power. Griffith uses the myth of the powerful black voter/legislator as much as he does the myth of the black rapist. In the film, individual white men re-empower white men as a group by relinquishing individual identities to form the "brotherly horde" of the Klan.[28] Electoral politics work similarly; one must have faith in a mystified system of democratic representation in which one vote is worth both nothing and everything – and in which one is reduced to being a voter in a group. In well-known philosophical narratives of the origins of the state, the brothers agree to relinquish individual power and go on to form a state. The mysticism of the imagined community of the nation yields to the mystification of the institutions of the state. Not so for Griffith – it is here that we see the degree to which twentieth-century concerns about the status of white male individual agency drive Griffith's representation of a nineteenth-century white man's problem as the need to assert a native, national identity against state institutions.

When we examine *The Birth of a Nation* from this perspective, two of its interests emerge as particularly striking. First, confrontation with state bureaucracy is what produces Klan nationalism. Second, Griffith focuses intently and sometimes contradictorily on elections and enfranchisement. The way these two things affect his aesthetic techniques, rather than the techniques themselves, should define Griffith's relation to history and his explorations of subjectivity and agency as modernist.[29]

The enfranchisement of black people reveals how the state has come to stage political existence in a way that suggests the abstract interchangeability of white and black men as citizens.[30] In the context of winner-take-all districting, citizenship is "the ultimate reflection of individual dignity and autonomy and ... voting is the means for individual citizens to realize this personal and social standing. Under this theory, voters realize the fullest meaning of citizenship by the individual act of voting for representatives who, once elected, participate on the voter's behalf in the process of self-government."[31] But since all representation is group rather than individual representation, this promise cannot be fulfilled.[32] By this logic, contrary to white men's claims, the black legislators technically represent the "helpless white minority," as Griffith calls them.

Griffith reaches back to Reconstruction, when the problem for white men was that black men were being enfranchised (theoretically) on equal levels. But he actually articulates and tries to solve a different problem: that enfranchisement didn't actually work as the liberal individualistic view of representative democracy claimed it did. His interest in grounding an elite individualist whiteness outside mass politics can be read as a response to what he does not overtly acknowledge: enfranchisement could be easily circumvented, suggesting that it was not the source of individual agency, responsibility, and identity it promised to be.

Griffith's depiction of African Americans as voters and legislators reiterates, if contradictorily, this sense of enfranchisement's power as illusory. After an election day on which "[a]ll the blacks are given the ballot, while the leading whites are disenfranchised," we see a black man placing two ballots in the box, while black and white men (carpetbaggers and men aligned with the character meant to stand for Thaddeus Stevens) prevent white men from placing their ballots. The next title reads: "Receiving the returns: The Negroes and carpetbaggers sweep the state."[33] The consequence of this sweep is a State House filled with black people who don't understand the point of being representatives: they eat peanuts and joints of meat, drink, laugh and take off their shoes while in session. Their bill to allow intermarriage of blacks and whites goes up alongside bills such as "all whites must salute negro officers on the streets."[34] Griffith meant the reference to racial intermarriage to be incendiary. In this, his claim is that franchise is powerful and black people can wield it effectively.

But Griffith also suggests that the franchise actually does not accomplish very much for black people in the long run. His depiction of the black State House shows the legislators to be petty and childish, rather than crafty and intelligent. They manage to pass the marriage bill only because it brings the same kind of childish satisfaction that requiring whites to salute them would. But since white women don't want to marry black men – Griffith shows that Lynch must kidnap Elsie, and Gus tries to rape Flora – that bill is useless. Their legislation has no potential to change their status as a group or to recognize their historical constitution as a group. The state legislature does not pass a bill for the "forty acres and a mule" that appears on a placard in an earlier scene of black protest. Griffith obscures this group constitution and links any remedy based on it to the close-up image of a black hand illegitimately putting in two ballots. Even more significantly, he portrays black people as uninterested in their groupness, that is to say, their authenticity as justification for their claims. Instead, they are eager to merge with the federal government's institutions and to marry out of their group.

Lynette Hunter writes in her analysis of George Orwell's doublethink novels that awareness of "the artificiality of the state and its public presence [lead to] the recognition that even in an empowered position the individual can do nothing to affect the workings of the state [and] generates the enervation, melancholy, paranoia and cynicism of postmodern theory."[35]

But in 1915 there are alternatives that seem "authentic." The places where the workings of the state are being most obviously contested are sites of imperialism, precisely those sites from which primitivist representations come. One of the ways *National Geographic* characterized populations or cultures as "native" (as opposed to "developed" or "modern") was by their inability to understand or unwillingness to accept modern systems of state management, including "government and its conceptual categories."[36] Both Britain (in the Fiji Islands) and the United States (in the Philippines) imagined "pacification," "civilization," "benevolent assimilation" and eventual accession to self-government in the early twentieth century as dependent on natives performing the kinds of acts that demonstrated the development of a self-consciousness connected to bureaucracy.[37] Griffith takes to heart Woodrow Wilson's assertion that "teaching" South American republics fair and free elections is the way to conquer them; this is why the film's determination to disenfranchise black people does not conclude with the enfranchisement of white people.

Although they succeed in first "Disarming the blacks" and then prevent them from voting entirely, the Klansmen do not themselves vote. Griffiths presents whites who are unfairly denied admission to the bureaucracy of the state, but Ben longs for a nation, not a state. After being denied the vote, being forced to allow a black man to behave rudely to "his" women and learning that blacks will outnumber whites in the state legislature 101 to 23, Ben sits on a hill and gazes at the landscape. The medium shot here encompasses Ben's upper body and the valley. "Title: In agony of soul over the degradation and ruin of his people. Ben enters left and stands on the riverbank looking out across the valley. He takes off his hat and sits on a rock, holds his clenched fists out in a gesture of helplessness, then gestures sweepingly with his left hand and bows his head."[38] The more expansive angle and gesture in this shot directly contrast the narrowness of the entry into participation in the bureaucratic state represented by the hole in the top of the ballot box. This is the affective linking of the land with the subject we find in nationalism. Those who corrupt the balloting process by slipping in double ballots or depriving white men of their votes can be seen only in part and the shots that depict them do not have the comprehensive sweep of Ben's gaze. The ballot box becomes a space of "forced social association" where Ben would, according to the visual logics I have just described, be reduced to fit into the tiny state-allotted civic space of the black ballot caster. In Griffith's logic, Ben must refuse the limited comprehension of the black citizen who thinks the franchise is something material handed out by the Freedman's Bureau. Instead, he embraces the limitless imagined expanse of the nation. Griffith characterizes Ben's defiance of the legislation of civil equality as postcolonial. He constructs Ben as a native complete with tribal dress that (unlike a modern Western uniform) robes his horse as well as himself, and is exotically effeminate in that it is a robe rather than trousers. He participates in rituals using blood and in ritual murder. After Flora kills herself, Ben exhorts the men to go after Gus:

MS: Ben holds up Flora's little Confederate flag and looks away as he dips it twice in a basin of water held by a fellow Clansman. He wrings it out and holds it aloft again. Title: Brethren, this flag bears the red stain of the life of a Southern woman, a priceless sacrifice on the alter of an outraged civilization. MS: ... Ben takes a burning cross from a Clansman behind him and holds it and the flag aloft. ... Title: Here I raise the ancient symbol of an unconquered race of men. ... I quench its flames in the sweetest blood that ever stained the sands of Time. MS: ... Ben quenches the fiery cross in the basin.[39]

Klan robes make of their wearers an ethnic group. "Looking ethnic," after all, emphasizes how much each member of a group looks like the others. The Klan is even more of a racial group because, as Michaels puts it, the whiteness of Klan robes makes their wearers more white than they could ever really be.[40] To weight whiteness with its own ethnicity through the idea of the native authenticates it as an identity in a way particular to Griffith's own era rather than to the one he depicts.

Griffith's imagery follows the early twentieth-century redefinition of the term "culture." From something akin to "civilization," it came to encompass the professionalizing American anthropological discipline's sense of a collection of recognizable, autonomous and consistent ways of thinking and acting that made a group of people distinguishable as a group – a way of life that was a "conceptual whole."[41] Michaels argues that after World War I, American discourse on racial and national identity took the form of a pluralism that emphasized cultural difference as the basis of identity – "the substitution of culture for race." His point is the significant shift away from justifying a group's practices based on its degree of deviation from a universal standard to making "the identity of the group ... grounds for the justification of the group's practices."[42]

With this in mind, it becomes easier to read Griffith's white tribalism as a form of authenticity mobilizing the tribal group against other tribes. He is not making a claim for a tribal (racialized) mass or crowd against elite (white) organization. *Birth of a Nation*, obviously, offers very little identification with unruly black crowds. Almost every critic of *Birth of a Nation* has drawn attention to the way Griffith visually contrasts the organized, (historically) sweeping white-sheeted lines of the gathered Klan forces with the chaotic milling of black people in the film. Griffith's understanding of the crowd or mass political mind differs from the British or European vocabulary of mass political participation.[43] For Griffith, the rise of the native is not the same as the alleged (British and European) working-class surge against power grounded in traditional top-down elite rule or parliamentary debate. Griffith refuses expanded political representation as a solution; in "culture's" terms this solution is unacceptable because it is inauthentic. It is not indigenous, so to speak, to the kind of (white) subjectivity he wants to endow with an unassailable right to exist. This conception of primitivism damns both the U.S. government and the black people who are to his mind so pathetically without the "culture" that would cause them to demand authentic and particular political rights that they are willing to assimilate themselves to a centralized government.

Woodrow Wilson's *A History of the American People* explicitly frames Griffith's film.[44] The constitutional philosophy that supported Wilson's decisions about imperialism in the Caribbean and the Pacific *and* his arguments for national self-determination in the peace settlements after World War I run through it implicitly. Although many current accounts of Wilson at the Peace Conference chronicle the many times he and other statesmen sacrificed the principle to protect the great powers' interests,[45] it was nonetheless true that national groups who wanted to establish their own nation-states took up the succinctly articulated concept and developed it.[46] The right to national self-determination required a collective identity. This, as Michla Pomerance points out, was the central problem of the doctrine that was never solved: identifying the "self" which would do the "determining."[47] Any debate about whether to grant a nation what was essentially an identity – a self – turned on questions of authenticity, whether the debate was about contiguous territory, community of speech, common rejection of "alien" rule or shared institutions. It required an assertion of a recognizable collective "whole way of life."

Hurston and Griffith's impulses toward ethnographic and cinematic genres create the intense "locality" of the native other (Hurston creates "the Haitian" and Griffith "the southerner/American") to express desire for and curiosity about the native mind not in terms of his or her presumed psyche but in terms of his or her politics as a culture. Questioning the significance of having a vote as much or more than he addresses the question of who should be a voter, Griffith creates a character who rejects "enfranchised subjectivity,"[48] that is, an understanding that his agency in the nation will be mediated by representation. Ben is "local" or "native," in contrast to the "cosmopolitan" colonial powers. Griffith uses his character's gaze to suggest that the primary object of public nostalgia in his movie is not merely slavery or the unburned South but also a particular mode of visualizing the relationship between governed and government.[49]

This is why, although one might think that this interest would inhere in the newly enfranchised group forging a new relationship with their nation, the focus is still on Ben and the Klan. Griffith makes sure black voters cannot be an object of fascination because they are not local or native. Irrevocably yoked to the U.S. federals by their willingness to wear uniforms and require salutes from whites, consenting to corruptible systems of representative democracy without having any strong belief in or understanding of them, black voters in Griffith's film are degraded state subjects. Griffith reverses actual power relations to make a claim for the oppressed status of southern whites relative to those newly (and, one might argue, barely) enfranchised.[50] This is consistent with primitivism: the primitivist laments his position of privilege/modernity and articulates envy for people who are materially or politically disempowered based on their supposedly more meaningful connection with intangible spiritual or sensual capacities. Ben's appropriations of the signs of tribal ritual are similarly constructed. "Natives" are in a position to have a greater capacity for understanding the agency and freedom of being more than a voter. Making the "problem" with the black voters a matter of inauthenticity implies that if the real (white) citizens of America do not resist state subjectivity, they will be colonized as black voters have allowed themselves to be.

Griffith here manages to make "native" a positive term and then to appropriate it for white supremacists. This is made possible by the work of intellectuals, such as Franz Boas, who during the debate about America's entrance into World War I were developing definitions of "culture" as coherent and autonomous. Griffith's movie does not "save" black people from being "uncivilized" but rather denies them the "value" of having their own culture. Boas himself made the claim that African

Americans did not have a unique culture and therefore should be assimilated into American culture as part of an anti-racist argument although the concept of culture he developed became part of African American twentieth-century discourses on race and power.[51]

Hurston is explicitly writing ethnography, a genre with the goal of producing and presenting a group by organizing an understanding of it through a defining cultural practice. But Hurston, like Griffith, creates her natives and their culture in terms of political theory. *Tell My Horse* first stages Haitian cultural practice as incompatible with modern state practices but then proceeds to find the practices themselves political, in a deliberate "use and abuse" of ethnographic conventions of the time. She begins with a claim that "lying" is a cultural practice:

It is safe to say that this art, pastime, expedient or whatever one wishes to call it, is more than any other factor responsible for Haiti's tragic history. Certain people in the early days of the Republic took to deceiving first themselves and then others to keep from looking at the dismal picture before them. ... They were trying to make a government of the wreck of a colony. ... They were trying to make a nation out of very diffident material. ... It must have been a terrible hour for each of the three actual liberators of Haiti, when, having driven the last of the Frenchmen from their shores, they came at last face to face with the people for whom they had fought so ferociously and so long. ... Perhaps it was in this way that Haitians began to deceive themselves about actualities and to throw a gloss over facts. Certainly at the present time the art of saying what one would like to be believed instead of the glaring fact is highly developed in Haiti. ... This lying habit goes from the thatched hut to the mansion.[52]

This analysis locates the origins of a culture's defining characteristic not in "traditional" practices independent of history but in the birth of the Haitian nation through revolution in 1804, the present economic problems of the country and its recent occupation by the United States.[53]

The lies of the hut and the mansion are different: "The upper class lie about the things for the most part that touch their pride. The peasant lies about things that affect his well-being, like work, food and small change."[54] The peasant, unlike the upper-class Haitian, will answer her questions about voodoo frankly, but not return with the change if paid to run an errand. The upper-class Haitian may be "the type of politician who does everything to benefit himself and nothing to benefit his country but who is the first to rush to press to 'defend' Haiti from criticism."[55] These people lie about the existence of voodoo "under the very sound of the drums claiming that all that has been written about it is nothing but the malicious lies of foreigners. ... Even if he is not an adept himself he sees it about him every day and takes it for a matter of course, but he lies to save his own and the national pride."[56] And finally, there are Haitians who "lie" to Hurston or to their fellow citizens about American involvement: why Americans invaded, how much money Haiti owed to foreign countries and who was responsible for the end of the American occupation.[57]

Although Hurston opens this section by structuring "lying" as an esoteric practice to be covered by ethnographic narrative as a "Haitian" thing to do, her descriptions of the lies she encounters are accounts of narrating the nation. "Culture" comes from the practices of nationhood rather than from practices existing independently of the modern world system. Lying is not narration incongruous with modernity but produced by a dispute over the multiple "truths" of European colonization and American imperialism. After recounting an argument she has with a Haitian about whether America has taken advantage of Haiti or whether the Americans saved Haiti from having to immediately repay its debt to France, Hurston concludes:

He was patently sorry for himself and all of the citizens who had suffered so much for love of country. If I did not know that every word of it was a lie, I would have been bound to believe him, his lies were that bold and brazen. His statements presupposed that I could not read and even if I could that there were no historical documents in existence that dealt with Haiti. ... I soon learned to accept these insults to my intelligence without protest because they happened so often.[58]

Hurston imagines these "lies" as told by and on behalf of an imagined community of nationalized citizens. They are "lies" because the "historical documents" would, she claims, support the American side. But in making a point of how often she must listen to these lies, Hurston emphasizes the unity "this man" has with "all of the citizens who had suffered so much for love of country." This is a classic postcolonial moment – explicit contestation over which narratives are properly credentialed as "history" and "truth" and can therefore compel action or indemnity.[59] Given the centrality of national debt to Haiti's history and current situation,[60] these conversations are not simply bits of local color. The contrast between "lies" and "historical documents" serves to outline the process by which "all the citizens" come to assert a national narrative; this process creates them as subjects of history. At the same time, Hurston alleges the imagined community of the nation (as opposed to the national state) as the site of an authentic "people" – also the ethnographer's object.

In the twentieth century, the ethnographer and the state have the same object. The chapter "Death of Leconte," about a presidential assassination, functions simultaneously as a redefinition of ethnography's "people" and as a discussion of the state's investment in creating its own people, often through the use of national narrative. As with her discussion of Haitian lying, Hurston compares official history to people's narrative:

This is the story of the death of President Leconte the way the people tell it. The history books all say Cincinnatus Leconte died in the explosion that destroyed the palace, but the people do not tell it that way. Not one person, high or low, ever told me that Leconte was killed by the explosion. It is generally accepted that the destruction of the palace was to cover up the fact that the President was already dead by violence.[61]

Hurston's account of ethnography, by focusing on the interviews she conducted in order to be able to tell her story "the way the people tell it," suggests that for her, the ethnographical "primitive" is functionally anti-state. The exotic beliefs of authentic natives center on modern political incidents. Like Griffith, Hurston paradoxically locates authenticity, or nativeness, as emerging from a hyperawareness of modernity, knowledge of the modern state's tricks and, she hopes, the ability to challenge these tricks born out of a history of colonial revolt and oppression.

Hurston and Griffith articulate the same problem (even if we might argue that Griffith willfully misconstrues himself as its chief victim): the state deceptively promises the power to ensure one's own freedom. Haiti is supposedly a self-determined government but this self-determination is constantly deformed by the need to defer to other countries' competing capital and foreign policy interests. Haiti's client presidents, U.S.-authored constitution, U.S.-controlled national budgets, and U.S.-established and U.S.-officered police reveal a conceptual vocabulary that could maintain the existence of "a people" without ensuring that their government represented their interests. The state creates the nation much as the ethnographer crafts a "culture."

Hurston sets government narrative against people's narrative. The government attempts to end "people's" narratives about Leconte. "When the daylight came they picked up something that nobody could say with any certainty was President Leconte and held a funeral. But then the way things were nobody could say the formless matter was not the late president either. So they held a state funeral and buried it."[62] Hurston's pronouns here indicate the flatness of the state narrative in comparison with the detail-packed, slightly folkish "people's version" she herself uncovered. She sees these unofficial versions not as rational disagreements among citizens about official reports but as manifestations of "the people" themselves. They establish themselves as a people by maintaining different political narratives. In this description, the Haitians lose the kind of specificity normally assigned to analyzing political identities among elite Westerners. These natives are united across high and low classes, a factor that contradicts her earlier analyses of divisions by race, education and class.

"Death of Leconte" reformulates "culture" around questions of political subjectivity. This may be where Boas's influence emerges despite their differences.[63] Susan Hegeman argues that Boas worked out his redefinitions of culture in political essays responding to World War I rather than in the scientific literature. Similarly, W. E. B. Du Bois, well aware of the way "culture" anchored political categories in the twentieth century,[64] published *The Negro* in 1915 to historicize Africa in a way that would give it a "self" with a right to "determination" in the face of a wave of colonization.[65]

In other words, modernism's preoccupation with imagining the conscious self should be understood as entangled with the twentieth-century's consolidation of subjects and communities that would be free and authentic yet also legible and malleable with regard to institutions that could coordinate, for instance, managed economies, migrant labor and the maintenance of international boundaries.

Modernist criticism dealing with the construction of natives often examines the "primitivist" response to empire as a fascination with reconstructing the individual psyche. Racial and cultural otherness, different kinds of art, artifacts and ritual, and the simultaneous threat and promise of "going native" stand in contrast to the internationalization, industrialization, commodification, homogenization and rationalization perceived as characteristic of modernity. The shared political vocabularies of *The Birth of a Nation* and *Tell My Horse* suggest, however, that modernist primitivism's "natives" are, unlike their creators, potentially freer *citizens* than the state subjects elite modernists must remain. Understanding modernist representations of "nativeness" or "blackness" in this way does not, of course, make primitivism any less of a fantasy that reinforces white, Western supremacy. However, it reveals the conditions of a politics of modernism that understands the problem of modernity as a problem of governance and allows us to see some of modernism's complex engagements with the "culture" not only of tribal peoples but also of liberal democracy.

AFTERWORD

Myths, monsters, modernization, modernism

My goal in writing this book has been to discuss the politics of modernism in a way that acknowledges the radical change postcolonial thought and other studies of subaltern agency have wrought in our accounts of modernization.

The question of modernism's politics has been raised, of course, in the context of the contemporary politics of its individual practitioners (Were they fascist sympathizers? Were they suffragettes? Did they support or oppose Empire?) and in the debates over whether particular literary techniques are "conservative/elitist" or "liberatory/egalitarian." Similarly, discussions about race and empire in modernism often debate whether the modernist use of material depicting non-Western or non-white people, as in primitivism or various strains of dialect or regionalist modernism, is racist, imperialist or appropriative or whether it is the case that modernists were radically open to Otherness and difference. I argue that the politics of modernism lie not in alignment with left or right but rather in modernism's conceptions of the political subject of history. Modernism is one account of modernization; rewriting the ideological implications and material histories of modernization should make a difference to modernist studies' account of modernism. What postcolonial studies has "done" to cultural histories of modernization is, first, to show that the West's others were not passively modernized but active participants in worldwide modernization, and, second, to show that "the West's" interactions with its colonized others were relevant not merely to those particular moments and locations but to global political and cultural development.

Another "politics of modernism" that has developed in modernist studies is akin to identity politics. Modernist studies scholars began to describe group modernisms such as "women's modernism" or "African American modernism." But if the very creation of such identity groups generated, as David Theo Goldberg argues, sites of state power and subject formation, then modernist studies must track back from this kind of group organization of modernism to examine state power and its effects on cultural politics. To do this I focused on selected texts, each of which could illuminate only a fraction of the far-reaching state bureaucratic structure. But in combination I found that across identity groups, across genres, across "high" and "low" cultural production the significance of the state and the uncertainty of the agency of the citizen emerged again and again.

The historical trajectory of this project arcs between two configurations of world power: Anglo-European imperial dominance just before World War I, when European powers held about 85 percent of the world's land mass, and American imperial and neo-imperial and economic dominance ("intervention," "spheres of influence") of the later twentieth century. One of my goals has been to suggest new foundations for the international study of modernism: the perspectives of geopolitics and globalization rather than of mere geography. "[E]veryone," as Eliot put it in 1928, "is conscious of nationality and race (our very passports impress that upon us)."[1] The invention and use of identification documents such as passports to distinguish between "citizens" and "aliens" increased markedly from the end of the nineteenth century to World War I, even as the movement of populations increased. During World War I, passport controls were described as necessary but provisional. However, they were not rescinded at the end of the war. Eliot has served as a biographical example of the modernists' transcendence of national identifications they supposedly made obsolete, but this claim highlights an unexamined complexity to modernist internationalism. National identity and consciousness of it had not been transcended but newly instantiated, and in new ways, by state power. The rise of the passport marked a change in the technologies and uses of citizenship categorization. It would not now maintain isolationism, but rather foster participation in a global economy that would reach tentacles into the most local of identities. Sociopolitical life internationalized in unprecedented, often traumatic ways. The history of the passport includes groups of people left geopolitically "stateless" in a world newly attuned to state power and national identity.

Internationalism in modernist studies once meant that modernism and modernist writers were in some sense *above* national boundaries and local specificity. Innovative style as an international language became a commonplace way to describe the relationship between history and aesthetics. Critics noted "modernist geographies" to demonstrate how little geographic lines mattered to these artists, though the act of crossing them – biographically or artistically – was vital. While William Faulkner and James Joyce were both intensely "local" artists who used avant-garde aesthetics, Joyce, unabashed expatriate, was unequivocally "modernist," while Faulkner was a great modern American writer. This mode of internationalism was paradoxically compatible with the formalist analysis of particular circles of artists because of its focus on the aesthetic expression of internationalism (geography) rather than on aesthetic form as one form in a related array of social forms (geopolitics).

Modernist studies seems to have shifted its emphasis away from both formal analysis and this definition of internationalism at the same time. Arguably, the decreasing emphasis on avant-garde style in modernist studies is connected not only to the feminist and cultural studies-led move away from formalist approaches but also to an increasing nationalization of Anglo-American modernist studies. By this I mean an increased tendency to have separate studies of "American modernism" or "British modernism," to subsume those under "twentieth-century American literature" or "modern British literature" and to assume that one national modernism can be studied without reference to the other. Opposition to a narrowly defined canon, and to an abstract internationalism that often authorized lack of attention to specific politics, has led to more culturally and historically focused studies; these would include both British "modernism and empire" studies and significant American modernism studies work emerging from the rise of American Studies (Susan Hegeman, Walter Benn Michaels, Michael Szalay). But this has led (somewhat humorously) to the label "transatlantic" or "transnational" being applied to critical studies that cover authors of different nationalities, as if the idea of conceiving modernism internationally is a novel and counterintuitive idea. Another consequence of the nationalization of modernism is that it allows for an unspoken preservation of the old doctrines of American exceptionalism within the field of modernist studies criticism.

I did not have space in this book to take up the work of Nella Larsen in particular or the way the Harlem Renaissance has been "fit" into the new modernist studies. But she is an example of an author whose work will suffer under an impetus toward nationalization of modernist studies.

In *Quicksand*, Helga Crane has "a fine contempt for the blatantly patriotic black Americans. Always when she encountered one of those picturesque parades in the Harlem streets, the Stars and Stripes streaming ironically, insolently, at the head of the procession tempered for her, a little, her amusement at the childish seriousness of the spectacle. It was too pathetic." Unlike Helga, who imagines that the only psychologically healthy existence for an African American might be traveling constantly between the United States and Europe, another of Larsen's heroines, Irene Redfield in *Passing*, is vehemently determined to remain in America despite both the promise Brazil seems to hold and the fact that she risks losing her husband, who wants desperately to expatriate. "[She would think of] ways to keep Brian by her side, and in New York. For she would not go to Brazil. She belonged in this land of rising towers. She was an American. She grew from this soil, and she would not be uprooted."[2]

Both of these textual moments can certainly be read in terms of American racial politics: the refusal to give up a claim to first-class citizenship, criticism of the failure of the United States to recognize black American contributions during World War I and criticism of those black Americans willing to overlook racism in the name of national loyalty. Such readings link her work to later African American texts such as Chester Himes's *If He Hollers Let Him Go*, which interrogates its protagonist's desire to be "an American." But despite the well-documented presence of international political movements in Harlem during the modernist period, there is very little discussion of Nella Larsen in terms of international black politics, of anti-colonial movements or of racialized global modernization. Larsen's mixed-race characters are not read, for instance, in the context of what David Theo Goldberg has documented as a global, state-managed "distinctively new manifestation of whiteness" at the turn of the twentieth century.[3] Nor is Helga's inability to settle read in terms of the ways in which racial (in)distinctions had the potential both to trouble and to reinforce the state's claim that it merely made official what were natural distinctions.

I am not arguing for a return to abstract internationalism and its prioritization of the avant-garde, to the theme studies treating a cultural phenomenon uniformly across "modernist geographies" or to accounts of modernists' travels. But nationalizing modernism ignores its fundamental connections to the history of globalization, including the construction of the Western subject in a political, economic and cultural context of imperial and neo-imperial modernization. The "modernist revolutionary subject," in other words, should be analyzed in terms of the competing discourses of differently conceived revolutions. Any analysis of modernism should theoretically take a postcolonial perspective.

But while writing this book, I found that the postcolonial or subaltern intervention that would make the world-historical significance of Haiti manifest *in modernist studies* in the way that, for instance, the Bolshevik

Revolution has been discussed, had yet to be recognized. In his examination of the discourses available across the spectrum of political positions in eighteenth-century Europe, Trouillot argues that there was literally no way for men and women of that time to comprehend the Haitian Revolution of 1804. It was "unthinkable" even as it was happening, for the political philosophy at the base of Haiti's founding was not accepted by public opinion until after World War II.[4] Even for the revolutionaries themselves, "discourse always lagged behind practice."[5] The revolution's subsequent erasure or trivialization even in postwar histories purporting to describe the world history of revolutions, Trouillot continues, is a symptom of a continuing refusal to acknowledge the centrality of race, slavery and colonialism to the making of the West(erner) at the methodological level of Western historiography.[6] Both modernists and modernist studies critics inherit this relationship to the epistemology of modern selfhood. I have had as a goal throughout this book to explore what it would mean to bring this perspective of postcolonial studies to modernist studies.

Modernism's myths and monsters limn these methodological and formal limits. As with all boundary markers, in the process of declaring some things impossible, they paradoxically establish their shadow existence. Trouillot's work allows for yet another reading of T. S. Eliot's description of Joyce's turn to myth to "give a shape" to the "futility and anarchy which is contemporary history."[7] Contemporary history is shapeless; the heart of darkness is ineffable. Let us read this problem not as the magnitude or unprecedented nature of globalizing modernity but rather as the presence of postcolonial narratives. As with Epstein's use of the metaphor of the "young black" surpassing his colonizers to describe the development of avant-garde art cinema, Eliot and Conrad respond not to the fact of momentous globalizing change (Conrad has Marlow point out that this has happened with the Roman Empire) but to a possible shift in the agents of that change. Thus, Eliot here describes a condition of modernist production (however unintentionally), in terms that resemble Trouillot's analysis of the unrecognizability of Haiti's world significance in accounts of modernity.

I turned to the zombie, a symbol associated with Haiti and one eagerly taken up by Western popular culture, not to claim its consistent appearance as a coherent figure in various modernist texts but to outline the ways in which its characteristics and the anxieties they raise about modern personhood persist in shadowy and irrational form in widely varying texts. The fear of zombie-like loss of agency, a condition in which one may not know the degree of one's agency (or lack thereof), stretches over the deliberately broad array of otherwise unrelated texts and authors I have discussed. Moreover, all of the texts I have discussed link, as Epstein does in the quote with which I began, uncertainty about the modern artist's method and vocation with political change in relations and methods of rule. The white zombie's whiteness underscores the way race, far from becoming obsolete, functions to anchor accounts of modernity and modernization. Discussing the racial foundations of Anglo-American modernism in terms of state-constructed administrable identities rather than assuming preconstituted racial groups has allowed for links between Hurston and Griffith and between Glasgow and Toomer on the basis of their shared if not identical apprehension of the significance of global modernization and its accompanying administrative technologies.

One of the conditions of modernist production is that, as Epstein puts it, "we no longer know, except that it is primarily a craft, what art is" and that "we" fear that apprentices to any craft surpass their masters ("us," that is, Western mastery) with "deeper skills." In this context, the modernist movement as summarized by Pound's injunction to "make it new" seems to partake of what Simmel describes as the desperate de-individuated person's attempt to fight the standardization of the (state-managed) money and labor economies:

> [O]ne seizes upon the qualitative differentiation in order somehow to attract the attention of the social circle by playing upon its sensitivity for differences ... man is tempted to adopt the most tendentious peculiarities, that is, the specifically metropolitan extravagances of mannerism, caprice and preciousness ... the meaning of these extravagances does not at all lie in the content of such behaviour, but rather in its form of "being different," of standing out in a striking manner and thereby attracting attention.[8]

Simmel's essay suggests, ironically, that to focus on modernist technique might be to neglect larger questions of form. In my readings I have tried to focus on the geopolitical forms rather than the aesthetic strategies of modernism.

In setting aside innovative aesthetics as a rubric for understanding modernism's internationalism, I wanted to align my study with modernist critical work that has established the significance of popular culture works and genres to modernism. However, I wanted to maintain an investment in claiming that modernism has identifiable formal interests. The history of modernist studies generally casts these as mutually exclusive critical commitments. Arguments for historical readings of modernist literature or for the study of non-canonical or popular culture works have often presented as challenges to formal(ist) analysis.

I have tried instead to historicize modernist writers' engagements with form. Bureaucratization and legalization generate governmental power by defining which *consistent* juridical, national and political identities will be recognized as valid. In other words, the twentieth-century state's emphasis on consistency, intelligibility and recognizability makes form an overarching element of state regulation. Information-gathering forms themselves exemplify the ways in which the state determines which knowledges will matter materially. In addition, we can see impulses to formalization emerging in cultural venues such as the establishment of professional intellectual disciplines at the turn into the twentieth century. I thus took my authors' attentions to form in the context of a broader cultural reliance on form and on the impetus to standardize such forms across national boundaries.

The scope and magnitude of the history of this aspect of twentieth century culture, multiplied the ways in which I could not hope to make this a comprehensive study of modernism's account of political modernization. I have sought instead to group a disparate set of texts in meaningful constellation around a monstrous condition they all, in various ways and to different degrees, apprehended. Nietzsche famously called the state "the coldest of all cold monsters." In the modernist context, the monster was not the state, but the citizen.

Notes

INTRODUCTION: WHITE ZOMBIES, BLACK JACOBINS

1 Michel Foucault, "The Abnormals," *Essential Works of Foucault: 1954–1984* Volume One *Ethics: Subjectivity and Truth* ed. Paul Rabinow (New York: The New Press, 1997), 51.
2 Jean Epstein, *"Bonjour Cinéma* and Other Writings" trans. Tom Milne. *Afterimage* 10 (1981 [1926]), 17.
3 T. S. Eliot, *The Waste Land*, ll. 60–7; Max Weber, "Bureaucracy," *From Max Weber: Essays in Sociology* ed. H. H. Gerth and C. Wright Mills (Oxford: Oxford University Press, 1946), 214.
4 Georg Simmel, "The Metropolis and Mental Life," *Simmel on Culture: Selected Writings* ed. David Frisby and Mike Featherstone (London: Sage Publications, 1997), 184.
5 Robert H. Wiebe, *Self-Rule: A Cultural History of American Democracy* (Chicago: University of Chicago Press, 1995), 113ff.
6 Eric Hobsbawm, *The Age of Extremes: A History of the World, 1914–1991* (New York: Random House, 1994), 29; Stuart Hall, "The State in Question," *The Idea of the Modern State* ed. Gregor McLennan, David Held and Stuart Hall (Milton Keynes: Open University Press, 1984), 10–11.
7 Nikolas Rose and Peter Miller, "Political Power beyond the State: Problematics of Government," *British Journal of Sociology* 43:2 (1992), 181–2.
8 Hobsbawm, *Age of Extremes*, 44–6.
9 See also Patrick J. McGrath, *Scientists, Businesses and the State, 1890–1960* (Chapel Hill: University of North Carolina Press, 2002) for a history of how the ideology of American government, as well as American social life, was shaped by alliances among scientific, corporate, military and political elites during the twentieth century.
10 Stuart Hall, "The State in Question," 11.
11 Wiebe, *Self-Rule*, 130.
12 Ibid., 137.
13 Michael Tratner, *Modernism and Mass Politics: Joyce, Woolf, Eliot, Yeats* (Stanford: Stanford University Press, 1995), 241.
14 Rose and Miller, "Political Power beyond the State," 191.

15 Lynette Hunter, "Blood and Marmalade: Negotiations between the State and the Domestic in George Orwell's Early Novels," *Rewriting the Thirties: Modernism and After* ed. Keith Williams and Steven Matthews (London: Longman, 1997), 202–16. Michael Tratner ties Woolf's famous comment about December 1910 not to the Post-Impressionist exhibit as many critics do, but to the date of the last election won by the Liberal Party, marking a shift to a contest between the Labour and Conservative parties rather than between Liberals and Conservatives. He reads *The Waves* and "Mrs. Bennett and Mr. Brown" in relation to the changes in Labour party structures and opportunities.
16 Lauren E. Goodlad, "Beyond the Panopticon: Victorian Britain and the Critical Imagination," *PMLA* 118:3 (2003), 539–540; Stuart Hall, "The State in Question," 11–12.
17 Wiebe, *Self-Rule*, 15.
18 Ibid., 26–7.
19 Goodlad, "Beyond the Panopticon," 542. In Britian in 1911, the receipts of registered philanthropies exceeded the state's expeditures on the poor law.
20 Rose and Miller, "Political Power Beyond the State," 187.
21 Barbara Cruikshank, *The Will to Empower: Democratic Citizens and Other Subjects* (Cornell: Cornell University Press, 1999), 43–4.
22 Rose and Miller, "Political Power beyond the State," 191.
23 Stuart Hall, "The State in Question," 10.
24 Rose and Miller, "Political Power beyond the State," 180.
25 Ibid., 191–3.
26 Cruikshank, *Will to Empower*, 7.
27 Rose and Miller, "Political Power beyond the State," 175.
28 Michel Foucault, "Governmentality," *The Foucault Effect: Studies in Governmentality* ed. Graham Burchell, Colin Gordon and Peter Miller (Chicago: University of Chicago Press, 1991), 20.
29 Cruikshank, *Will to Empower*, 48.
30 Rose and Miller, "Political Power beyond the State," 191–2.
31 Michel Foucault, "The Subject and Power," *Michel Foucault: Beyond Structuralism and Hermeneutics* ed. Hubert L. Dreyfus and Paul Rabinow (Chicago: University of Chicago Press, 1982), 221.
32 Rose and Miller, "Political Power beyond the State," 179.
33 Hilary McD. Beckles, "Capitalism, Slavery and Caribbean Modernity," *Callaloo* 20:4 (1997), 777–9.
34 Ibid., 785.
35 David Theo Goldberg, *The Racial State* (Oxford: Blackwell, 2002), 48.
36 See Toni Morrison, Chapter 1, "Black Matters," *Playing in the Dark: Whiteness and the Literary Imagination* (Cambridge, MA: Harvard University Press, 1992) for a discussion of the significance of the birth of the "new white male" in eighteenth-century North America.
37 Beckles, "Capitalism, Slavery and Caribbean Modernity," 782.

38 Michel-Rolph Trouillot, *Silencing the Past: Power and the Production of History* (Boston: Beacon Press, 1995), 72–3.
39 Susan Buck-Morss, "Hegel and Haiti," *Critical Inquiry* 26 (Summer 2000), 835–6.
40 Ibid., 837.
41 Ibid., 842ff.
42 Beckles, "Capitalism, Slavery and Caribbean Modernity," 784.
43 I am taking this excerpt slightly out of context; Epstein is theorizing cinema. See Rachel Moore, *Savage Theory: Cinema As Modern Magic* (Durham: Duke University Press, 2000), 23.
44 Bonnie Kime Scott, *The Gender of Modernism: A Critical Anthology* (Bloomington: Indiana University Press, 1990), 562.
45 Ellen Glasgow, *Barren Ground* (New York: Hill and Wang, 1984 [1925]), vii.

1. WHITE ZOMBIES IN THE STATE MACHINERY

1 *White Zombie*, dir. Victor Halperin, 74 min., *Bela Lugosi Collection* Volume II, Triton Multimedia 2001 [1932], DVD. See also Michael Price and George Turner, "*White Zombie* – Today's Unlikely Classic," *American Cinematographer* (February 1988), 34–40.
2 As Beaumont enters the office, the view behind him is of the machinery he has just passed through. This shot makes it apparent that the mill is not as large, and that its floor plan is not as complicated, as the earlier shots suggest.
3 Paul Gilroy, *The Black Atlantic: Modernity and Double Consciousness* (Cambridge, MA: Harvard University Press, 1993), 73; 55.
4 In addition to Gilroy's work, see also Patrick Williams, "'Simultaneous Uncontemporaneities': Theorising Modernism and Empire," *Modernism and Empire* ed. Howard J. Booth and Nigel Rigby (Manchester: Manchester University Press, 2000) and Rey Chow, Chapter 3, "Postmodern Automatons," *Writing Diaspora: Tactics of Intervention in Contemporary Cultural Studies* (Bloomington: University of Indiana Press, 1993).
5 Halperin consistently makes the point that voodoo and zombies are not "native." For instance, stereotypical "voodoo" drums are heard outside on the night of Madeline's wedding; we know that it is Lugosi's character who is outside waiting and Beaumont who will poison her. Neil and Bruner, a missonary, go off to rescue Madeline with Bruner claiming her zombification is "native work"; again, we know that the person they should be chasing is the zombie master.
6 For this history see Mary Renda, *Taking Haiti: Military Occupation and the Culture of U.S. Imperialism, 1915–1940.* (Chapel Hill: University of North Carolina Press, 2001). The United States occupied Haiti for nineteen years. The marines installed a U.S.-chosen and U.S.-controlled president, dissolved the legislature at gunpoint, censored the newspapers and wrote a new constitution for Haiti which specifically reversed the nation's rules limiting

foreign ownership of land (enacted after the revolution, for obvious reasons) and foreign investment. U.S. officials and marines seized the palace, and the customs houses, took control of the banks and began to manage Haiti's debt. During the occupation the marines used a system of forced labor and reorganized and strengthened the Haitian military – it was officered by U.S. marines during the occupation. The marines waged war against anti-colonial forces in the countryside for several years.

7 Barbara Cruikshank, *The Will to Empower: Democratic Citizens and Other Subjects* (Ithaca, NY: Cornell University Press, 1999), 39.
8 Lynette Hunter, "Blood and Marmalade: Negotiations between the State and the Domestic in George Orwell's Early Novels," *Rewriting the Thirties: Modernism and After* ed. Keith Williams and Steven Matthews (London: Longman, 1997), 202–16.
9 Hans H. Gerth and C. Wright Mills, "Introduction," *From Max Weber: Essays in Sociology* trans. H. H. Gerth and C. Wright Mills (New York: Oxford University Press, 1946), 70.
10 Max Weber, "Politics As a Vocation," *From Max Weber: Essays in Sociology* trans. H. H. Gerth and C. Wright Mills (New York: Oxford University Press, 1946), 82.
11 Max Weber, "Bureaucracy," *From Max Weber: Essays in Sociology* trans. H. H. Gerth and C. Wright Mills (New York: Oxford University Press, 1946), 225–6.
12 Weber, "Politics As a Vocation,"
13 Ibid., 82; 77 (italics in the original).
14 See Wendy Brown's discussion of how consent both marks and legitimates the subordination of the consenting party, especially with regard to gender, in *States of Injury: Power and Freedom in Late Modernity* (Princeton: Princeton University Press, 1995), 162–4.
15 Linda Williams, *Hard Core: Power, Pleasure and the "Frenzy of the Visible"* (Berkeley: University of California Press, 1989) 39–40.
16 This is true for Neil as well. After Madeline's "death," Neil turns to drinking in a local bar and sees and hears Madeline in a pool of liquid spilled on his table and hovering in the air before him. He tries to embrace the images. This scene is self-conscious about the idea of capturing the image – the other patrons are shot as their own shadows and Madeline's image appears as film within the film. Thanks to William Flesch for the piano image.
17 Brown, *States of Injury*, 164.
18 As Rhodes notes in his book on *White Zombie*, there were certainly film reviewers who read the zombies in the context of U.S. labor disputes and government opposition to unionization. See Gary D. Rhodes, *White Zombie: Anatomy of a Horror Film* (Jefferson, NC: McFarland & Company, Inc., Publishers), 45.
19 Nancy F. Cott, *Public Vows: A History of Marriage and the Nation* (Cambridge, MA: Harvard University Press, 133–4.

Notes to pages 34–39

20 For instance, Margaret Fuller (*Women in the Nineteenth Century*) and Charlotte Perkins Gilman (*Women and Economics*) both focused on how women became subordinated in marriage in ways that men did not; neither accepted the idea that women's agreements to contract themselves in marriage meant that they could demand an equal contract or had equal power to contract.
21 Michael Grossberg, *Governing the Hearth: Law and Family in Nineteenth-Century America* (Chapel Hill: University of North Carolina Press, 1985), 86.
22 Cott, *Public Vows*, 149–51.
23 Rita Felski, *The Gender of Modernity* (Cambridge, MA: Harvard University Press, 1995), 13.
24 Brown, *States of Injury*, 17.
25 Ibid., 27.
26 Max Weber, "Religious Rejections of the World and Their Directions," *From Max Weber: Essays in Sociology* trans. H. H. Gerth and C. Wright Mills (New York: Oxford University Press, 1946 [1915]), 347.
27 See also Vicente L. Rafael's work on Filipino overseas contract workers and immigrant laborers. Such workers, he argues, can be understood as taking on the characteristics of spectral presences insofar as they return to the Philippines, citizens to the nation, in the form of remittances from their labor. *White Love and Other Events in Filipino History* (Durham, NC: Duke University Press, 2000), 204–205.
28 Based on my reading of articles on Haiti 1915–34 in the *Chicago Tribune*, the *Savannah Tribune*, *The New York Times*, *The Independent*, *The Outlook*, *The Nation*, *The World's Work*, *The National Geographic Magazine*, and *The Chicago Defender*.
29 The history of the development of the cinema and its theorists echoes this dual investment in photographic realism and the idea that what the film captured was more than a mere record of reality.
30 For a full account of the importance of the primitive to early film theory, see Rachel O. Moore, *Savage Theory: Cinema As Modern Magic* (Durham, NC: Duke University Press, 2000).
31 Williams, *Hard Core*, 37–9.
32 These lines were also featured as part of the film's pressbook – a catalog for posters, handbills and other advertising materials that also contained suggestions for theater managers to use in promoting the film. Among other strategies, the booklet suggested making an enlargement of the penal code ("Here's something while terrifying still has a showmanship quality about it that will create tremendous interest in the picture at your theatre") or distributing 5 × 7 cards with a picture of Lugosi as Legendre on the cover and the penal code printed inside ("The Penal Code of the Republic of Haiti, Article 249, plays an important part in the motivation of WHITE ZOMBIE. On Page 3 you will see the actual wording of this article."). See Rhodes, *White Zombie*, 258ff.
33 Moore, *Savage Theory*, 13.

34 Rey Chow, "Postmodern Automatons," *Writing Diaspora: Tactics of Intervention In Contemporary Cultural Studies* (Bloomington: Indiana University Press, 1993) 60.
35 Moore, *Savage Theory*, 93–4.
36 Cott, *Public Vows*, 150.
37 Jean Epstein, "*Bonjour Cinema* and Other Writings," trans. Tom Milne. *Afterimage* 10 (1981), 34.
38 Rhodes, *White Zombie*, "Appendix G: Reviews of White Zombie," 265–8.
39 Williams, *Hard Core*, 38–9.
40 Chow, "Postmodern Automatons," 60.
41 *The New Yorker* (August 6, 1932), 41–2.
42 Moore, *Savage Theory*, 117.
43 See Suzanne Clark, *Sentimental Modernism: Women Writers and the Revolution of the Word* (Bloomington: Indiana University Press, 1991), 1–9.
44 The first quote is from the 1919 review "Kipling Redivivus," *The Athenaeum* (May 9, 1919), 297–8; the second from the 1959 transcript of Eliot's toast "The Unfading Genius of Rudyard Kipling," *The Kipling Journal* (March 1959), 9–12. The other critical essays are "The Idealism of Julien Benda," *The New Republic* (December 12, 1928), 105–7; "Rudyard Kipling," Introduction to *A Choice of Kipling's Verse Selected With An Essay On Rudyard Kipling By T. S. Eliot* (London: Faber and Faber, 1941), 5–36. Eliot also wrote an essay for a course at Harvard in 1909, "The Defects of Kipling," now published with commentary in *Essays in Criticism* 51:1 (January 2001), 1–7. For an account of the reaction to Eliot's edition of Kipling (mostly unfavorable refusals to reconsider Kipling, whose cause was not helped, in 1941, by Eliot's reputation for conservatism and anti-Semitism and the turn to psychological criticism of Kipling) see Maurice Hungiville, "A Choice of Critics: T. S. Eliot's Edition of Kipling's Poetry," *Dalhousie Review* 52 (1972–3), 572–87.
45 Eliot, "Kipling Redivivus," 298.
46 Ibid., 297.
47 Ibid., 298.
48 Ibid.
49 Ibid. And see Peter Nicholls, *Modernisms: A Literary Guide* (Berkeley: University of California Press, 1995), 194, on Pound, Eliot and Lewis's view that formal experimentation was a sign of coming of age for the individual artist.
50 Eliot, "The Idealism of Julien Benda," 106–7.
51 Eliot, "Rudyard Kipling," 6.
52 Ibid., 6; 15; 17.
53 Ibid., 17.
54 Ibid., 23.
55 Ibid., 30.
56 Eliot included, for instance, "Ave Imperatrix! (Written on the occasion of the attempt to assassinate Queen Victoria in March 1882)," "Our Lady of the Snows (Canadian Preferential Tariff, 1897)" and "The Veterans (Written for

the Gathering of Survivors of the Indian Mutiny, Albert Hall, 1907)" in the volume.
57 Eliot, "Rudyard Kipling," 7.
58 Ibid., 18.
59 Ibid., 15.
60 Ibid., 12.
61 Ibid., 34–5.
62 Ibid., 21.
63 Ibid., 16.
64 Ibid., 18.
65 Ibid., 19.
66 Ibid., 26.
67 See Valentine Cunningham, "The Age of Anxiety and Influence; or, Tradition and the Thirties Talents," *Rewriting the Thirties: Modernism and After* ed. Keith Williams and Steven Matthews (London: Longman, 1997), 21; and Jane Tompkins, *Sensational Designs: The Cultural Work of American Fiction 1790–1860* (New York: Oxford University Press, 1985). Louis Menand also has used Eliot's work on Kipling to support larger arguments about how current critical understandings of modernism must be covering over contradictions. See *Discovering Modernism: T. S. Eliot and His Context* (Oxford: Oxford University Press, 1987), 159.
68 Eliot is summarizing Benda here. "The Idealism of Julien Benda," 105.
69 T. S. Eliot, "The Man of Letters and the Future of Europe," *Sewanee Review* 53 (1945), 333–4.
70 Eliot, "The Idealism of Julien Benda," 106.
71 Eliot, "The Man of Letters," 336.
72 Ibid., 339.
73 Ibid., 340.
74 Ibid., 335.
75 See Partha Chatterjee, *Nationalism and the Colonial World* (London: Zed Books, 1986); Benedict Anderson, *Imagined Communities: Reflections on the Origin and Spread of Nationalism* (London: Verso, 1991); Etienne Balibar, *Race, Nation, Class: Ambiguous Identities* (London: Verso, 1995); Chungmoo Choi, "The Discourse of Decolonization and Popular Memory: South Korea," *The Politics of Culture in the Shadow of Capital* ed. Lisa Lowe and David Lloyd (Durham: Duke University Press, 1997).
76 Lowe and Lloyd, "Introduction," *The Politics of Culture in the Shadow of Capital* ed. Lisa Lowe and David Lloyd (Durham: Duke University Press, 1997), 7.
77 Eliot, "The Man of Letters," 341.
78 Eliot, "Rudyard Kipling," 17.
79 Ibid., 27.
80 Ibid., 24.
81 For discussions of modernist interest in the "local," "regional" and "primitive" see Susan Hegeman, *Patterns for America: Modernism and the*

Concept of Culture (Princeton: Princeton University Press, 1999); Robert L. Dorman, *Revolt of the Provinces: The Regionalist Movement in America, 1920–1945* (Chapel Hill: University of North Carolina Press, 1993).
82 Eliot, "Rudyard Kipling," 30–2.

2. SET IN AUTHORITY: WHITE RULERS AND WHITE SETTLERS

1 Patrick Williams writes that the term "empire" generalizes many specific forms of colonial rule, even within one nation's projects. "Questions which then arise include: do these different modes of colonialism incite or inhibit different modes of modernism; and would the different forms, processes, and practices involved mean that, for example, there would be a specifically white settler modernism?" See "'Simultaneous Uncontemporaneities': Theorising Modernism and Empire," *Modernism and Empire* ed. Howard J. Booth and Nigel Rigby (New York: St. Martin's Press, 2000), 15. While picking up Williams's term, I am not using it exactly the way he means it; I do not analyze the differences between colonial projects in India and New Zealand with the attention for which he calls.
2 Edward Said, *Culture and Imperialism* (London: Chatto & Windus, 1992), 6.
3 Fredric Jameson, "Modernism and Imperialism," *Nationalism, Colonialism and Literature* ed. Seamus Deane (Minneapolis: University of Minnesota Press, 1990), 44.
4 Michael North, *Reading 1922: A Return to the Scene of the Modern* (Oxford: Oxford University Press, 1999).
5 Said, *Culture and Imperialism*, 227.
6 Jameson, "Modernism and Imperialism," 45.
7 Astradur Eysteinsson, *The Concept of Modernism* (Ithaca, NY: Cornell University Press, 1990), 16.
8 Ibid.
9 See Eysteinsson, *Concept of Modernism*, 73ff and Chapter 5, "Realism, Modernism and the Aesthetics of Interruption"; Amy Kaplan, "Introduction: Realism and 'Absent Things in American Life,'" *The Social Construction of American Realism* (Chicago: University of Chicago Press, 1988).
10 Kaplan, *Social Construction*, 13.
11 Louis Menand, *Discovering Modernism: T. S. Eliot and His Context* (Oxford: Oxford University Press, 1987), 101; 111.
12 Ibid., 104–6.
13 Ibid., 118.
14 Ibid., 112.
15 Menand, *Discovering Modernism*, 102; Levenson, *Genealogy*, 31.
16 Levenson, *Genealogy*, 23–30.
17 Ibid., 34.
18 Ibid., 8.
19 Ibid.

Notes to pages 60–69

20 David Trotter, "The Modernist Novel," *The Cambridge Companion to Modernism* ed. Michael Levenson (Cambridge: Cambridge University Press, 1999), 74–80.
21 Mansfield (1888–1923) was born in New Zealand to a third-generation colonial family. She went to London at the age of fourteen and attended Queen's College for three years. She returned to New Zealand for two years, and went to London again in 1909. She traveled in Europe, but never returned to New Zealand.
22 Sydney Janet Kaplan, *Katherine Mansfield and the Origins of Modernist Fiction* (Cornell: Cornell University Press, 1991), 103.
23 Nicholas Thomas, *Colonialism's Culture: Anthropology, Travel and Government* (Princeton: Princeton University Press, 1994), 165–7.
24 Katherine Mansfield, *The Short Stories of Katherine Mansfield* (New York: Ecco Prees, 1983), 125.
25 Ibid., 129.
26 Ibid., 131.
27 Ibid., 129.
28 Mary Louise Pratt, *Imperial Eyes* (New York: Routledge, 1992), 201; 209.
29 Thomas, *Colonialism's Culture*, 157.
30 Mansfield, *Short Stories*, 129–30.
31 Ibid., 130.
32 Ibid., 127.
33 Ibid., 143–4.
34 Ibid., 132.
35 Ibid., 133.
36 Ibid., emphasis added.
37 Ibid., 124. It is important here to realize that this is not a case of "going native," a paradigm that, however alarmingly it broadcasts the possibility that, as Thomas puts it, the settler might be altered rather than alter the landscape, does not question the ultimate stability of whiteness as a category.
38 See Ann Laura Stoler, "Making Empire Respectable: The Politics of Race and Sexual Morality in Twentieth-Century Colonial Cultures," *Dangerous Liaisons: Gender, Nation and Postcolonial Perspectives* ed. Anne McClintock, Aamir Mufti and Ella Shohat (Minneapolis: Minnesota University Press, 1997), 344–73, on the state and corporate regulation of European sexual behaviors in the colonies and for a discussion of the discourse of the eugenic "otherness" of Europeans living in the colonies.
39 Thomas, *Colonialism's Culture*, 159–60.
40 See Sara Suleri, Chapter 4, "The Feminine Picturesque," *The Rhetoric of English India* (Chicago: University of Chicago Press, 1992).
41 Sara Jeannette Duncan, *Set in Authority* ed. Germaine Warkentin (Peterborough, Ontario: Broadview Press, 1996 [1906]), 72.
42 In Chapter 3, I discuss a similar but later cultural moment. Rebecca West describes the World War II traitor William Joyce as being more attached to the rituals (such as the carrying in of the mace) expressive of national

authority than are the court officers who exercise the state power procedurally to sentence and execute him.
43 Bernard S. Cohn, "Representing Authority in Victorian India," *The Invention of Tradition* ed. Eric Hobsbawm and Terence Ranger (Cambridge: Cambridge University Press, 1983), 166.
44 Ibid., 167.
45 Duncan, *Set in Authority*, 219.
46 Ibid., 133.
47 Ibid., 76.
48 Thomas, *Colonialism's Culture*, 5.
49 Herbert's mother ceases to worry about Herbert when she gets a last request from him for an amount of money that "suggested ... with curious pertinacity the cost of a steerage passage to America. ... To America she would resign her son with something like confidence ... and in the relief of this conviction Mrs. Tring's head, as fair and fluffy as ever, was soon bent with its accustomed absorption over the evening paper. America, after all, had been open to him whether he had gone there or not" (74). Duncan here mocks Mrs. Tring, as throughout, for understanding British politics and economics in terms of her own convenience.
50 Duncan, *Set in Authority*, 97.
51 Ibid., 129.
52 Joseph Conrad, *Heart of Darkness & The Secret Sharer* (New York: Signet, 1983 [1910]), 76.
53 Ibid., 70–1.
54 Max Weber, "Bureaucracy," *From Max Weber: Essays in Sociology* trans. and ed. H. H. Gerth and C. Wright Mills (Oxford: Oxford University Press, 1946), 198; 228.
55 Duncan, *Set in Authority*, 84.
56 Cohn, "Representing Authority," 188; 184.
57 Duncan, *Set in Authority*, 110.
58 Trotter, "Modernist Novel," 71.
59 Levenson, *Genealogy*, 8.
60 Thomas, *Colonialism's Culture*, 155.
61 Trotter, "Modernist Novel," 70.
62 Duncan, *Set in Authority*, 79–80.
63 See Michael Silvestri, "The 'Thrill of Simply Dressing Up': The Police, Disguise, and Intelligence Work in Colonial India," *Journal of Colonialism and Colonial History* 2:2 (2001). See Thomas, *Colonialism's Culture*, 117, for an analysis of the difference between British rule of the natives of Fiji resident in villages and British policy with regard to Fiji Indians brought to Fiji as indentured plantation labor. Village residents were subject to regulation based on what the British studied and then defined as their "customary order" through social regulations such as sanitation and building codes, while plantation laborers were violently punished. "So far from Indians being a specific population that required understanding and definition, administrative

attitudes manifested a "fear of culture" appropriate to a proletarianized population." In *The Burnt Offering* (1909), Duncan explores more explicitly how these approaches to "culture" connect with ideologies of rule through representative democracy.

3. SOLDIERS AND TRAITORS: REBECCA WEST, THE WORLD WARS AND THE STATE SUBJECT

1 John Torpey, *The Invention of the Passport: Surveillance, Citizenship and the State* (Cambridge: Cambridge University Press, 2000), 7; Benedict Anderson, *Imagined Communities: Reflections on the Origin and Spread of Nationalism* (London: Verso, 1991 [1983]), 115.
2 Torpey, *Passport*, 92. See especially his Chapter 3 for an analysis of the causes and effects of increased freedom of movement in the nineteenth century, and the implications of this for modern state infrastructure.
3 Ibid., 7.
4 Carl Rollyson, *Rebecca West: A Saga of the Century* (London: Hodder and Stoughton, 1995), 247–50.
5 Victoria Glendinning, *Rebecca West: A Life* (New York: Alfred A. Knopf, 1987), 228.
6 Bonnie Kime Scott, *The Gender of Modernism: A Critical Anthology* (Bloomington: Indiana University Press, 1990), 562.
7 See Glendinning, *Rebecca West*, 197. West developed *The Meaning of Treason* from articles she wrote for *The New Yorker* covering the trials of William Joyce and John Amery. The book consolidated her reputation in the United States and was a success in both England and the United States. She was featured on the cover of *Time Magazine*, and the Viking edition sold a thousand copies a day when it first appeared.
8 Janet Oppenheim, *"Shattered Nerves": Doctors, Patients and Depression in Victorian England* (New York: Oxford, 1991), 309.
9 Ibid., 151.
10 Elaine Showalter, *The Female Malady* (New York: Pantheon, 1985), 171.
11 Rita Felski, *The Gender of Modernity* (Cambridge, MA: Harvard University Press, 1995), 40–1.
12 Ibid., 41.
13 Rebecca West, *The Return of the Soldier* (New York: Carroll & Graf, 1980), 122–3.
14 Ibid., 147.
15 Wendy Brown, *States of Injury: Power and Freedom in Late Modernity* (Princeton: Princeton University Press, 1995), 190.
16 West, *Return of the Soldier*, 99–100.
17 Ibid., 91.
18 Ibid., 91–2.
19 Ibid., 98.
20 Ibid., 132.

21 Ibid., 110–11.
22 Ibid., 145.
23 Ibid., 63–4.
24 Ibid., 115–16.
25 Ibid., 12.
26 Ibid., 134.
27 Ibid., 19–21.
28 Ibid., 9–12.
29 Ibid., 55–8.
30 Ibid., 58.
31 Ibid., 181.
32 Felski, *Gender of Modernity*, 63.
33 According to Eric Hobsbawm, World War I was the first war to be fought as a zero-sum game. Imperial economies meant that "international political rivalry was modeled on economic growth and competition, but the characteristic feature of this was precisely that it had no limit." Companies such as Standard Oil, the Deutsche Bank or the De Beers Diamond Corporation were limited only by their own capacities. See *The Age of Extremes: A History of the World, 1914–1991* (New York: Vintage, 1994), 28–30.
34 West, *Return of the Soldier*, 154.
35 Sandra M. Gilbert and Susan Gubar, *No Man's Land: The Place of the Woman Writer in the Twentieth Century* Volume 2 (New Haven: Yale University Press, 1988), 315.
36 Laura Stempel Mumford, "May Sinclair's *The Tree of Heaven*: The Vortex of Feminism, the Community of War," *Arms and the Woman: War, Gender and Literary Representation* ed. Helen M. Cooper, Adrienne Auslander Munich and Susan Merrill Squier (Chapel Hill: University of North Carolina Press, 1989), 168.
37 Susan Kingsley Kent, "The Politics of Sexual Difference: World War I and the Demise of British Feminism," *Journal of British Studies* 27:3 (July 1988), 252.
38 Ibid., 248–50.
39 Ibid., 234–5.
40 Ibid., 236.
41 Ibid., 238.
42 West, *Return of the Soldier*, 21.
43 Ibid., 125.
44 Ibid., 126–7.
45 Karen R. Lawrence, "Gender and Narrative Voice in *Jacob's Room* and *A Portrait of the Artist as a Young Man*," *James Joyce: The Centennial Symposium* ed. Morris Beja, Phillip Herring, Maurice Harmon and David Norris (Urbana: University of Illinois Press, 1986), 34–5.
46 West, *Return of the Soldier*, 109.
47 Masami Usui, "The Female Victims of the War in *Mrs. Dalloway*,"*Virginia Woolf and War: Fiction, Reality and Myth* (Syracuse: Syracuse University Press, 1991), 152–3.

48 West, *Return of the Soldier*, 13.
49 Frederic Jameson, "Modernism and Imperialism," *Nationalism Colonialism and Literature* ed. Seamus Deane (Minneapolis: University of Minnesota Press, 1990), 51.
50 Virginia Woolf, *A Room of One's Own* (New York: Harcourt Brace and Company, 1981 [1929]), 97.
51 Harold Perkin, *The Rise of Professional Society: England Since 1880* (New York: Routledge, 1989), 173.
52 West, *Return of the Soldier*, 151; 187.
53 Lisa Lowe and David Lloyd, "Introduction," *The Politics of Culture in the Shadow of Capital* ed. Lisa Lowe and David Lloyd (Durham, NC: Duke University Press, 1997), 18.
54 Wyndham Lewis, ed., *Blast 1* (Santa Rosa: Black Sparrow Press, 1989 [1914]), 151.
55 Janet Lyon, *Manifestoes: Provocations of the Modern* (Cornell: Cornell University Press, 1999), 121. See also James Longenbach, "The Women and Men of 1914," *Arms and the Woman: War, Gender and Literary Representation* ed. Helen M. Cooper, Adrienne Auslander Munich and Susan Merrill Squier (Chapel Hill: University of North Carolina Press, 1989), 97–123.
56 Lyon, *Manifestoes*, 110.
57 Karen Piper, *Cartographic Fictions: Maps, Race and Identity* (New Brunswick, NJ: Rutgers University Press, 2002), 37.
58 Barbara Cruikshank, *The Will to Empower: Democratic Citizens and Other Subjects* (Cornell: Cornell University Press, 1999), 47.
59 T. S. Eliot, Letter to Ezra Pound April 15, 1915. *The Letters of T. S. Eliot Volume I 1898–1922* ed. Valerie Eliot (New York: Harcourt, Brace Jovanovich, 1988).
60 Cruikshank, *Will to Empower*, 191.
61 Wendy Brown, *States of Injury: Power and Freedom in Late Modernity* (Princeton: Princeton University Press, 1995), 192–3.
62 West, *Return of the Soldier*, 183.
63 "Really the composition of this war, 1914–1918, was not the composition of all previous wars, the composition was not a composition in which there was one man in the center surrounded by a lot of other men but a composition that had neither a beginning nor an end, a composition of which one corner was as important as another corner, in fact the composition of cubism." From Gertrude Stein, *Picasso*, as cited and discussed in Stephen Kern, *The Culture of Time and Space, 1880–1918* (London: Weidenfeld and Nicolson, 1983), 290ff.
64 Lowe and Lloyd, "Introduction," 6.
65 Alan Sinfield, *Literature, Politics and Culture in Postwar Britain* (Berkeley: University of California Press, 1989), 8–10.
66 Brian Currid, "The Acoustics of National Publicity: Music in German Mass Culture, 1924–45" (diss., University of Chicago, 1988).

67 Francis Selwyn, *Hitler's Englishman: The Crime of Lord Haw-Haw* (London: Routledge, 1987), 221.
68 Rebecca West, *The Meaning of Treason* (London: Virago, 1982 [1949]), 13.
69 Ibid., 15–16.
70 Ibid., 16.
71 Ibid., 43.
72 Ibid., 50.
73 Ibid., 16.
74 Ibid., 42.
75 Ibid., 44.
76 Ibid., 28.
77 Ibid., 34.
78 Ibid., ix; 166.
79 Ibid., 71–2.
80 Ibid., 141.
81 Ibid., 55.
82 Ibid., 144–5.
83 David Lloyd and Paul Thomas, *Culture and the State* (London: Routledge, 1998), 7.
84 West, *Meaning of Treason*, 56–7.
85 Ibid., 24.
86 Ibid., 26.
87 Ibid., 54.
88 Ibid., 53–4.
89 Torpey, *Passport*, 3.
90 Ibid., 166.

4. WHITE TURKEYS, WHITE WEDDINGS: THE STATE AND THE SOUTH

1 Wendy Brown, *States of Injury: Power and Freedom in Late Modernity* (Princeton: Princeton University Press, 1995), 163.
2 Nancy Cott, *Public Vows: A History of Marriage and the Nation* (Cambridge, MA: Harvard University Press, 2000), 16.
3 Paul Bové, *Mastering Discourse: The Politics of Intellectual Culture* (Durham, NC: Duke University Press, 1992).
4 Ellen Glasgow, *Barren Ground* (New York: Hill and Wang, 1984), v.
5 T. E. Hulme, "Romanticism and Classicism," *Critical Theory Since Plato* ed. Hazard Adams (New York: Harcourt Brace Jovanovich, 1971 [1924]), 767–74.
6 Bové, *Mastering Discourse*, 128–9.
7 Ibid., 135.
8 See Robert Langbaum, *The Poetry of Experience: The Dramatic Monologue in Modern Literary Tradition* (Chicago: University of Chicago Press, 1985 [1957]).

9 Bové, *Mastering Discourse*, 137–9.
10 See also my argument on Wyndham Lewis and the suffragettes above.
11 Glasgow, *Barren Ground*, 11.
12 T. S. Eliot, "The Love Song of J. Alfred Prufrock" l. 49.
13 Glasgow, *Barren Ground*, 280.
14 B. C. Southam, *A Guide to the Selected Poems of T. S. Eliot* (New York: Harvest/HBJ, 1968), 69.
15 Donna Haraway, *Primate Visions: Gender, Race and Nature in the World of Modern Science* (London: Routledge, 1989), 352.
16 Glasgow, *Barren Ground*, 133.
17 T. S. Eliot, *The Waste Land*, l. 252.
18 T. S. Eliot, "*Ulysses*, Order, and Myth," *Selected Prose of T. S. Eliot* ed. Frank Kermode (New York: Harcourt Brace, 1975), 177–8.
19 William Faulkner, *Absalom, Absalom!* (New York: Vintage, 1990 [1936]), 65.
20 Ibid., 5.
21 Ibid.
22 Glasgow, *Barren Ground*, 209.
23 Ibid., 242.
24 I am indebted here to Michael North's reading of Claude McKay's "The Tropics in New York," *The Dialect of Modernism: Race, Language and Twentieth Century Culture* (Oxford: Oxford University Press, 1994), 111–12.
25 Glasgow, *Barren Ground*, 270.
26 Ibid., 269–70.
27 Ibid., 13.
28 Ibid., 14.
29 See Robert L. Dorman, *Revolt of the Provinces: The Regionalist Movement in America, 1920–1945* (Chapel Hill: University of North Carolina Press, 1993), for an account of how different currents of regionalism sometimes supported and sometimes debunked the frontier myth in the service of arguments about American exceptionalism. The agrarian ideal of small independent landholders as a way of retaining regional self-sufficiency, of course, ignores the "problem" of losing forced labor in the south, as does Glasgow's jump to mechanized acres. See my discussion below.
30 Glasgow, *Barren Ground*, 172.
31 Angela Hewitt, "'The Great Company of Real Women': Modernist Women Writers and mass Commercial Culture," *Rereading Modernism: New Directions in Feminist Criticism* ed. Lisa Rado (New York: Garland, 1994), 362.
32 Glasgow, *Barren Ground*, 171.
33 Ibid.
34 Ibid., 157.
35 Ibid., 224.
36 Ibid., 226.
37 Jane Tompkins, *Sensational Designs: The Cultural Work of American Fiction 1790–1860* (Oxford: Oxford University Press, 1985), xvii.

38 Suzanne Clark, *Sentimental Modernism: Women Writers and the Revolution of the Word* (Bloomington: Indiana University Press, 1991), 2.
39 Elizabeth Freeman, *The Wedding Complex: Forms of Belonging in Modern American Culture* (Durham, NC: Duke University Press, 2002), 74.
40 Glasgow, *Barren Ground*, 369–70 (italics added).
41 Katherine Jellison, *Entitled to Power: Farm Women and Technology* (Chapel Hill: University of North Carolina Press, 1993), 2–16; 25–34.
42 Astradur Eysteinsson, *The Concept of Modernism* (Ithaca, NY: Cornell University Press, 1990), 26.
43 See Michael Grossberg, *Governing the Hearth: Law and Family in Nineteenth-Century America* (Chapel Hill: University of North Carolina Press, 1985), Chapter 2, for the history of the jilt.
44 Georg Simmel, "The Metropolis and Mental Life," *Simmel on Culture: Selected Writings* ed. David Frisby and Mike Featherstone (London: Sage, 1997), 177.
45 Glasgow, *Barren Ground*, 275.
46 Ibid., 284.
47 Ibid., 300.
48 Simmel, "The Metropolis and Mental Life," 175; Colin Gordon, "The Soul of the Citizen: Max Weber and Michel Foucault on Rationality and Government," *Max Weber, Rationality and Modernity* ed. Scott Lash and Sam Whimster (London: Unwin Hyman, 1987), 297.
49 Dorman, *Revolt*, 50.
50 Ibid., 98.
51 Ibid., 95.
52 The colloquialism "nigger in the woodpile" described a "white" family having mixed-race members.
53 Glasgow, *Barren Ground*, 12.
54 Ibid., 364.
55 Ibid., 363.
56 Kirstie McClure, "The Issue of Foundations: Scientized Politics, Politicized Science, and the Feminist Critical Practice," *Feminists Theorize the Political* ed. Judith Butler and Joan W. Scott (New York: Routledge, 1992), 345.
57 Jean Toomer, *Cane* (New York: Liveright, 1993), 64.
58 Toomer, *Cane*, 2.
59 Werner Sollors, "Jean Toomer's *Cane*: Modernism and Race in Interwar America," *Jean Toomer and the Harlem Renaissance* ed. Genevieve Fabre and Michel Feith (New Brunswick, NJ: Rutgers University Press, 2001), 22–3.
60 Toomer, *Cane*, 3.
61 McClure, "The Issue of Foundations," 344.
62 George Hutchinson, "Identity in Motion: Placing *Cane*," *Jean Toomer and the Harlem Renaissance* ed. Genevieve Fabre and Michel Feith (New Brunswick, NJ: Rutgers University Press, 2001), 48.
63 Sollors, "Jean Toomer's," 30.
64 Toomer, *Cane*, 64.

5. MODERNIST (PRE)OCCUPATIONS: HAITI, PRIMITIVISM, AND ANTI-COLONIAL NATIONALISM

1 Elazar Barkan and Ronald Bush, "Introduction," *Prehistories of the Future: The Primitivist Project and the Culture of Modernism* ed. Elazar Barkan and Ronald Bush (Stanford: Stanford University Press, 1995), 3.
2 See Vicente Rafael's analysis of the Philippines census in *White Love and Other Events in Filipino History* (Durham, NC: Duke University Press, 2000). See also Benedict Anderson, "Census, Map, Museum," *Imagined Communities: Reflections on the Origins and Spread of Nationalism*; and Matthew Hannah, "The Spatial Politics of Governmental Knowledge," *Governmentality and the Mastery of Territory in Nineteenth-Century America* (Cambridge: Cambridge University Press, 2000).
3 Howard S. Abramson, *National Geographic: Behind America's Lens on the World* (New York: Crown, 1987), 62.
4 Philip J. Pauly, "'The world and all that is in it'; The National Geographic Society: 1888–1918," *American Quarterly* 31 (1979), 517.
5 Abramson, *National Geographic*, 119–120.
6 Pauly, "'The world,'" 517.
7 Instructions for the 1880 U.S. national census from just twenty-five years earlier reveal that resistance to the census was probably common. See Hannah, *Governmentality*, 121–3.
8 Hilary McD. Beckles, "Capitalism, Slavery and Caribbean Modernity," *Callaloo* 20:4 (1997), 3–4.
9 I do not have the space to discuss this here, but representations of revolutionaries and anarchists often seem to partake of the "primitive," for instance, in Conrad or in descriptions of Bolshevik revolutionaries.
10 See, for example, Marie-Denise Shelton "Primitive Self: Colonial Impulses in Michel Leiris's *L'Afrique fantôme*," *Prehistories of the Future: The Primitivist Project and the Culture of Modernism* ed. Elazar Barkan and Ronald Bush (Stanford: Stanford University Press, 1995).
11 Widely circulated and associated with Woodrow Wilson, though not originating with him, the principle of "national self-determination" was intrinsically inconsistent and nearly impossible to define in practical terms. Moreover, the concept was overdetermined by the administration's *realpolitik* needs. For instance, as Michla Pomerance points out in her analysis of the Wilsonian version of this concept, it was implicitly anti-imperial, yet Wilson could use it to justify "intervention" in Mexico on the grounds that the state that the nation had chosen was not run on the principle of "self-government." See "The United States and Self-Determination: Perspectives on the Wilsonian Conception," *American Journal of International Law* 70 (1976), 21.
12 Anderson, *Imagined Communities*, 113.

13 Derek Heater, *National Self-Determination: Woodrow Wilson and His Legacy* (New York: St. Martin's Press, 1994), 19; Frank Ninkovich, *The Wilsonian Century: U.S. Foreign Policy Since 1900* (Chicago: University of Chicago Press, 1999), 52.
14 *The Nation* (April 27, 1899), reprinted in Eric S. Foner and Richard C. Winchester, eds., *The Anti-Imperialist Reader: A Documentary History of Anti-Imperialism in the United States* Volume I (New York: Holmes and Meier, 1984), 386.
15 *Kansas City Times* (July 27, 1899), reprinted in Foner and Winchester, *Anti-Imperialist Reader*, 374.
16 Foner and Winchester, *Anti-Imperialist Reader*, 363–421.
17 *The Nation* (May 18, 1899), reprinted in Foner and Winchester, *Anti-Imperialist Reader*, 397.
18 Heater, *National Self-Determination*, 38.
19 Heater, *National Self-Determination*, 22–43; Lloyd E. Ambrosius, *Wilsonianism: Woodrow Wilson and His Legacy in American Foreign Relations* (New York: Macmillan, 2002), 125–9.
20 Ambrosius, *Wilsonianism*, 128.
21 Hannah, *Governmentality*, 114–15.
22 Ninkovich, *The Wilsonian Century*, 52.
23 Previewed as *The Clansman* January 1 and 2, 1915, Riverside, California; first shown February 8, 1915, Los Angeles as *The Clansman*; world premiere March 3, 1915, New York, under the permanent title *The Birth of a Nation*. See Robert Lang, ed., *The Birth of a Nation* (New Brunswick: Rutgers University Press, 1997), 39. Quotes/descriptions from the film with page numbers are from Lang's edition of the continuity script. Quotes/descriptions from the film without page numbers are from my viewing of the film on VHS (Republic Pictures Home Video, 1991 [1915]).
24 Tom Gunning, *D. W. Griffith and the Origins of American Narrative Film: The Early Years at the Biograph* (Urbana: University of Illinois Press, 1991), 66.
25 See Michael S. Rogin, Chapter 7, "'The Sword Become a Flashing Vision': D. W. Griffith's The Birth of a Nation," *Ronald Reagan The Movie and Other Episodes in Political Demonology* (Berkeley: University of California Press, 1987); Walter Benn Michaels, "Anti-Imperial Americanism," *Cultures of United States Imperialism* ed. Amy Kaplan and Donald E. Pease (Durham, NC: Duke University Press, 1993); Amy Kaplan, *The Anarchy of Empire in the Making of U.S. Culture* (Cambridge, Massachusetts: Harvard University Press, 2002).
26 In June 1993, the state of North Carolina elected only its second black congressman in the twentieth century.
27 Lang, *Birth of a Nation*, 103–4.
28 Rogin, "Sword Become a Flashing Vision," 223.
29 Nationalism itself, Anderson writes, has as one of its characteristics the "formal universality of nationality as a socio-cultural concept – in the

modern world everyone can, should, will, 'have' a nationality, as he or she 'has' a gender." Anderson describes the classical nation-state project as forging a relationship among social habits, culture, attachment and political participation. There is more to say about Anderson's use of gender as the anchor of naturalness, particularly given women's historical relationships to citizenship, but my point is that paradigms of nation as underwriting identity and subjectivity can be historically tracked alongside the "modernist era." See *Imagined Communities*, 5.
30 As Lani Guinier points out, the right to representation is not the same as the right to vote. A voter doesn't actually have to vote in order to be represented; living in the district is sufficient. See *The Tyranny of the Majority: Fundamental Fairness in Representative Democracy* (New York: The Free Press, 1994), 126.
31 Ibid., 124.
32 Under a theory of liberal individualism, voting rights supposedly belong to individuals and not to groups. But when opponents of race-conscious districting attack the idea of group representation using the liberal idea(l) of one-man, one-vote, their "emperor has no clothes"; that is, they ignore the fact that all representation is based on groups in a system of geographical districting. Moreover, "they ... reveal a bias toward the representation of a particular racial group rather than their discomfort with group representation itself." See Guinier, *Tyranny*, 121.
33 Lang, *Birth of a Nation*, 107.
34 Ibid.
35 Lynette Hunter, "Blood and Marmalade: Negotiations between the State and the Domestic in George Orwell's Early Novels," *Rewriting the Thirties: Modernism and After* ed. Keith Williams and Steven Matthews (London: Longman, 1997), 209.
36 Nicholas Thomas, *Colonialism's Culture: Anthropology, Travel and Government* (Princeton: Princeton University Press, 1994), 106.
37 In the Fiji Islands, the British attempted to institutionalize what they thought were recognizable hierarchical social institutions that could be turned into "government." Using both newer anthropological and older social evolutionary racial categories, they created systems of administration through land ownership. The British Governor's instructions to these chiefs included directives to record and transcribe everything that happened in their districts on paper, exhortations not to "play" at "cross-purposes" among themselves, and a description of the laws of the country as "a net of very fine meshes, nothing can escape: it will cover all alike." Thomas reads these instructions and other British creations of "order" in Fiji as significant not because of the actual information written reports to the Governor produced but because they constituted the agency of a state and its subjects. See *Colonialism's Culture*, 107–12. The Philippines census similarly functioned "as a stage on which Filipinos were to be represented as well as represent themselves as

subjects of a colonial order: disciplined agents actively assuming their role in their own subjugation and maturation." See Rafael, *White Love*, 26.
38 Lang, *Birth of a Nation*, 114.
39 Ibid., 128–9.
40 Walter Benn Michaels, *Our America: Nativism, Modernism, and Pluralism* (Durham, NC: Duke University Press, 1995), 21.
41 Susan Hegeman, *Patterns for America: Modernism and the Concept of Culture* (Princeton: Princeton University Press, 1999), 64; George W. Stocking Jr., "The Ethnographic Sensibility of the 1920s and the Dualism of the Anthropological Tradition," *Romantic Motives: Essays on Ethnographic Sensibility* ed. George W. Stocking Jr. (Madison: University of Wisconsin Press, 1989), 212–20.
42 Michaels, *Our America*, 14.
43 Robert Nye describes the way that modernist reactions to the phenomena of modern European crowds and masses conceptualized them as non-logical, non-discursive, atavistic and full of the energy an enervated modern society could no longer produce. These "masses" became mass politics – challenges to legitimate authority and liberal elites – and audiences that avant-garde artists both manipulated and longed to imagine themselves in union with as an alternative to taking up traditional artistic authority and the conventions that went with it. Michael Tratner argues that modernists conceived of mass politics, mass movements, and extensions of the franchise in the early twentieth century as an "unconscious" erupting into society; this often took the form of imagining a "working class" element to their elite consciousnesses. See Nye, "Savage Crowds, Modernism and Modern Politics," *Prehistories of the Future: The Primitivist Project and the Culture of Modernism* ed. Elazar Barkan and Ronald Bush (Stanford: Stanford University Press, 1995); and Tratner, *Modernism and Mass Politics: Joyce, Woolf, Eliot, Yeats* (Stanford: Stanford University Press, 1995).
44 See Rogin, "Sword Become a Flashing Vision," for an account of Griffith's use of Wilson's writing in the film's titles and of the connections among Dixon, Griffith and Wilson.
45 While Wilson was negotiating at the Paris Peace Conference, the United States, as a result of its brutal forced labor regime, was fighting Caco soldiers rebelling against the occupation. Representatives of the Haitian opposition to the occupation went to Versailles to try to meet with Wilson as he advocated for the rights of small nations to self-determination, to no avail. Haiti had consequences for Ireland and vice versa – Britain and the United States traded silence about each. See Renda, *Taking Haiti*, 33; 139; and Heater, *Self-Determination*, 75.
46 Heater, *Self-Determination*, 46.
47 Pomerance, "United States," 16.
48 Lynette Hunter's phrase. See "Blood and Marmalade."
49 Of course, race is part of that relationship. In his April 10, 1915, letter answering the *New York Globe*'s editorial attack on *The Birth of a Nation* as

"capitalizing on race hatred," "pandering to depraved tastes" and "fomenting race antipathy," Thomas Dixon (the author of *The Clansman*) asserted that a "jury" of "representative clergymen" of New York had viewed the film and declared that it (among other things) reunited the country, taught boys (*sic*) the history of the nation and prevented lowering of the standard of citizenship through miscegenation ("Reply to the *New York Globe*," *The Birth of a Nation* ed. Robert Lang [New Brunswick: Rutgers University Press, 1997], 166–7).

50 See also Catherine Jurca, "Tarzan: Lord of the Suburbs," *Modern Language Quarterly* 57:3 (September 1996), for a discussion of the American rhetoric of "reverse colonization" in another context.
51 Hegeman, *Patterns*, 48–51.
52 Zora Neale Hurston, *Tell My Horse: Voodoo and Life in Haiti and Jamaica* (New York: Harper & Row, 1990 [1938]), 81–2.
53 The occupation ended three years before Hurston's trip.
54 Hurston, *Tell My Horse*, 82.
55 Ibid., 80.
56 Ibid., 83.
57 Ibid., 84–5.
58 Ibid., 85–6.
59 Hurston's tone and position are, as in nearly all her works, difficult to track because of the degree to which it is possible to read *Tell My Horse* as a mixture of colonial and anti-colonial styles and genres, a technique she uses elsewhere. It is possible to support an argument that Hurston supported the occupation in *Tell My Horse*. For a recent example see John Carlos Rowe, *Literary Culture and U.S. Imperialism: From the Revolution to World War II* (Oxford: Oxford University Press, 2000). As other critics have argued, the fact that she titles the book after a phrase used by a Haitian god to challenge the socially powerful or to allow a person to express otherwise socially unacceptable opinions while "possessed" can be taken as a hint to read her as the ironic trickster she discusses in *Mules and Men*. Certainly, *Tell My Horse* is not openly critical of the occupation or of the United States in the way that James Weldon Johnson, Langston Hughes or C. L. R. James (whose *Black Jacobins* was published the same year) were. My juxtaposition of *Tell My Horse* with *The Birth of a Nation* is not a claim that the two authors share a politics of white supremacy. Rather, I mean to emphasize the way narrating state and national subjectivity in "cultural" terms constitutes a common discourse.
60 After the revolution in 1804, Haiti entered a period of political isolation, with most nations refusing to recognize it as a nation until the French did. At the time the French were still threatening to retake the island; Haiti did not get French recognition until 1825 and it was on the condition that it pay an indemnity of 150 million francs to the French planters who had lost "their" land. With little export income and low credit, Haiti had to borrow the money from France, which led to European and then to American

intervention in and control of Haiti's economy and factional struggles among Haitian politicians playing different foreign governments off against each other. American bankers became more involved in U.S. Latin American policy under Presidents Taft and Wilson; in 1914 U.S. marines took $500,000 of Haitian government funds via gunboat to the National City Bank in New York. The Haitian Bank changed its French flag for an American one. See Renda, *Taking Haiti*, 50–3; 99. Wilson certainly knew the significance of this. In 1919, he said, "A country is owned and dominated by the capital that is invested in it ... the processes of capital are in a certain sense the processes of conquest." See Pomerance, "United States," 15. James Weldon Johnson attacked the motives and consequences of American financial transactions and the profits of the American banks in his report to the NAACP and his articles for *The Nation* and *The Crisis*. See *The Selected Writings of James Weldon Johnson* Volume 2 ed. Sandra Kathryn Wilson (Oxford: Oxford University Press, 1995), 207–52.
61 Hurston, *Tell My Horse*, 103.
62 Ibid., 110.
63 Hazel Carby argues that *Tell My Horse*'s ethnographical approach allows for the expression of an imperial vision and that her definitions of "the folk" cause her to "displace" the political issues of her time. More recently, Leigh Anne Duck has argued that far from being apolitical, Hurston's work in Haiti is a reasoned and deliberate rejection of cultural nationalism. See Hazel Carby, "The Politics of Fiction, Anthropology, and the Folk: Zora Neale Hurston," *History and Memory in African-American Culture* ed. Genevieve Fabre and Robert O'Meally (New York: Oxford University Press, 1994); and Leigh Anne Duck, "'Rebirth of a Nation': Hurston in Haiti," *Journal of American Folklore* 117:464 (Spring 2004).
64 Hegeman, *Patterns*, 50.
65 David W. Blight, "W. E. B. Du Bois and the Struggle for American Historical Memory," *History and Memory in African-American Culture* ed. Genevieve Fabre and Robert O'Meally (New York: Oxford University Press, 1994), 52–3.

AFTERWORD: MYTHS, MONSTERS, MODERNIZATION, MODERNISM

1 T. S. Eliot, "The Idealism of Julien Benda," *The New Republic* (December 12, 1928), 106.
2 Nella Larsen, *Quicksand and Passing* (New Brunswick: Rutgers University Press, 1986), 96; 235.
3 David Theo Goldberg, *The Racial State* (Malden, MA: Blackwell Publishers, 2002), 175.
4 Michel-Rolph Trouillot, *Silencing the Past: Power and the Production of History* (Boston: Beacon Press, 1995), 88.
5 Ibid., 89.

6 Ibid., 98.
7 T. S. Eliot, "*Ulysses*, Order and Myth," *Selected Prose of T. S. Eliot* ed. Frank Kermode (New York: Farrar, Straus and Giroux), 177.
8 Georg Simmel, "The Metropolis and Mental Life," *Simmel on Culture: Selected Writings* ed. David Frisby and Mike Featherstone (London: Sage, 1997), 183.

Index

Abramson, Howard S. 185
agrarians 117, 118—19, 134
agriculture, U.S. 118, 132—3, 138
Ambrosius, Lloyd 186
Amery, John 80
Anderson, Benedict 146, 147, 149, 175
Andrews, Bert 80
Arnold, Matthew 48
Atkinson, Edward 148
authority 67, 71, 75

Balibar, Etienne 175
Barkan, Elazar 145
Beckles, Hilary McD. 9, 185
Benda, Julian 48
Blast 56, 99, 100
Blight, David W. 190
Boas, Franz 157, 161
Bové, Paul 117, 118—19
Brown, Wendy 32, 36—7, 102, 116
Buck-Morss, Susan 11
bureaucracy 1, 74, 79—80, 102, 105, 168
Bush, Ronald 145

Carby, Hazel 190
Caribbean 150
  modernity in 9—10
Chatterjee, Partha 175
Choi, Chungmoo 176
Chow, Rey 39—40, 43, 44
cinema, camera in 43—4
citizenship 6
  expansion of slavery and 10
  gender and 83, 96, 98—9
  marriage and 116
  race and 10
Clark, Suzanne 174
Cohn, Bernard S. 70, 75
Conrad, Joseph 47, 58—60, 166
  compared to Sara Jeannette Duncan 71—6
  Heart of Darkness 57

consent 5, 24, 29, 34, 41, 116
Cott, Nancy 34, 35, 42, 117
Crane, Hart 119
Cruikshank, Barbara 101, 172
culture, defined in twentieth century 155, 156, 157—8
Cunningham, Valentine 49
Currid, Brian 105

Davis, Fred 83
democracy 3—4, 6, 28, 80, 110, 149, 152, 157
design 138, 142
Dixon, Thomas 151
Dorman, Robert L. 137, 176
Du Bois, W. E. B 142, 143
  Negro, The 161
Duck, Leigh Anne 190
Dulles, Allen 80
Duncan, Sara Jeannette 14, 68—78
  compared to Joseph Conrad 71—6
  Burnt Offering, The 179
  Set in Authority 68—78

Eliot, T. S. 1, 2, 4, 12, 13, 101, 118, 122, 163, 166
  defining political imagination 47
  "Love Song of J. Alfred Prufrock, The" 120
  man of letters and 49—52, 74
  and Rudyard Kipling 15—16, 45—9, 52—4
  Waste Land, The 1, 56, 120, 121, 122, 134
Epstein, Jean 1, 12, 42, 147
Eysteinsson, Astradur 57, 184

Faulkner, William 122, 126, 164
  Absalom, Absalom! 123, 130, 131
  As I Lay Dying 123
  Sound and the Fury, The 122
Felski, Rita 36, 91
fifth column 79, 104
Ford Madox Ford 76

Index

Foucault, Michel 1, 5, 8, 135
  governmentalization 8
franchise 6, 28, 29, 151
  American 3
  British 4
  women's suffrage movement 93–4, 101
Freeman, Elizabeth 131
Fuller, Margaret 173

Gilbert, Sandra M. 92
Gilman, Charlotte Perkins 173
Gilroy, Paul 25
Glasgow, Ellen 14
  Barren Ground 19–20, 118, 119, 120–32, 134–6
Glendinning, Victoria 179
Goldberg, David Theo 10, 162, 165
Golden Bough, The 121
Goodlad, Lauren E. 170
Gordon, Colin 135
Griffith, D. W. 13
  Birth of a Nation, The 150–7
Grossberg, Michael 35, 184
Grosvenor, Gilbert 146
Gubar, Susan 92
Guinier, Lani 187
Gunning, Tom 150

Haiti 9–12
  debts of 159
  and Revolution 10–12, 166
  and modernity 9, 10
  U.S. media depiction of 38
  U.S. occupation of 4, 5, 27, 148, 171
Hall, Stuart 169
Halperin, Victor 4
Hannah, Matthew G. 150
Haraway, Donna 121
Harlem Renaissance 138, 164
Heater, Derek 186
Hegel, Georg 11, 12
Hegeman, Susan 161, 164, 176
Hewitt, Angela 184
Himes, Chester 165
Hiss, Alger 80
Hobsbawm, Eric 3, 180
House Committee on Un-American Activities (HUAC) 80
Hulme, T. E. 120
Hungiville, Maurice 174
Hunter, Lynnette 6
Hurston, Zora Neale 14, 158–61
  definition of culture by 161
  use of ethnography by 158, 160

Tell My Horse 150
Hutchinson, George 185

I'll Take My Stand 115
imperialism 146–7, 154, 163
  British 70, 75, 87, 95, 108, 154, 179, 187
  gaze of 62
  governance under 77
  modernism and, *see* modernism, empire and 62–3, 65, 68
  representation of authority under 71
  U.S. 5, 27, 148, 150, 154
  whiteness and 66
  women and 66

James, C. L. R 9, 10, 147
Jameson, Fredric 56, 96
Jellison, Katherine 133
jilt, *see* marriage, breach of contract of
Johnson, James Weldon 190
Joyce, James 164
  Ulysses 56, 122
Joyce, William 81
  Twilight over England 105
  passport of 112–13

Kant, Immanuel 10
Kaplan, Amy 151, 176
Kaplan, Sydney Janet 60
Kent, Susan Kingsley 93
Kern, Stephen 104
Kipling, Rudyard 15–16

labor:
  disputes 3, 5
  race and 125, 136, 138–40
Langbaum, Robert 119
Larsen, Nella 164, 165
  Quicksand 164
  Passing 165
Lawrence, Karen 95
Levenson, Michael 59
Lewis, Wyndham 99
Lloyd, David 51, 99, 104, 111
Longenbach, James 100
Lowe, Lisa 51, 99, 104
Lugosi, Bela 4, 21
Lyon, Janet 100

Mansfield, Katherine 14, 60–8
  "Millie" 64
  "Woman at the Store, The" 61–8
  national imagery 64

Index

marriage 116–17, 135, 143
  American history of 34–5
  breach of contract of 133–4
  in literature 115, 117, 131, 136
  modernity and 36, 116, 118
  state and 35, 36, 116
Marx, Karl 27
masculinity 83, 103–13, 109
  white 4, 25, 152
McGrath, Patrick J. 169
Menand, Louis 58–9, 175
metropolis 1, 5
Mexico 87
Michaels, Walter Benn 151, 155, 164
Miller, Peter 6, 7, 8
modernism:
  alienation in 2
  empire and 13, 17–18, 55–7, 59, 74, 150, 162
  gender and 92–3, 99–102, 122, 126, 128
  identity politics and 162
  internationalism in 163
  nationalization of criticism in 164
  postmodernism and 58
  psychoanalysis and 97
  realism and 55, 57–8, 74, 76–7, 78
  self-consciousness of 8, 123
  style of 37, 100, 164, 167
  white settler 55, 66
modernity 1, 2, 134, 135
  anti-colonial 12
  defined 36, 117
  gender and 91, 141
  monstrosity and 37
  natives and 12, 20, 156
  race and 25–6, 139, 165
  uneven 116, 140, 142
  World War I and 91
modernization 2, 6, 36, 126, 136–7, 139, 140, 145, 162, 165
Monroe Doctrine 147
monstrosity 37
  and automation 39
Moore Rachel O. 173
Morrison, Toni 170
Mumford, Laura Stempel 180
Muybridge, Eadweard 31, 38

National Geographic 146–7, 154
New Age 60
New Yorker, The 44–5
Nicholls, Peter 175
Nietzsche, Friedrich 168

Ninkovich, Frank 186
Nixon, Richard M. 80
North, Michael 56, 183
nostalgia 83
Nye, Robert 188

Oppenheim, Janet 179

passport 79–80, 112–13, 163
Pauly, Philip J. 185
Perkin, Harold 97
Philippines, U.S. censorship of news and mail during war with 148–9
Piper, Karen 181
plantation 9, 147
Pomerance, Michla 156
Posnock, Ross 143
postcolonialism 13, 162, 165, 166
Pound, Ezra 101
Pratt, Mary Louise 62
Price, Michael 171
primitivism 20, 145, 147, 150, 154, 156, 157, 161, 162
propaganda 105
psychoanalysis, Freudian 82
  use by state 97–8

radio 105–6
Rafael, Vicente L. 146, 173
Ransom, John Crowe 137
realism, *see* modernism and realism
reform, social 6–7, 8
regionalism, American 19, 117, 122, 123–5, 131, 136–8, 143
Renda, Mary 171, 190
Rhodes, Gary D. 173
Rhythm/Blue Review 60
Rickover, Hyman G., Admiral 80
Riley, Denise 101
Rogin, Michael 151
Rollyson, Carl 179
Roosevelt, Theodore 132
Rose, Nikolas 7, 8
Rowe, John Carlos 189

Said, Edward 56
Scott, Bonnie Kime 18, 81
Selwyn, Francis 105
sentimentalism 42, 43–4, 118, 126, 130, 136
Shelton, Marie-Denise 186
Showalter, Elaine 179
Silvestri, Michael 179
Simmel, Georg 2, 4, 5, 12, 135, 167

Sinfield, Alan 182
slavery 10
    modern racial dimensions of 10
Smith–Lever Act of 1914 132
Sollors, Werner 143
South America 117, 118, 137, 143
Southam, B. C. 183
state:
    bodies and 107
    cinema and 39–40
    culture and 111–12
    determination of identity by 75, 79–80, 81, 165
    documentation by 81
    ethnography and 160
    form 28, 29, 117, 168
    gender and 111
    marriage and 35
    narrative and 61
    nation and 92, 105, 107, 147–8
    prerogative power of 84–5
    social management by 7, 8, 101, 142
    subjectivity generated by 60, 75, 80, 95, 98–9, 105, 113, 162, 167
    welfare 7
    women and 101–2
Stein, Gertrude 104
Stoler, Ann Laura 177
Szalay, Michael 164
subject:
    agency of white male 31
    enfranchised 6
    imperial 70, 77
    liberal 31–2, 36
    modern 9–10, 60, 74, 99
    national 92
    state 60, 80, 94, 101
suffrage, *see* franchise
Suleri, Sara 68
Swinburne, Algernon 46

Taft, William Howard 146
Tate, Allen 119
Thomas, Nicholas 61, 62, 67, 77, 187
Thomas, Paul 111
Tompkins, Jane 131, 136, 175
Toomer, Jean 13
    Cane 20, 136, 138, 140–3
    "Her Lips Are Copper Wire" 143
    "Reapers" 143
Torpey, John 80, 81, 113

Tratner, Michael 172, 188
treason 85, 104–5
    masculine 108
Trotter, David 60, 76
Trouillot, Michel-Rolph 166
Turner, George 171

urbanization 6
Usui, Masami 96

voting, *see* franchise

Weber, Max 1, 2, 4, 7, 12, 28–9, 36, 74
West, Rebecca 14, 18, 80–114
    Black Lamb and Grey Falcon 80
    Meaning of Treason, The 80, 81, 103–13
    Return of the Soldier, The 80, 81–98, 102–3
whiteness 66, 138–9, 155, 156, 165
White Zombie 4, 5, 9, 15, 21–34, 38–45, 117, 139, 143
    aesthetics of 37, 38
    critical reception 42, 44–5
    use of close-up in 40, 42
    use of natives in 171
    pressbook 174
Wiebe, Robert 4, 6
Williams, Linda 31, 44
Williams, Patrick 171
Wilson, Woodrow 132, 147, 154
    History of the American People 155
    "Inquiry, The" 149
    national self-determination 149–50, 156
Women's Social and Political Union (WSPU) 93
Woolf, Virginia 96, 172
    Jacob's Room 92, 94, 95
    Mrs. Dalloway 82, 96
    Room of One's Own, A 97
World War I 3, 81, 93, 147, 180
    and imperialism 87
    shell shock in 82–3

Yeats, William Butler 122

zombie 5, 22, 37, 92
    bride 5, 32–3, 40
    gendered 30–1
    political symbolism of 5, 9, 12, 15, 26–7, 29, 30, 166, 173

Made in the USA
Lexington, KY
19 November 2013